Capitalism 101
My Tea Party Principles

by

Leon A. Weinstein

TELEMACHUS
PRESS

Capitalism 101: My Tea Party Principles

The publisher does not have any control over and does not assume any responsibility for author or third-party websites or their content.

Cover designed by Telemachus Press, LLC

Cover art copyright © iStockPhoto #4501306 Stock Exchange Concept

Published by Telemachus Press, LLC
http://www.telemachuspress.com

Visit the author's website at http://www.leonweinstein.com

ISBN #978-1-937387-60-0 (eBook)
ISBN #978-1-937387-61-7 (Paperback)

Version 2011.10.23

Printed in the United States of America
10 9 8 7 6 5 4 3 2 1

Good Wishes to the Author

"I wish you and the book the best of luck—keep up the good work"
Karl Rove

"I have a particular interest in this book's subject matter" *Michele*
Bachmann, member of the US House of Representatives & Republican
Presidential contender

"I look forward to an opportunity to read your book" *Michael S.*
Steele, Chairman, Republican National Committee

"God bless you" *Sarah Palin*

Opinions about Leon Weinstein's action-adventure novel "Looking for Hugh: The Capitalist Guidebook"

"... *fascinating story about Capitalism in an Orwellian style.*" Kevin McCullough, Radio Host

"*I think it's altruistic and noble to try all means possible to restore American traditions of individualism, self-responsibility, and entrepreneurship.*" Herb Walberg, Chairman, The Heartland Institute

"... *it is a masterpiece!*" Phil Hendren "Dizzy Thinks book review, London, GB

"... *terrific.*" Burt Prelutsky, conservative columnist and bestselling author

"... *thoughtfulness...*" Rudolph W. Giuliani

"... *highly recommended.*" Mike Everling, Senior Facilitator, Karl Hess (Libertarian) Club

"... *we love it...*" Sandra Needs, Chairman 49th AD Republican Central Committee

"*Leon Weinstein has masterfully and creatively written an adventure-fantasy which reminds me of both "Animal Farm" and "Alice in Wonderland."*" Terry Gilberg, Talk Radio Host

About This Book

The opinions and views expressed in this book are solely those of the author and are provided here for your entertainment. This book is intended to amuse, amaze and, most importantly, cause you to think.

You are encouraged to express your opinions and support of this book by leaving a review on Amazon http://amazon.com or leaving a message on Facebook http://www.facebook.com or following Mr. Weinstein on Twitter http://www.twitter.com

Table of Contents

Introduction

"In the beginning was the word...."

I HAVE TO confess, I am one of them. I am one of those terrible people who think that the government shouldn't take from us what it pleases whenever it pleases. I am one of the terrorists who are obnoxiously sure that a paycheck is better than all unemployment benefits combined. I am one of those monsters that have the audacity to insist that the government can spend only what the productive citizens agreed to give it and not one cent more. I am also not sure it is a good idea to allow people who never contributed to the society and didn't pay any taxes to vote on how much to take from others and how to distribute the money. I personally think that "No representation without taxation" (if you do not pay taxes, you can't decide what to do with them) would be a good starting point to change what is not good in America today.

I think that a capitalist economy can't support a socialist welfare state and that if we will not change our ways very soon, the American economy and its political system will collapse. Please do not say it is impossible. No one would believe a mere thirty years ago that the Soviet Empire would crumble during our lifetime. It is however gone and our children will know it only from the history books.

Liberalism, Progressivism, Socialism are easy to explain. Gifted demagogues can throw well-crafted slogans and lead masses to national suicides as it already happened in Russia (Lenin), China (Mao), Germany

i

(Hitler) and in many smaller countries such as Vietnam, Cambodia, Hungary, Czechoslovakia, Romania and the list goes on and on.

Capitalism is much less attractive to mobs, especially to the young and restless. It looks to them (from an arrogance of their age and absence of real life experiences) as an egoistic, pragmatic and in-humane life philosophy. The more people prosper under capitalism, the more their children and others who benefit from the work of capitalists incline to call it their enemy and oppressor.

At a certain point, I began to fear that masses in America don't know what other realities look like. That they may choose to go the way of "social justice" and destroy the best country in the world.

During the last years it looked to me that ... *America was going down the predictable path of wealth re-distribution and self-destruction. It looked like it was impossible to stop or even slow this process.*

And suddenly there was the Tea Party. Thousands upon thousands of people who showed that they listen, understand and are not ready to put up with the "fundamental changes" to their beloved country, the definitely and without doubt the best place in the world for individuals, for you and me.

I was fascinated. I went to the first Tea Party meetings in the streets of my city. I found mostly old folks who came to fight for the future of their children and grandchildren. Everyone whom I met was fed up with the system.

I didn't believe at first how many people there saw the same slide into socialism I feared so much. We talked, argued pros and cons, exchanged emails and continued to stay in touch. I told many of my fellow Tea Partiers about the book I was writing and received their inputs and advice. I might say that "Capitalism 101" is a collective effort, an essence of what we as a movement believe in and are fighting for.

The book was greatly influenced by works of Jay Stuart Snelson. In 1965-1978 Jay created a course of lectures for the Free Enterprise

Institute in Los Angeles. The lectures introduced the "Property Theory" by astrophysicist Andrew Galambos, the founder of the institute. Jay's book "Taming the Violence of Faith" and his Win-Win Theory of social interaction gave me an additional boost in my understanding of how to explain capitalism and freedom to the very people who created and built it—to the Americans.

"Capitalism 101" presents a case-by-case study of volitional science (science of co-existence of volitional beings—people). Certain thoughts and ideas in this book can be traced to Ayn Rand, Milton Freedman, Karl Hess, F.A.Hayek, Frederic Bastiat and especially Ludwig von Mises. I would also like to thank Harold Fleming for his "Ten Thousand Commands. A story of antitrust laws," John Longenecker for "Transfer of Wealth/Safe Streets" and F. A. Harper for "Why Wages Rise." Those authors and their books were sources for invaluable information and thoughts for me.

As a newcomer I have an advantage of a "fresh look" on the society, its trends and developments. I emigrated in 1974 from the then-USSR, known to its population as a "Prison of Nations." I can't say I didn't like it. I hated it passionately. I am still trilled that my family and I were allowed to escape. It all happened because of you, my fellow Americans. You purchased our freedom with wheat that Soviets badly needed at that time. To you goes my love and gratitude.

However being from the country of the "well developed socialism" as the leaders of the Soviet Union used to call their society, I am very sensitive to any even small manifestations of socialism and its twin sister—fascism. This is why I believe that it is of utmost importance to convince the population of the United States of America that they have to stop taking their great lives for granted.

If you will not resist with all your might, a terrible decease called "socialism" will topple America and very possible that the world as we know it will perish. It will take under its ruins the ideals of the American Revolution, capitalism and liberty.

If we will not understand and appreciate our values, if we will not pass them to the next generation, if we will not teach our children and grandchildren to cherish those values and defend them, we are doomed.

The American dream is not about a small house and a backyard with vegetables, but about leaving to the next generation a world that is a little bit better than it was when the previous generation arrived. A little bit better from many different points of view.

If we want our kids to live a better life, we need to teach them how to distinguish right from wrong, utopias from reality, how to stand for what they believe in. We need to teach them to think, not to follow.

Below is a statement of my beliefs—a hypothesis that I will try to prove in this book:

Capitalism and Liberty is the best yet invented way for the human society to coexist ... because it is proven to be the best for individuals, leads to prosperity and unlike other social structures might (just might) stop the mutual destruction of the humankind.

I believe that those two concepts (capitalism and liberty) are not implemented to their fullest extent in any modern (contemporary) society. I also believe that there is a need to bring to social sciences the precision and the clarity of the physical sciences.

I came to a conclusion that governments that govern our lives are as bad an idea as an idea of a "Just King" or in effect of any King. Both resemble an invitation for a cat to baby sit a little mouse.

At the dawn of the American Revolution Thomas Paine wrote his "Common Sense" where he proclaimed that Monarchs are not necessary and that life can be much better without them. It was a total break from the millennia old tradition of trusting kings to take care of their subject's lives and an unheard of revolutionary idea. Let me proclaim one of my own—a government that has power over lives of the citizens is as counterproductive and unnecessary as Kings, Monarchs,

Rulers, Strongmen, Shahs or Tsars. We will talk about it at length in this book. But let's leave conclusions for the end and start back at the beginning.

But before we begin our journey I want to give my very special thanks to my fellow "reformed Liberal," the Pulitzer Prize-winning author of Glengarry Glen Ross David Mamet. Mr. Mamet recently published a book "The Secret Knowledge: On the Dismantling of American Culture" and an article "Why I Am No Longer a 'Brain-Dead Liberal.'" Thank you Sir! You and I went different ways but arrived at the same checkpoint.

Preface

"A fool and capitalism will soon part"

Leon Weinstein

I WAS BORN in the Soviet Union in the majestic St Petersburg, one of the most beautiful cities in the world. I knew it was majestic because all the history and guide books were saying the same thing—that St Petersburg is a jewel of the world, it is beautiful beyond imagination and has no comparison anywhere.

My grandfather was telling me stories about the city as well. How beautiful it was when he first came there in 1916 to practice law after his graduation from a law school. I believed him more than all the history books combined.

In fact, St Petersburg of my youth was a grey, quite boring and enormously dirty city. All its palaces, sculptures and other wonders were covered by thick layers of dust and corrosion. We lived in a historical center of the city and my grandfather (in Russian you call your grandfather for short "Deda") often took me around and told me about buildings with marble walls, sculptures on the roofs and grandiose stores that once dominated the area. I loved his narrative about the closest shopping district situated on a street called in my time "Pestelja." The name was of a revolutionary aristocrat, who took part in the 1825 failed military coup attempt against Tsar. I do not believe the street had the same name under the Tsar's rule.

Deda would take me, a 6-year old boy, by the hand and we would walk the street and he would tell me: "Here was a great food store where dozens of different kinds of sausages were sold, some from Ukraine, others from Germany and Austria, birth place of the very best sausages in the world." And near them in a cheese department there were at least thirty different types of cheeses, not including cottage cheeses from around Russia, Estonia and Finland. "The entrance"—he would reminisce: "… was majestic, at the door I recall there was a huge man in a uniform who would help older clients to climb two stairs up to the store and handed out small bits of baked goods to passing by children. In the store there were great chandeliers, a lot of light, it was clean, with a great smell of bakery and hot chocolate, and there was always someone who would come to you and offer to help to find anything you need or carry goods to your home."

It sounded like a fairy tale, and what child doesn't like fairy tales?

While Deda was talking to me about those ancient times when he was young, we were standing in front of the entrance of a crummy and bad smelling food store. On its' dirty and broken steps were usually a couple of drunks begging for small change to buy a drink. In the smelly dairy department there were no cheeses from Finland and in the stronger smelling meat department there were no sausages from Germany.

The store was never renovated or repaired since the communist revolution, and it was well known for its personnel that would always cheat by adding on weight to products and under-giving the change. When you would say something about it, the employees of the store would gang up on you, start yelling and practically run you out of the store. To call the police was useless; since they used to give the policeman small presents and the peace officers were always on their side.

Another great story about Deda during his youth was the famous barbershop with the "best in the whole city" men's hair stylists. At his time the place had a small private bar (free to the clients), newspapers from around the world could be found there, cigars and a host who would entertain clients while they were waiting in deep leather armchairs smoking cigars, reading newspapers and talking about news and politics.

I knew the place pretty well—I used to go there to get haircuts, but my recollection of the place was somehow different. The barbershop in my time had a smell of a gym; there were four half-broken chairs where you would get a haircut, but no cigars, no leather, no host, no free newspapers and above all no talk about politics. The big brother was listening and everyone knew that!

The place was cheap, fast, bad haircuts, no complaints, and no pleasure. We were told during my childhood that haircuts are not for pleasure; but they are a necessity like water. A real Socialist shouldn't think about such things as personal beauty. Real socialists for example love each other not because of their looks, but because of their mutual interests in social issues, their love of the country & willingness to sacrifice everything to the Greater Good of the Motherland.

As a matter of fact, we didn't have hot water during my childhood for about 3-4 months every year. Every time it happened, the government called it "maintenance." Probably hot water wasn't a necessity, but a luxury and as such the citizens of the greatest Socialistic country in the world didn't need it all the time.

My Deda died when I was seven. He had a heart attack when he was taken (for the third time) to the KGB headquarters. He was told that he would be proclaimed an "Enemy of the State" and as such will be shot, unless he signed a false statement that two of his attorney colleagues approached him and suggested to form a group of kamikaze to kill Stalin and other leaders of the communist party. Deda didn't sign the paper. He outwitted the KGB and died in their interrogation rooms.

Many years after that time, in 1973, the United States Senate voted to attach a little provision to the bill regarding sales of wheat to the Soviet Union. In exchange for the help so much needed by the Soviets, the Jackson-Vanik provision required the USSR to allow free immigration. As a result of the deal the Soviets made with the US government about fifty thousand "minority citizens" (Germans, Jews and Pollack) left the country. My family was one of the lucky ones. We remembered the words of my beloved Deda—"If in the fence surrounding the USSR will open even a smallest crack, run your heads off." We did.

Just before I left, I visited the Pestelja Street. Nothing changed from the days of my childhood. Same dirt, same nauseating smell, same drunks (or maybe they were the children of the drunks I knew during my childhood).

Then came Ronald Reagan, the destruction of the Berlin wall, and the end of the Soviet Union. Already as a US citizen I visited the place of my birth and was on Pestelja in 1989, then in 1995. Same dirt, a bit less smell, and a bit more products on the shelves. I was told that the stores, apartments and buildings were being privatized. People who lived there were afraid: "Those new Russians, those capitalists are thinking about themselves and themselves only. We will die without food and goods, they wouldn't care…" I kept hearing these words from my ex-neighbors all my words that capitalism is good in producing wealth for everyone were taken with healthy skepticism.

In 2003, eight short years later I visited the street again.

Where are you, my beloved Deda! Maybe I was dreaming? The walls of almost all the buildings on the street were decorated with marble. The whole block of my childhood was filled with stores, some of which were selling food, some designer clothes, some antiques or electronic gadgets and video games. On the second floors of the buildings were law offices and physical therapy cabinets, offices of travel companies and evening classes for adults. The street was clean, smelled of perfume and was filled with families shopping their heads off. On many stores I saw a sign "7x24." The shopping district worked seven days a week, twenty-four hours a day!

At the entrance of the main food store, in front of two perfectly repaired steps was standing a huge African man in a uniform, smiling to passersby, helping older people to get in, and handing pieces of baked goods to children. WOW! On top of the building was written in golden letters "Proudly owned by Rybakoff family for 150 years." And quite suddenly I remembered—I was in the same class with Anatoly Rybakoff who once, we think as a joke, said that his grandfather owned this store. He got it back and now brought it to its past glory. Something that neither managers nor employees were able (or wanted) to do while it was owned by the state.

I rushed to see the barbershop. Six deep leather armchairs were standing in a beautifully designed waiting room. I didn't notice cigars, however the drinks, the newspapers and the talk about politics was on and heated as ever.

Why does everything that the state touches (even when attempting to do good for people), go sour. In contrast, when a person attempts to make his living, when his motivation is pure greed, it turns out for the good of all?

For seventy years Russia's socialist government was saying that it was trying to achieve this Greater Good for all the people. The books and TV programs, lecturers at work and teachers at schools were educating citizens of Russia to help each other, to share, to think about their neighbors and participate in the variety of programs for this elusive Common Good. They took all the surplus produced by the state and gave it back to the people. They nationalized (seized) all the factories, universities, banks, hospitals, communications and natural resources and distributed profits among the people.

The results were devastating.

Actually this experiment of taking property and wealth-producing enterprises from private hands to distribute it among other groups of people, was a huge economic and social failure in every country it was ever imposed. When capitalism came back, in less than a decade, the world the Soviets lived in for seventy years was magically changed, and all of the society (not only newly rich) benefited from it.

Look at what the pursuit of happiness does. America is the most capitalistic and at the same time the most prosperous society in the world. This prosperity was built during a mere two hundred years. And in the

USSR capitalism cured problems that were incurable under socialism for all those years the socialists were in charge.

Care to hear another personal story about capitalism? My younger brother and his family live in Israel in a place called Mevaseret Zion, on the edge of the Greater Jerusalem. Mevaseret is on one side of a hill, and an Arab village called Abu Gosh is on the other. Abu Gosh is famous for their hummus, and the villagers live from the restaurants they built to accommodate thousands of Jerusalemites coming every day to eat great Mediterranean food or take out tons of hummus, tahini and falafels.

Then starts the intifada, Arabs began to blow up Jews in the busses and restaurants, throw stones at children, and the Israelis stopped going to restaurants as much and are not taking out food from Abu Gosh like they used to. The main source of income for Abu-Gosh was food purchased by Israelis. No Israelis, no income.

The elders of Abu Gosh sat down to think how to protect their livelihood. They thought and thought and thought and came up with a solution. From this day on, for all the years of intifada on a road from Mevaseret Zion to Abu Gosh, every seven-eight hundred yards was placed a chair. In those chairs from dusk till dawn seven days a week were seated Arabs from Abu Gosh facing the Arab side of the hill with rifles in their hands. They were ready to shoot anyone who would interfere with the business. They knew exactly where the interference might come from and were ready to shoot nevertheless. There has not been one single incident in Abu Gosh during all the years of intifada. Israelis started coming to the area even more often because it was the safest place in Israel to eat great food and take families on weekends. Viva capitalism!

A miracle, simple and unlike global warming is completely manmade!

Yet, if this thing called capitalism is that good, if it helps some to amass fortunes, and more importantly, if it allows most of the population to live better lives than under any other known politico-economical system, then we should all work hard to preserve it and teach our kids how to cherish and defend the system.

Why then in our kindergartens and schools do we not spent time teaching kids this vitally important aspect of our lives? If for six thousand years of recorded history, all the other systems were only able to produce misery for most of the population, if prior to capitalism the common people were treated like dirt, killed at will, their property and privacy invaded … and under capitalism it all changed, than we shall pray that capitalism will last long enough to benefit our children and grandchildren.

Our ancestors were smart; they proved it by building the best society that ever existed on the planet. Now we need to learn how not to lose it, how not to become fools that soon part with the wealth we inherited from our parents and grandparents.

The very first riddle

Let me start now with the first riddle. There will be plenty of them in this book.

Not long ago I wrote a novel for kids and teenagers called "Looking for Hugh" and dedicated it to my grandson Nikolas who at that time was an eleven years young six-grade student of a middle school in Northridge, California. When the book was published, I gave him a signed copy.

The next morning Nik called me. "Gran" he said "I am on a break, reading your book, and a kid here is asking me where he can get a copy? I said I will ask you."

"Is he your close friend?" I asked.

"Not really" was a reply, "We play soccer together from time to time."

I explained to Nikolas that his buddy can purchase "Looking for Hugh" at the book's site, at Amazon.com, at a couple of book stores in the area or he can buy it directly it from me.

After short consultation with the boy, Nik asked me to put aside a copy and he would pick it up after school.

Two days later I received from Nick an agreed ten dollars and gave him the book. I also took one dollar bill and handed it to Nik. "What's that?"—He asked. I explained that I believe that every job shall be paid for and that selling a copy of my book on which I made profit is a job and it shall be compensated.

The idea appealed to Nik and two days later I received another call from him and was asked to put aside one more copy. Later I learned his sales technique. During the long break instead of playing soccer as he and a bunch of crazy fans like himself did every day, Nik was positioning himself in the middle of the school yard with the book in his hands pretending to be deeply in reading. It was only natural that his friends, who were obviously astonished by this view, were one by one stopping by to find out what he was doing. They were told that THIS book is even better than soccer.

After the third sale I initiated a serious conversation with my grandson. "Look" I said "Your school might not be that happy with a student selling something on the campus."

Nikolas thought about the subject. "What if I sell books outside of the campus?" he asked. Then on another thought "I have a question too" he mused. "I noticed that the book is sold online for more than the ten dollars that you charge. Why do you sell it for less than the price printed on the back of the book?"

I explained to Nikolas that when online bookstores sell my book, they charge me a fee for their services and I am getting from them about nine dollars. Nikolas thought about it. Then "Can I sell it for …say, eleven dollars?"

"Sure" I said "I do not care what you are getting from your customers."

"And how much do you want me to give you if I sell it for eleven dollars?" he said.

"Nine," I replied.

Another pause, hard thinking and then … "Wow!"

After that day, Nik sold about fifteen books. I never asked what he charged. I was getting my nine dollars and was happy. Instead I asked my daughter, his mom what he spends his money on. She told me that Nik dreams about an Apple laptop and recently struck a deal with her about doing some house chores in exchange for monetary compensation. She said that he proposed a table of absolutely unrealistic, over the roof prices that he would get for washing dishes, sweeping floors and baby-sitting his sister. My daughter said that Nik was a tough negotiator and that he argued that changing diapers is not only humiliating but is also a hazardous job. But, she said, he told her that if she doesn't have money but needed him to sit with his sister, he will do it for free. One thing I will not do for free, he warned her is diaper changing. They concluded their negotiations and struck a deal. My daughter was very proud of him.

Nik bought his laptop under a "50% credit deal" he negotiated with me. Here is how it was done. When he earned and saved up half of the money needed for the computer, he came to me and asked for a loan. We discussed the terms and he is now paying me back with a small interest. He doesn't know that I am depositing the money he pays me into his college savings account.

I now have a couple of questions for you dear readers. What do you think about this story? Was it right in your opinion to allow an 11-year old boy to sell books to his peers, to make money in order to buy the things that he wants? I should add that pursuant to our conversations Nikolas purchased a box of candies at Costco and sold them retail to his classmates making about hundred per cent profit on each.

Q1. Is it OK to pay your child for domestic chores? Is it OK to allow children to make, spend or save money? And finally is it OK to loan money to your kids and charge interest, teaching them in the process how to calculate payments that include principle and interest?

You can use multiple answers covering most of possible opinions:

A. We shall never mention words like "profits," "earnings," "taxes" and shall not allow children to earn money. When they need something, they shall come to parents and ask. We, the parents, shall control all aspects of their lives and shield them from life's ugly realities.

B. Kids shall know their responsibilities, and they have to study, help parents, share and care without ever thinking about compensation. The idea of unselfish faith is well articulated in the Book of Job for example, and we shall take our clues from the Book.

C. We need to prepare kids for the real world. We need to show them the real value of money, and the amount of time one needs to earn it and the amount of effort you need to invest in making even a small profit. And most of all we need to teach them values.

D. Other _____ (what?)

If your answer is "A" you most probably will hate this book. If you will hate this book, why should you buy it for yourself or for your child, right? Put it back.

If you answered "B" I would try to turn you into a believer in Freedom of Choice and Free Markets.

If you answered "C" you and I are of the same blood.

If your answer is "D" then at least it is not "a." I would offer to try to resolve our differences.

Comment of a Progressive / Socialist: A child is supposed to have a happy childhood, which means an absence of responsibilities or worries of an adult. Happy childhood excludes money. Money is evil, right next to weapons. Also it is unfair that some children have money and others do not. The US constitution says that all men are created equal.

Money makes people un-equal and therefore having excess amounts of money is against the American constitution. One person will be able to buy something he wants and another cannot. Where is the equality promised by the founding fathers? It is absolutely not important if one person was working hard and using his brains and muscles to make money, and another was watching TV all the time while the first one was working.

Your grandson Nik shall be punished (not encouraged) for selling books and candies on campus or anywhere else. Profits are the evil of our society. The money Nik earned shall be given to the principal in order to distribute among those that need them most.

<u>Comment of a True Liberal / Capitalist</u>: Way to go Nik!

And now—to the book!

The Foundation

HUMAN BEINGS (US) have to eat in order to live, have to wear clothes in order to stay warm, have to build houses in order to survive bad weather. Someone has to prepare food, make clothes, build houses, and do thousands of other things that we either absolutely need, or just want to have.

One person makes food, sells it and buys what he needs or desires with the money he made by selling food. Another person makes clothes, sells them and buys what he needs with the money he made selling clothes. A system when you make what you want (no one tells you what to do) and sell to whoever you want; a system when you are paid for the product or service you offer to people and where other people are free to buy it from you or to buy it from any other person; a system when you keep what you earned and make your own decision to do whatever you want with the money you earned , is called capitalism.

There are a number of other systems of those "socio-economic relations" between people who make products and the users of their products or services. For example a system that was dominant for centuries almost all around the world is called "monarchy." Under this system, the life and happiness of the citizens were totally dependent on the whims of the head of the state called Monarch, Tsar, King, Ruler, Prince or Shah.

Monarchs took from people anything they wanted to and anytime they wanted to.

Monarchs imprisoned people for things you would not believe—for example you could've gone to prison for talking or even looking at the Ruler without his permission.

Monarchs went to wars when they felt like it, and thousands of people were killed or crippled just because their kings wanted to fight. "I am the state," the kings were saying. That meant simply "I do not care what others want. I do as I please." The good of the King was the law under monarchies.

Q1 - Do you think the Kings cared much about the rest of the country? Below are two possible answers to this question:

a) Yes, I think most of the Kings cared a lot about people who lived in the countries they ruled.

b) No, it looks like they cared mostly about themselves.

Socialism is another system in which a group of people who govern the state tells working people (we call them Producers) what they shall produce and what portion of their earnings they can keep.

Socialists usually take from the Producers either part or everything they produce and give to someone else, disregarding whether this person worked to produce anything or not.

It is like if during your childhood years your Mom would tell you that if you will clean the house, mop the floors, run to a supermarket and take garbage out, she would pay you three dollars for this job. You work hard, did everything you agreed to, but when you come to get your pay she gives you one dollar.

When you ask your Mom where are the remaining dollars she tells you that in order to be fair to your younger siblings she gave one dollar to your sister who did nothing and was playing dolls all the time you worked, and gave the last dollar to your toddler brother who was in a cradle and obviously wasn't able to help with the domestic chores but wanted to get a dollar as well. So, Mom concludes, I gave exactly the agreed amount of money but I <u>re-distributed</u> (gave away) your money to be fair to everyone.

Do you think this is fair to you, the person who did the job?

Capitalism is the only system that is fair to producers, to the people who do the job.

If you want to do nothing, and wait for someone to give you a bit of that and a bit of this, go for socialism. Capitalism is not for you.

Let's now talk about a different subject. Let's talk about fear.

Under Monarchy everyone is afraid of the King. He is the one that can take everything from you, including your freedom or even your life without any reason whatsoever. He is the boss with unlimited powers. Kings build beautiful palaces for themselves with other people's money, but do not really care about the people.

Under socialism everyone is afraid of the government. The government can give you less or more and can ruin your business and life. The government can allow you to go to a trip abroad, or decide not to let you go. The government can decide what ethnicity will get student loans and who will be accepted at prestigious jobs, and what ethnicity will not. Under socialism, the city where the government presides has abundance of everything (socialists take things and money from everyone in the country and bring the goods to where they themselves live), while the rest of the country often struggles without simple necessities. Socialists usually build great capitol cities and do not care about anything else.

What do you think the producers are afraid of under capitalism?

Under capitalism, producers are afraid of one and only one thing—to lose their customers. Customers are the kings. This is why producers build beautiful stores, landscaped entrances and surroundings, and smile every time you enter their stores. In many other countries people do not smile as much. They do not really care about their customers. They care, but are (afraid) of the kings or the government. To them they smile.

Americans prefer capitalism because it is fair to the ones who work hard (most of the population of the country), because it is working well and because there is no better system yet invented to create wealth for so many people and in a record short period of time.

I am sure there will be people who will advocate just an opposite view. I do not want you to take anyone's word for it. The idea of this book is to let you come to your own conclusions and not because someone tells you what you shall believe in, but because you yourself thought hard and made your decision.

Let's together examine some real situations and you, you and only you will decide what is better for you, your family and friends, and which system is more honest and fair to live under and to enjoy life.

We will start our examination with a very strange question. Here it comes. The question is "Who owns you?"

Capitalism 101
My Tea Party Principles

Chapter I
Who owns you?

WHEN I WAS a small child I used to ask lots and lots of questions. I bugged my parents, their friends, our neighbors, teachers at school, distant relatives, salespeople at the stores my parents shopped at and even passerby who happened to be in close proximity. I used to ask them "why does the sun always rise from the west" and "how many legs do the caterpillars have" and "what causes hiccups" and the most important of all "whom THIS belongs to?"

You see, my parents used to tell me "THIS belongs to this boy or that girl and you can't touch it without their permission," or "THIS belongs to your aunt Maggie..." or "THIS belongs to the school..." in short "THIS IS NOT YOURS!"

So what is MINE? What belongs to me? What I can touch without permission from anyone? And why I shall not touch their things and they shall not touch mine? Looks like everything belonged to someone. All that was very confusing to me. Very very confusing.

I didn't know where to start to unravel this mystery and decided to concentrate on the most important question: "Whom I belong to? Who owns me? Do I own my own self or does it belong to someone else?"

Let's talk about it. When your mom or dad (again in your childhood) told you "march to your room" your body went to another room, right?

So the body is yours but someone else is in charge. If someone else controls your body, then it doesn't entirely belong to you ... Like it is your car, but whoever drives it does with it what he wants. You can say "this is my car," but then your car is already two blocks away from you.

You were under your parent's control until age eighteen, but the day you turn eighteen you are getting full control of your own body. Until that day you have guardians who are guarding you and helping you to navigate the world you happened to be born in. Because of that they have partial control of your body.

At age 18 you can sign up for the army or the navy and voluntarily hand control over your body to your commanders.

However generally after this wonderful and scary day—your eighteenth birthday—you shall be in total control of where to move your body, how to dress it and what to put in it (I mean food and drinks).

Why this moment is wonderful is obvious—if you want to go to the movies, you tell your body to get out of the bed, get dressed and walk or drive to a movie theater. If you want an ice cream, a new video game, a doll, a dress or a great Swiss army knife ... you can get it without asking anyone's permission. You can go and get what you want.

It is scary because together with the rights come the responsibilities. Among them—if you are an adult then you have to earn your living. If you want to go to the movies, you have to buy a ticket and it is YOU who are supposed to earn money for this ticket. And if you want a new dress or a Swiss army knife ... you have to pay for it YOURSELF.

You will have to think about cars that break, food that needs to be bought and cooked, about going to work, paying bills ... brrrr ... At the moment you will start doing what you want to do you will have to act as an adult. And believe me, I know many people who come to this juncture in their lives, their eighteenth birthday with mixed feelings ... and I even met some who were ready to give up control over their lives in exchange for food and shelter. That's how much they didn't want to take all those responsibilities upon themselves.

But what does that mean—control over your own life—you might ask. To understand that, let's try to examine together what is really yours, and what is not.

Your family probably owns furniture, probably a car, a TV set, clothes, books and you can sell anything you own, right? Can you sell a car that you are not happy with? Of course you can. Can you sell books or furniture or shoes? Yes. Can you sell a dog or a cat? Yes you can. There is no assurance anyone would want to buy your old shoes or an unfriendly cat, but you CAN sell them.

However you can't sell a child and can't exchange a child for a set of new kitchen appliances or an old vacuum cleaner.

You can sell anything you purchased or found, or received as a gift, but a child wasn't purchased, not found or even given as a gift. A child was born and was lucky to be born in the United States of America where selling humans is strictly prohibited.

Once people used to sell each other and it was called slavery. This practice was going on from Biblical times to the end of the XIX Century, and even a bit beyond. In the XXI Century at least in the civilized world where you and I live the Biblical type of slavery is prohibited by law. There is still a hidden slavery, and people are enslaving each other right and left, but it looks slightly different and we will talk about it later.

Parents have responsibilities toward their children and limited rights until they are eighteen … but their children are not their property.

You are a property of one and only master and this master is … you yourself! Everything I am saying here I say in total respect to any belief in God you might have. It is not about God, it is about you and the world around you. It is about responsibility, slavery and freedom.

You belonged to yourself since the day you were born; but maybe you just didn't know that. If you are curious by nature, you might look up a document called "The Declaration of Independence" and read about your "unalienable rights" that every American (you included) has or is supposed to have, and check who gave us those rights. Was it a monarch, or a government or a bunch of other people who can grant you this right and then decide to take it back? Go ahead and check.

What else is yours? How about your thoughts and ideas? Are they yours or do they belong to someone else? I guess they are yours. At least mine are mine. If I want, I share them with other people. If I do not want, I do not share and no one knows about them.

One of Thomas Edison's inventions was an electrical typewriter. This wonderful and very useful invention was a direct result of his thinking, his ideas and his ingenious implementation. He invented it and this was HIS invention. Many millions of people were using this and other inventions from Edison, they were buying products based on his inventions and he became rich and famous because of his creations.

Q1 - Is it good in your opinion if someone invents something very useful such as loaf of bread or car wheels that many people use and enjoy? So what do you say?

   a) Yes?

   b) No?

I think it is good for everyone—for me, for you and for the inventor. Can you imagine if there would be no wheels in the world? That means no cars to drive, no planes would be able to land and would stay in the skies forever, and handicapped people will not be able to move without having wheel chairs to help them.

Q2 - Is it OK in your opinion to compensate a person who invented something that is good for you? Without such people there wouldn't be cellular phones and computers, high rise buildings and railroad engines. Do inventors deserve to be compensated? I think there are only three possible answers—and you will decide by yourself which one is yours:

a) Yes

b) No

c) I do not know

Edison invented a light bulb and you and I can read books at night and look for lost things under beds and in dark corners. We can see entrances to stores and planes at the night skies. Many people bought products based on his inventions and Edison he got rich and famous. Everyone was praising him and rushing to buy electrical lights, electrical typewriters and many other products he invented.

An Inventor (if he is successful) gets to be rich and famous and it is good for him to invent and sell things to us. You get the light and he gets paid for that. You get the speed to move around your town or universe and he is getting things that he always dreamed about. Everyone wins, right?

Two college age guys invented Google and many millions of people are using this invention. Google is a very fast and convenient way to gather information. The inventors became rich and famous.

Q1 - Is it good for you and me that those guys invented a very fast way to look for things on the Internet?

a) Yes?

b) No?

What do you think?

If you would invent something like how to fly faster than light, go to a distant star and come back before lunch, this would be your invention. If you would want, you would share it with others. If you wouldn't want, you can keep it a secret. It is yours; you do with it what you want.

Or let's say you invented a cure for a terrible disease and many people can be saved and cured because of you. Do you think you deserve the pay from all those people who used your medicine to cure them and their loved ones? You worked hard for many years to invent it and did not know you would get good results at the end. You went through long periods of looking, finding, being disappointed and even depressed but finally you hit the right answer.

Q1 - Do you think you deserve to be famous for that?

    a)   Yes?

    b)   No?

What do you think?

This is how powerful our thoughts and ideas are—they lead to our ability to light up and heat our houses, to fly from one continent to another, to cure people who otherwise would be sick for life or die. Those ideas were created by people like you and I. They originated in their heads and they belong to them. They could have kept those ideas to themselves, gave them to anyone they wanted to as a gift, or shared them with the world at large or if they are lucky to sell and benefit from them.

OK, your thoughts and ideas belong to you. Anything else?

Things of course! You have your things. Books and pens, games and clothing, your old Teddy Bear and a new electronic gadget ... How did you get them? Some you received as gifts from people close to you. Some of them you bought with the money you earned, and some you might have won in a lottery.

Where else you could you get things? You can exchange something that was yours with a friend who gave you something that you wanted. What else? You could find an old treasure. You could inherit stuff ... or you could've stolen something, right?

Let me define stealing. Stealing is getting something without permission from the rightful owner. For example, a person came to a store and secretly took something without paying for that. Or a person came to a friend and took something without telling him or her about it. A person asked a friend to loan a book or a game or a toy and didn't return it despite the promise and despite all the friend's reminders. A person attacked another person and took something from him by force. A person overheard an idea of another person and used it to get something for himself without compensating the inventor. All these examples are stealing. Add violence to theft and you have robbery, which is stealing combined with violence.

We will talk about stealing in greater detail later. By now I wanted to just list ways you can get things and ideas—receive them as a gift or inheritance, earn, find or exchange, or steal them. If you steal them they are not exactly yours. You will probably need to hide them because if the owner will see them, then you will be forced to return them and most probably will be punished (and rightfully so). You can use them in hiding, you can even control them (a thief stealing a car and driving it) but they are not yours.

Yours are your own body, your thoughts and ideas, plus things that you got without coercion (stealing, cheating, and robbing). All that together we call your <u>belongings</u> or sometimes your <u>property</u>.

<u>Your body, your ideas and your things belong to you</u>. Remember that—it sounds like a very simple concept, but it is a very important foundation for many other things in your life and relations with people around you. This happened to be the very First Postulate of a branch of human knowledge called "Volitional Science."

Riddle #1 - On The Remote Island

In the middle of the Pacific Ocean there was a nice island called Bu-bu. It had lots of coconut palms and other tropical greenery, lots of good water, plenty of sun, fish and birds, even small animals different from any place in the world. In short it was a great place for islanders to live, except for one small thing. There was no medical doctor on the island.

There was a larger island several miles from Bu-bu that had a doctor, but he was very busy and he was alone, and never was able to come to Bu-bu.

Children on Bu-bu Island were constantly sick, many of adults were limping and people were sick for weeks when a influenza or other bacilli would come to the island.

And one day a miracle happened.

Dr. Jeremy Doe was on a cruise with his wife and kids. He couldn't sleep in a cabin, went for a midnight stroll, and fell overboard completely unnoticed by anyone. He felt an impact of the cold ocean water and lost consciousness. When he regained his senses he found himself on the Bu-bu Island in the middle of nowhere.

The islanders were very nice and receptive to him, but when they learned that Jeremy was a surgeon who was able to perform miracles and save lives even using primitive islanders' tools, they went bananas.

Jeremy was happy to help, but all his thoughts were about how to let his wife know that he is alive. The islanders didn't have any phones, radio or other means of communications with the outside world.

Jeremy asked islanders to bring him to the big island several miles from Bu-bu. Jeremy saw small planes taking off and landing there. When Jeremy was asking islanders to take him there, they either didn't understand what he was talking about or didn't want to understand. The waters around the island were infested with sharks and swimming was out of the question. Jeremy hoped that one day someone from the islanders would need to go to the big island or someone from the big island would visit them here.

Despite the fact that Jeremy felt desperate and frustrated, he didn't stop helping islanders with their medical needs. There were ten thousands of them on the island and someone constantly was sick or had an accident and badly needed medical help.

One day Jeremy saw that a large yacht sailed from the big island and headed toward them. Jeremy had a feel that his wife was on this boat looking for him. The islanders also saw the yacht and showed Jeremy all the signs that they are happy for him. They danced around him, sang songs and even brought a tropical punch they drunk together with him praising his deeds and thanking him for the things he did.

The moment Jeremy drunk the punch he felt asleep and woke up only when the yacht was long gone. The islanders hid him in a hole in a ground and covered him with green leaves so no one would find him. They knew that if they will let him go there will be no more doctors on their island and hundreds of them will be sick again and many small children would die.

Thinking out loud:

Q1 - Jeremy helped many islanders and even operated on some and saved their lives. If Jeremy would go many islanders would be sick or die. Was it for the good of the island and the islanders to keep Jeremy over there? What do you think?

   a) Yes?

   b) No?

Q2 - Who has a right to decide should Jeremy stay or go? What do you think?

   a) Jeremy belongs to Jeremy. The only person who makes decisions about him staying or going is Jeremy.

   b) If Jeremy can help so many natives and without him many will die or be sick, the islanders have a right to keep Jeremy on the Island.

Comment of a Progressive / Socialist: The good of ten thousand people is more important that one person's good. Ten thousand is much more than one, actually ten thousand times more. It is sometimes painful to make sacrifices for the good of your country or your island, but we are not animals. We do not need to do what we want, but what is necessary. Do not ask what your island will do for you; ask what you can do for your island!

Comment of a True Liberal / Capitalist: Jeremy is supposed to decide by himself if he wants to sacrifice his life or not. No one can decide for him.

Q1 - a

Q2 - a

Riddle #2 - Catchy Song

Jim was a student at a musical school. He played piano and composed music. He was always very critical of himself and said to his friends that he yet can't show his pieces to anyone. But one day, he kept repeating, one day I will write something great. You will see.

And one day he wrote a great song. The melody was really good, both catchy and deep. Jim was very proud of his song. He recorded the music and sent it to his favorite famous composer, whose work he adored and listened to every day. Jim wanted to hear from the composer if his song was as good as he thought it is.

The famous composer was at that time working on a main song for a Hollywood movie. He was frustrated—the deadline approached and he had nothing to show to the director and producer of the movie. And suddenly he got Jim's melody. He loved it instantly. He played it several times and felt it is exactly what was needed. The composer showed this music to the crew and everyone especially the leading actress loved it so much that she began to perform it in concerts.

The film was a smashing success and the composer got an Oscar for his work, and got paid tons of money from the sales of the single with his now famous song.

Jim got nothing, not even a note from the composer. Jim couldn't continue his musical career. He had to start making money and he became a maintenance man for a large building downtown. He says that he hates music and he never listens to anything except news and sports.

<u>Thinking out loud</u>:

Q1 - Who shall be paid for this song?

a) The composer—without him no one would know about it

b) The lead actress—she sang it and made it famous

c) Jim—he created it.

d) You—for doing nothing, just because you would love to buy this new sleek computer but do not have enough money

<u>Comment of a Progressive / Socialist</u>: Capitalism is a very bad system. In capitalism the only thing people are after is money. They want money so much that they begin to steal and cheat. It would be much better if everything would belong to everyone and no one would be paid for a specific deed. People would do what they can and would receive what they need. Wouldn't that be wonderful?

<u>Comment of a True Liberal / Capitalist</u>: If you create a song, this is your creation and it belongs to you. You are the owner; you can do with it what you want. You can give it away; you can sell it or give as a gift. It is YOURS.

<u>Author's opinion—Right answer is</u>:

Q1 - c

Chapter II
Do people want to be happy or do they want to be unhappy?

IF YOU WOULD have a choice, what would you chose—to eat chocolate or to be frozen in the snows of Siberia? How about a choice between being bitten by mosquitoes or to fly a jet as a pilot? If you would have a choice, what you would prefer—to lose things or to find them? To hear people praising you or cursing you? Personally, I prefer things that make me happy. How about you?

Do you think other people would prefer to feel good or be sad and miserable? Do you think other people want to feel happy or do they prefer to feel unhappy? Most of the people I know prefer to be happy.

Let's try to find out what makes you happy. Does getting presents that you dreamed of make you happy? How about meeting new friends with whom you do things that you love to do—for some it is playing basketball, for some discussing books, for some building models of ships, or dressing dolls, or cooking exotic foods? How about winning trophies? Will these make you happy?

What makes you sad? If you lost your cell phone, would it make you sad? When someone steals your bag, would it make you sad? Would winning a bike race make you sad?

When you accidentally cut your finger and feel pain, does it make you sad and miserable or does it make you happy?

Now tell me what is better in your opinion—to feel happy as often as possible or to feel sometimes happy and sometimes miserable?

Are you looking forward to an interesting day that will bring you happiness—your birthday for example, or the first day of summer? Are you looking forward to a day when you will be given an achievement award? If this is so, it looks like **happiness is what you are really looking forward to**? Am I right?

I personally love swimming in cold water. This makes me happy. Does it make you happy? Is it possible that what makes me happy is not what makes you happy?

A friend of mine is collecting stamps. One day he came to me and said that this is the happiest day in his life. When I asked why, he showed me a stamp he got after two years of dreaming about it. I said I am happy for you, but this stamp or any other stamp wouldn't make ME happy.

So one person thinks that getting a rare stamp is happiness. Another person thinks that swimming in ice cold water is happiness. Everyone has his or her own happiness and wants to achieve HIS or HER particular happiness.

This is exactly exactly exactly what is written in the Declaration of Independence—all Americans (including you & I) have a right to own their own lives, be free and <u>pursue their own happiness</u> the way they themselves understand it!

If you are happy to fly a jet, you can try to become a pilot. If you want to create foods that will be both tasty and good for your body, you can do it. If you want to become a gardener and make people happy, you can do it. If you want to become a gardener and tend to your own garden, and make yourself happy, this is also OK. No one can tell you what shall make you happy and what not, and no one can stop you from achieving your goal. All is in your hands. This is America, the best country in the entire world! We are SOOOO lucky to live here!

Americans allow each other to pursue their own happiness the way each of us understands it. There is one point to remember however—you have no right to interfere with the other person's pursuit of happiness. It sounds easy, but for some reason most of the people on the planet do not get it. I hope you will.

Riddle #3 - My Friendly Weapon

This happened in your city. Actually not far from you, but not on your street. You were at the middle school at that time. There was a boy whom you probably knew at least by sight. His name was Miki.

Miki was small and thin. He had two stomach surgeries when he was at an elementary school and he even went through a full year of home schooling. Now he was OK, but was smaller by a full head than this brown haired girl with a pony tail in his class that he had a crush on.

Miki had a problem and his problem had a name. Actually it had two names—twin brothers Bob and Dob. They were quite big for their age, and constantly wanted to prove that they are powerful and smart. And they thought that they can do it by bullying Miki.

They didn't do it out in the open, but every day they would find a moment when Miki was alone, and they would push him, or squeeze him, or do something else that would make him feel miserable. On top of everything, every day they took away his special lunch that his mom prepared for him because he couldn't eat regular food. They thought that taking lunches from Miki was funny.

Miki was scared of the twins. He was dreaming about getting sick again and spending another year at home, about Bob & Dob's dad getting a job in another galaxy, or about a miracle that would free him from those evil brothers.

And one day a miracle happened. Miki met and befriended Weapon. Actually his name was John Allan Weapon, but everyone called him simply Weapon. He was two years older than Miki, tall and HUGE!

I will meet you after school, he said to Miki after learning about his Bob & Dob problem.

This was the best day in Miki's life. When the twins saw Weapon they ran away as fast as they could. From time to time Weapon would come to Miki's school, shake Miki's hand, walk him home and smile to everyone around. Weapon never said or did anything to the twins, but they were so afraid of him that they avoided Miki and ran away every time they saw him.

Miki began to enjoy school. He was a good student and loved to learn new things. Interesting, he thought, I never "used" my friend Weapon but the mere fact that I had such a friend changed my life.

And then one day Miki saw Bob & Dob's dad talking to his mom. Your son befriended a dangerous person, he was saying to her. He is so huge, he is much older than Miki and who knows what this huge guy wants from him. Other kids are afraid of him as well, for example my sons. This older boy comes often to Miki's school and looks danger-ous. He is so big and powerful that he might harm our kids.

And Miki's mom forbade Miki to see Weapon. This is it, she told Miki; there is no Weapon in your life any more. And what a terrible name you call him by! No more Weapon either here or there.

Bob & Dob again began to bully Miki and every day took his spe-cial lunches that his mom prepared for her sick son. They made him jump, sing silly songs and yell cock-a-doodle-doo as many times as they wanted. You do not have your Weapon any more, they laughed. Now we can do with you whatever we want.

Thinking out loud:

The story has three parts—before Miki befriended Weapon, during the time Weapon and Miki were friends and after Miki's mom forbade him to see his new friend. Miki's life was miserable before and after. He was happy only during the time Weapon was with him. Notice that Weapon never said or did anything to the twins. So here are the ques-tions and some of the possible answers:

Q1 - Why didn't the Twins bully Miki during the time Weapon and Miki were friends?

a) Because they were sick?

b) Because they were busy with something else?

c) Because they were afraid that if they would bully Miki he would use Weapon to harm them?

d) Because their dad was an executive in a local school district?

Q2 - Why did the Twins resume their attacks on Miki?

a) Because they were abused by their grandmother when they were small?

b) Because Miki didn't have Weapon anymore?

c) Because Miki was provoking them by bringing tasty lunches to school?

d) Because Miki had rich parents?

Q3 - The twins forced Miki to give them his lunch and were holding him even when he wanted to be left alone. What in your opinion were they doing to Miki?

a) Stealing from him?

b) Enslaving him at those moments?

c) Humiliating him

d) All of the above

Q4 - If someone would be bullying you every day, pushing you around, taking away your belongings—would you feel:

a) Happy?

b) Unhappy?

What would you feel?

Q5 - If someone would be bullying you every day, would you like to have Weapon on your side?

a) Yes

b) No

c) I do not know

Would you?

<u>Comment of a Progressive / Socialist</u>: If you have a problem you shall go to authorities. Authorities will always know better how to resolve everybody's problems than people themselves.

<u>Comment of a True Liberal / Capitalist</u>: When you have a weapon, hoodlums will think twice before attacking and humiliating you.

<u>Author's opinion—Right answers are</u>:

Q1 - c

Q2 - b

Q3 - d

Q4 - your choice

Q5 - your choice

And now I have a tricky, tricky question. Do you like winning lotteries? If yes, let me tell you a story about one lottery. I hope you will enjoy it.

Riddle #4 - Lottery

Once upon a time there was a group of tropical islands somewhere in the middle of the ocean. The sunsets were beautiful, the palms were full of coconuts, and fishing was great. But the islanders were not happy. They saw that on other islands people lived better lives and had more time for fun. They were making washing machines that made their lives a bit easier, creating drugs that made many illnesses go away and invented air conditioners and heaters and made winters and summers more bearable.

The islanders were puzzled by why others were doing those smart things while they don't. They were told by their neighbors that it is because they didn't have good education on their island.

The islanders decided that they have to build a school and a university, bring very good professors and teach young islanders how to do those and many other useful things that they didn't have but wanted so much.

However to hire professors would require lots of money. The islanders didn't know where to make the money until someone said a magic word "lottery."

If every islander would buy even one ticket every month then we will get lots of money, the elders of the island thought. But how we can make everyone buy lottery tickets? We can't force them. And they came with a smart idea—to offer islanders a chance to win a huge prize. If one million islanders will buy one million tickets of one dollar each, then the lottery will receive one million dollars every month. One half will be used for paying professors and another half will be given to the winner.

All islanders loved the idea. Each month they bought one million lottery tickets and from this million exactly one half was paid to the teachers and professors and the second half given to the winner. Everyone was happy. The islanders hired the best professors and many of the young began to study to become engineers, doctors or teachers.

People were eagerly anticipating each lottery round, were buying lots of tickets and for a long time were talking about winners and what they did with their fortune. Very often the islanders were saying to each other or even to themselves "When I will win ..." And their eyes would become soft and dreamy.

One winner used his money to build a house on the top of the tallest hill in the middle of the island. Another opened a furniture factory; a third bought a plane and began to travel the world. A fourth drunk for two months in every pub and bar and was hospitalized with amnesia in a local hospital.

There was a boy on the island by the name Iggi who badly wanted to win. His mom was sick and he heard that there are places in the world that can cure her illness. He dreamed about winning the lottery in order to take her there and be able to pay for the surgery.

Iggi was so eager to win that he used his lunch money and all his pocket money to buy tickets and he did it day after day, month after month. And one day he looked at the winning numbers and almost fainted. He was the winner of the grand prize, of a half million dollars. His dream came true.

Iggi ran to the place where the elders were counting lottery money and waiting for the winner to arrive. He was warmly greeted by the elders. "Here is your money," said the chief elder after he examined the ticket, "Use it wisely," and he handed Iggi a small stuck of bills. "But it is much less than half a million" said Iggi.

"Yes" said the elder: "And there is a reason which I am sure you will understand and appreciate. We looked how unwisely people used their winnings and we decided that since we, the government of the island, are much smarter than the average folks, it is our obligation to help you to spend such large sum of money the right way."

First we took some of the money that you won to help the wives of fisherman who were killed during the recent storm, he continued. I am sure you will approve of such noble use. Second we needed to buy some fishing gear for our island's fisherman and didn't have money so we took some of yours. I am sure you will understand how important it is for all islanders to continue getting fresh fish. Also we charged you a "night lighting tax" since we all need to have some light at night, a "repair the elders hall tax" and a very small "islands finances stabilization fund tax." I hope you do understand the word "tax" and understand why it is needed for our great island?

Those are very noble and very important things that will be done with the money you won. You shall be proud to be able to do so many good things with your money. And the remaining amount we gave you and it will be enough to buy a huge ice cream with lots of syrup.

"But" said Iggi "That was my money; I won it fair and square. I want the money, not a story of how you used it."

"You are a bad and an insensitive person" the elders told him "We do not want to talk to you anymore. You are thinking only about yourself and your needs. You shall start thinking about other people as well. You shall start thinking about the Good of the Island which is much more important then your personal needs and desires."

Iggi left them hating the elders and the lottery, thinking that if he won or earned money, he and not the elders is supposed to decide what to do with them. He never ever purchased a lottery ticket again.

The word about taxes and fees that the elders now take from the winnings spread throughout the island and one by one people stopped buying lottery tickets and the lottery died. Since there was no more money to pay to the professors, they all left and the University died as well. The island still has no washing machines, medical supplies, air conditioners, heaters or people who can build them. Elders blame all that happened on the stupid islanders who suddenly and without any reason stopped buying tickets.

Iggi left the island and never came back … So did many others, who had hoped that life would improve on the island, but somehow lost this hope.

<u>Thinking out loud</u>:

Q1 - Why did the islanders stop buying lottery tickets?

   a) Because they were stupid?

   b) Because they hated gambling and lotteries?

   c) Because the dream of winning big was stolen from them?

   d) Because they didn't like the University?

What do you think?

Q2 - Who is supposed to decide what to do with money won at lotteries—people who win or people who didn't?

   a) The government shall decide what to do with the money since the people who are in the government are smarter and more knowledgeable than the average folks.

   b) The people who earn or win shall do what they please with the money. They can give it to charity or build huge houses; they can spend it on taking their Moms to good hospitals or build businesses. It is their money. No one can touch them.

Is this a "brainer" or a "no-brainer"? What is you opinion?

Q3 - The elders took Iggi's money to help families of dead fisherman and to buy fishing gear so the islanders would be able to fish and feed their families. Was it noble to help those people?

   a) Yes?

   b) No?

Q4 - The islanders now knew that they will not receive big prizes and stopped buying lottery tickets. The lottery died and the school and the

University died as well. Was it smart to reduce the prize and kill the lottery?

a) Yes?

b) No?

<u>Comment of a Progressive / Socialist</u>: The best way to build a just society is for the government to get all the money and goods the islanders earn and establish committees to distribute them among the islanders according to each person's needs. It is not necessary to have a lottery to start a University. Since the elders will be distributing all the money anyhow, they can spend a part of it to establish a university or use them for any other purpose they will agree on.

<u>Comment of a True Liberal / Capitalist</u>: If you decided that what Elders wanted to do with Iggi's money was seemingly honorable (YES answer to Q3) but led to the end of the lottery ... and because of that wasn't very smart (NO answer to Q4), then you yourself figured out the essence of what is called "equal distribution of wealth" or socialism. Socialists, Marxists and progressives usually have seemingly honorable intentions, but when you implement their ideas you see that they are really really stupid and kill both freedom and prosperity. This is what happened with the lottery on Iggi's island. The Elders (the government of the island) probably had honorable intentions but what they did was unjust and dumb. "Looks honorable but is actually stupid" is the middle name of progressivism often called socialism or Marxism.

<u>Author's opinion—Right answers are</u>:

Q1 - c

Q2 - b

Q3 - a

Q4 - b

Once I was driving through a small town and stopped at a coffee-shop near the main road. The place was empty and we got to talking with a nice woman who happened to be the shop's owner. Her name was Susan and she was the only person working in the shop. She cooked, cleaned, washed dishes, served the tables and took out the garbage all by herself. "Once I was rich," she told me. Since I got interested, she told me her story.

Her mom owned this small sandwich and coffee place. This was the place where she did her homework, played with dolls and when her mom was sick or absent, used to manage the place since she was a small girl. One day she got sun burned and decided to cook herself a sun screen cream. She experimented with dozens of ingredients and came up with a great remedy.

First she tried it herself and loved it. She then gave some to her siblings and friends and they loved it as well. Then she gave a bit of her cream to her school mates and their friends. Then a rumor about her great sun screen began to spread and people from all over the valley came to buy her magic stuff.

At first Susan was taken aback by the idea of selling her cream, but then she instantly liked it. She cooked the cream and her mom sold it in her coffee shop.

Every day people from all over the region would stop by the shop to get the cream, and they also got sandwiches and coffee and her mom's famous steaks as well. The representatives of a regional pharmacy chain came to Susan and offered to sell her cream at their two hundred stores.

Soon Susan and her Mom were making tons of money. Susan was happy. Her mom was happy. Two of Susan's small sister's were very very happy. They got many beautiful things that no one in the town could afford before.

The neighbors however were not happy. They told Susan that she is becoming a greedy capitalist and that no one in the town will talk to her or even look in her direction. They told her that it is a shame that she makes so much money at the time when they struggle in their day to day life.

Susan was so much affected by this talk that she stopped making her cream.

Her family was disappointed. The people who used to buy her cream were disappointed. The pharmacy chain that had a big success with selling the cream was disappointed. The only people who were happy were Susan's neighbors. She was now as poor as they are.

End of story.

The Second postulate of the Volitional Science is "Each and every human being wants to be happy." What makes different people happy can be very different. It depends on each person's preferences, thoughts and ideas. The very same thing one person can consider "good" another can consider "bad." However human beings will move toward what they consider good and happy and away from what they consider bad, dangerous and unhappy. One can argue that an instinct can sometimes override this rule (for example a mother running into a burning house to save her child), but on a deeper level this is what a mother wants above all—to assure safety of her offspring.

Chapter III

What is freedom?

Why it is mentioned in the Declaration of Independence?

I HAVE A very important and urgent question for you. Do you think stealing is OK?

a) Do you think "Yes, it is OK," or

b) "No, it is not OK?"

Let's assume you said NO, it is not OK. But maybe it is OK to steal a little bit? If you need something badly and another person has plenty of it, maybe it is OK to steal? He has so much that he will not notice ... Do you think is it OK to steal a little bit when you want or need it badly?

a) Maybe it is OK if the person whom you stealing from has plenty, more than he needs? or

b) No, never?

What do you think?

What if someone is stealing from you? Is it OK to steal from you?

a) Yes?

b) No?

Maybe if you have two cars and someone has no cars, it is OK to steal from you because he has none and you have more than you need?

Maybe you do not like people stealing from you because it makes you unhappy? And we already postulated that each and every person should be left alone to pursue his or her own happiness and that people shall not interfere with what other people are doing?

But maybe I made a wrong assumption about you and you think that stealing is sometimes bad but sometimes it is not THAT bad?

So, is it OK to steal sometimes, or are you dead set against it under any circumstances? Let's try to examine this strange sounding question.

Let's say that you got a new fancy model of an Apple (or Watermelon) computer that no one of your friends, colleagues or neighbors have. Dream of all dreams! Envy of the whole town! The Apple computer that is faster, sleeker and smarter than any computer ever sold on the US or World markets!

Then one day a neighbor who also wanted to have this miracle of the computer, but was not as lucky as you are breaks into your room and steals it from you!

Do you think it is OK if a person breaks into your room without your permission and takes your things? Does it make you happy or unhappy? There are three possible answers to this question:

a) It makes me happy

b) It makes me unhappy

c) I do not care

If it makes you happy or if you do not care, then you are a superman!

How about if he did it after asking his best friend—and took your computer with this friend's permission? Does it make it OK to take it without your knowledge and permission if he asked his best friend and got his permission? Or you still would call it a theft?

I would still call it a theft. How about you?

How about if the thief went to everyone in your neighborhood and asked <u>their</u> permission to take your computer without <u>your</u> permission—and they said: "Yes, you can take this toy without getting the permission of the rightful owner." Would you still consider it a theft? I would.

Would you still feel unhappy about the fact that he asked so many people which would it make it OK to take it from you without your permission?

Would it make you happy to lose your computer to know that the whole city except you (the owner) had told him—go ahead, take this wonderful computer without the owner's permission?

In your fair opinion, would it still be called theft or not? Remember, the whole city told him to go ahead and take the computer...would you consider that OK, or you still would call it—theft? I still think that even if the whole city said it is OK, taking my things without my permission is theft.

How about if the whole country told the thief—you can go, break into this room and take the computer without the owner's permission? Is it OK now or do you still think that they shall ask you, the owner, not the other people? Do you know the answer or you need to think about it?

What if the thief is poor—is it OK to steal if his parents were poor? Are you feeling better or the same if the thief's parents were poor? Here are two possible answers to this question. Which one is yours?

a) I feel better now. If the thief is poor, he can steal my things all day long

b) No, there is not much difference. Stealing is stealing. He can come and ask, but not take without my permission.

How about—is it OK to steal if his parents are from Denmark or Turkestan? Also would it be less theft if your parents were Yugoslavs and you would be considered a Yugoslavian-American? Below are two possible answers:

a) Yes, if the thief's parents are from one of those countries, that makes a lot of difference.

b) No, it doesn't really matter where his or my ancestors are from. If he or she took things without the owner's permission, it is called theft.

How about—would you feel better about the loss of your computer if the thief's father beat the guy who stole it when he was young?

a) Yes

b) No

Or would it be OK to steal if his father left the thief's mother when he was a small child?

a) Yes

b) No

Would you call it stealing if the thief is handicapped?

a) Yes, it is theft

b) No, if the thief is handicapped and on top of that he is a minority, then stealing is OK

Hmmm, How about if a truck driver or a gardener would fake a check and take from the bank all the money you were saving? Would you consider that a theft?

a) No, first I need to know the details and only then I can tell if it is a theft or not

b) Of course it is theft

How about if a thief would go to a teller and say—hey, I want to take money from this guy's or gal's account without their permission ... and the teller would say "sure, go ahead"—would it make it OK to take the money from your account without your permission? There are actually two possible answers to this question:

a) Yes, it is OK to take my money without my permission if the teller said that it is OK

b) No, it is not OK. It is not the teller's money. He can't give it away or take it himself. The money belongs to my family and me.

Now let's go up the ladder—would it be less theft, more theft or about the same amount of theft if the bank's manager would say it is OK to take your money from your account without your permission?

What is your opinion? You can choose one from listed below or come up with something else:

a) It would be less theft

b) It would be the same amount of theft

c) It would be more theft

How about if the City's Chief Engineer or Chief Planning Officer would say "Let's take this money without the owner's permission because we need it to repair the freeway that we all, including the owner of the money use? Does it make it less theft?" I came up with two answers to this question. Here they are:

a) Yes, if the Chief Engineer or especially if the City Council in its entirety said it is OK, it makes it less theft, especially if the money were used for a cause.

b) No, it is still theft. My family and I are the only people who can give away my money.

What do you think? Maybe you have different answers?

How about if the President of the country would say: "No problem! You can take his money without his permission!" Would it be less theft or about the same amount of theft if the money would be taken from you or from your bank account without your permission?

How about if the President not only said that but also issued a Presidential Order allowing to take your money without your permission and called it a "special taxation decree." Would you consider it OK if your money would be taken without your permission if this "operation of appropriating your money" would be called "special taxation?"

a) Yes, now I comprehend and am fully happy. I am ready to work hard and make money in order to allow the President to do with MY money whatever HE wants.

b) t doesn't change anything, it is still a theft

c) It would be even more theft

d) I do not like it but I am OK with that.

Which one is your answer?

When you do not agree to give something that belongs to you but it is taken from you without your permission by the government, it is called "legalization of crime."

Regular thieves, con artists or bandits rob you by using coercion or force. Government thieves do it by issuing decrees and laws. But if you will not give what they want from you, they will do the very same things robbers do—they will force you to do what they want. They can put you in prison for not giving them money, and if you will try to resist they might kill you.

Do you think that if something was taken from you without your permission by a decree signed by a treasury secretary or a president, it is still theft or now you are OK with it and will not call it theft?

a) Yes, it is called theft even if the President signed the order to take my belongings from me.

b) No, if the President will order to take it from me without my permission, it is OK.

To take your money or any other belongings without your permission is crime. When it is done by President's orders, it is called socialism. This is what progressives, Marxists and socialists want. To take your belongings and do with them what they (not you) want. It is all about money and things. They want to have what is yours and since they can't get what is yours without committing a crime, they issue orders and laws. This is what socialists do—they take from you your money and other property and give it to other people (not forgetting themselves in the process).

Here is what a very smart person by the name Frederic Bastiat wrote in his book "Law": *"Socialism is legalization of crime to benefit one group on an account of another."*

Riddle #5 - Mountain Bike

Let's say that you are working overtime in order to buy a bike for your son. He was dreaming about a mountain bike and you decided to give him this great present for his birthday. You work additional hours, you are tired, you do not go to movies with your wife, and even missed two of your son's baseball games—all that to buy him his dream bike. And both you and he are looking forward to the day you will get the paycheck and will go to a store to get the bike.

The big day finally comes. You get the paycheck, go to the bank, get cash … but on the way home two people with a knife force you to give them a big portion of the money you were carrying home. Actually they took more than the third of what you earned, and this was exactly the amount that you had for the bike. Thanks God you put money for the bike separately and convinced the robbers that this is what you have. Now there is no money to buy the bike.

Would you be happy that instead of your son getting the bike those two unknown people will now buy what they want with the money you earned? Please choose between two answers below:

a)   Yes. I will be happy

b)   No, I will not be happy

My guess is that you wouldn't be happy. In fact, most probably you would be upset as hell.

Would it make it OK if those two people who robbed you from the money you earned would ask one of their friends about robbing you and he would say—"yes, go ahead rob him?" Would you feel better about not being able to buy a bike for your son if there was an additional person who agreed that you should be robbed?

a) Yes, I would feel better

b) I do not care

Which one is your answer?

How about if those two people would ask ten (or even maybe twelve) friends if it is OK to force you to give them one third of the money you earned? Would it make it less theft and robbery, more theft and robbery or about the same theft and robbery if they would ask ten friends? Would you change your mind and say

a) Yes, now I really feel good about the robbery, or

b) No, do not touch my money even if you have asked a thousand friends!

How about if they asked the whole world, every person in the world, and they all said—sure, take money from this guy, would it make it OK for them to force you to give them a third of the money you earned? Would it be less theft and robbery, more theft and robbery or about the same amount of theft and robbery?

a) Yes, it is less theft if they asked Guatemalans and Ethiopians and they all agreed that the robbers can take part of my money without me agreeing to that.

b) It is the same amount of theft

c) It is now even more theft, because now it is a Global Theft and Robbery

How about if those thieves were working for the US government? Would it make it less theft, more theft or just about the same amount of theft?

a) Yes, it is less theft

b) It is the same amount of theft

c) It is now more theft

So, which one of those three is your opinion?

What if the mayor of the city you live in decided to take that money from you to build a new park for children? Would it make you happier if you would know that you will not get the bike because the mayor decided to use the money to create a new park?

a) Ask me first what I want to do with the money I earned—to build the park or buy a bike for my son.

b) Yes, it is OK if the Mayor wanted to build a park, you can rob me now. It is OK to rob people if you have a good cause.

How about if the Governor of your state would decide to take this money from your family in order to help sick children in Portugal? Would it be less painful for you to lose the bike if you would know that the money went to buy medicine for the Portuguese children? Would it make this "forcing money out of you" less theft, more theft or about the same amount of theft? Think before answering. You already know my answer, but maybe yours will be different?

Please choose from those three possible answers:

a) Yes, it is less theft

b) It is the same amount of theft

c) It is now more theft

Thinking out loud:

Q.1 - Are there any circumstances under which a person or a group of people, or a government can take away your belongings without asking your permission?

    a) Yes

    b) No

Comment of a Progressive / Socialist: If the society has an urgent need to finance important social programs, it has an obligation to take as much money or property from the citizens disregarding if they agreed to that or not. There are many things that are more important than "wants" or "desires" of individuals, even if those individuals are the ones who earned the money.

Comment of a True Liberal / Capitalist: no one can take money or other belongings of another person without his consent. It is called robbery, theft, extortion and shall be punished by law. If the government wants something from me it shall come to me and ask. And if I will decide that it is important enough in my view, and that I have enough resources, I will help. We are paying the salaries of all those government workers, including the President, and they are supposed to serve us, not make us serve them and do things THEY think are important.

Author's opinion—Right answer is: b

Riddle #6 - Island of ABDUG

Two families lived on an island called ABDUG. One family was called AB and another DUG. The AB family of seven loved to work and worked many hours every day. Their side of the island was green, with large trees, fountains, nicely done place for picnics, secluded corners to read books, watch sunsets or just sit alone and dream about anything you want.

The DUG family of twelve loved to have a good time but didn't like working the land or at any other place. Their side of the island was covered with dirt, broken furniture, garden hoses, auto parts and pieces of glass. When asked, they usually told everyone that nothing would grow on their land and hinted that ABs got a much better deal than them.

Sitting at home and watching Abs work, DUGs laughed at them joking that the purpose of their lives was to work. But everything suddenly changed when DUGs saw a new ABs fruit garden. ABs planted every imaginable fruit in the garden, and suddenly every tree began to bear fruits and berries. It was more than what the DUGs could take.

One night they dressed in black and went to fetch fruits from the ABs garden. Much to their surprise they met two huge and very scary dogs who didn't like the invaders.

Next day DUGs went to ABs and asked to sell them the fruits promising to pay a couple of days later. ABs said that they would love to sell the fruits to them, but first they want to see the money. DUGs again went home empty-handed

They gathered in the family room of their large but always dirty house to think how to get the fruits. We can't steal the fruits at night, they were saying to each other. We can't trick ABs into giving us fruits for a promise to pay in the future. We can't rob them—they will report us to police and we will be punished. What do we do? And then it dawned on them! They found the best way to get what they want.

Next day DUGs invited ABs to an all-island meeting. On this meeting they offered everyone to vote on the right of DUGs to use ABs garden and take from it anything they want. Guess what—the twelve DUGs voted "yes" and the seven ABs voted "no." The new law was approved by twelve to seven votes. Now it was legal to steal and rob the ABs.

This legal way of stealing was a result of the Island's democracy. Lots of people love democracy and call their countries "democratic," mostly those that can vote for something they want from others but can't get without cheating, stealing or robbing.

From this day on DUGs went to the garden whenever they wanted and took any fruits they wanted. They even forbade ABs by another vote to sell the fruits to the jam making company as ABs were planning to do all along.

We are the good guys DUGs were saying to ABs, we didn't forbid you to use the garden. We are not selfish. You are welcome to use it as well. We could've done that but we wanted to be just. We made the garden a communal property and allowed all the people without discrimination by race, gender or age to enjoy the same fruits that you enjoyed but didn't want to share.

Thinking out loud:

Q1 -What do you think happened to the garden during next two years?

> a- ABs will continue working in the garden, will take good care of the fruit trees, and the trees will give more and more fruits every year

> b- DUGs will begin working in the garden and will make it the best garden ever

> c- No one works anymore in the garden. It will give less and less fruits every year and one day the trees will all die.

Comment of a Progressive / Socialist: DUGs made a mistake. After making the garden a communal property they were supposed to obligate AB to continue working and developing the garden.

Comment of a True Liberal / Capitalist: People work hard when they receive fruits of their own labor. Take it away from them and the gardens will die.

Author's opinion—Right answer is: c

Riddle #7 - Making Decisions

Let's say a boy made a small bottle of medicine to cure a very severe disease ... and he is not sharing the medicine with anyone. Is he a good person or a bad person?

a) Good

b) Bad

c) I do not have enough information to decide

The reason he didn't give it to anyone is because in order to make this cure he had to get up early in the morning, go ten miles to the nearby mountain, climb up to the top, find a certain flower that is blossoming only in the early spring and only several mornings a year ... and he went there ten times and finally found it, and made this medicine ... because his mom is sick and he has only a small bottle that will be barely enough for her ... so he just can't give it away or share it with anyone...

Now, was it fair to make a decision about him being a bad or good person before you know all the details?

a) Yes it is fair because I am smart and I do not need facts to make up my mind

b) No it is not fair—next time someone accuses another person, I will first find out all the details and only after that will jump to a conclusion

Now let's continue with this story ... a neighbor whose Dad was sick with the same illness crawled into the boy's house and stole the cure ... Do you think it is OK? Will it make it less theft, more theft or about the same theft if the thief's Dad is sick with the same illness?

How about if two opera singers decided to take this boy's medicine without his permission to give it to their older friend—are they thieves and robbers or it is OK for the opera singers to steal, especially if they are stealing for a friend?

What if the robbers gave this medicine to a very famous actress? Will it make it less robbery and theft, more robbery and theft or about the same robbery if the intended recipient of the medicine was a good person or a bad person?

Would the boy's mom be happier to know that she wasn't cured because the medicine was given to a good and famous person?

Would the boy be happier if the medicine that was stolen from him was given to a person who won the Boston marathon, or would he be as angry as when it was stolen to give it to a person who suffered from a brain tumor?

How about if this medicine was needed for the President of the United States? Does it make it OK to take this medicine without the boy's permission and leave the boy's mother without cure, if the intended user is the President of the United States?

Would it be less robbery and theft, more robbery and theft or about the same amount of robbery and theft?

Thinking out loud:

Q1 -Whose medicine it is? Who is the owner of it? Who can do with it as he pleases? Is it the person who prepared and produced it? Or his neighbors? Or well dressed people from the city hall? Or people from the West Coast? Or people from Washington? Maybe it is The President of the Russian Federation? Maybe it is China's ambassador to the United Nations? Or do you think that the medicine belongs to the Congress of the United States of America?

Who has the right to do what he wants with the medicine?

a) The person who has more power and can take it without its creator's permission

b) The one that is in the highest position in the government of the country

c) The highest court of the country

d) The person that created and made it.

e) The person who needs it the most

Comment of a Progressive / Socialist: we are all equal, but some people are more important than others. Who will get the cure shall be decided by the government representatives or by the court.

Comment of a True Liberal / Capitalist: the one and only person who has any rights to anything he produced is the person who produced it, if he did it without coercing other people.

Author's opinion—Right answer is: d

So, do you think it is important to think before making conclusions and acting? Do you think the decisions and actions should be based on proven facts and observed principles or on rumors and imagination?

Let's say that you became the President of the United States. You are now in charge of the National Defense and millions of lives of your fellow Americans depend on the actions you will take. One day you get briefing by your military advisors and they say that a Bad Guys nuclear submarine that was dangerously close to the American coast just disappeared and they are afraid that it is heading toward the New York City. "Maybe" one of them says: "It is planning to nuke New York?"

You say "If they sent their nuclear submarine to our coast, we will send ten of ours to their coast. To every nuke they have, we have ten."

A day later the Bad Guys learn that ten American nuclear submarines changed their course and are heading toward their country. An hour later they are sending twenty Bad Guys nuclear planes to fly in the direction of the United States.

You, the President say "This is it, they want to nuke us! I knew that all along," and you order a nuclear attack on the Bad Guys that would annihilate half of their country and damage their continent beyond repair.

Bad Guys, in turn, order an attack that will retaliate by nuking half of America … You get the picture, right?

All that was about to happen because you came to a conclusion that a Bad Guys submarine went silent because it was sent to attack the United States. Did you have enough evidence? Did you have enough facts? You had only your hunch, right?

Based on this conclusion half of the world would be destroyed … and after it was destroyed and millions of lives lost you learn that the Bad Guys submarine went silent because … they had an electrical problem. A nuclear holocaust happened based of a wrong assumption that wasn't based on a proven facts conclusion.

Would you agree that it is quite important for the US and the world to have the President who is not jumping to conclusions without understanding and examining facts?

Now let me tell you a story about something that just happened in America. One evening a police station in Cambridge, Massachusetts got a 911 call that two people are attempting to break into the front door of a house of a well-known college professor. A police car was dispatched to the place and the police officers saw that there are indeed two people doing something in the dark at the porch of the professor's house.

Officers got out of the car and ordered the people to stop whatever they were doing and identify themselves. Instead of following the instructions, one of the men began to yell and curse the policeman. He was so rude and offensive that the police officers decided to arrest him for interference with the police duties and waking the whole neighborhood up.

The man turned out to be the owner of the house and a professor in the university. He lost his keys and attempted to force the door open but was a bit drunk and couldn't do it. Instead of thanking the police for keeping the neighborhood safe and checking on the safety of his house, he decided to curse and offend them.

The next day the President of the United States who personally knew the professor, said that he thinks that the police acted "stupidly" and that the professor was absolutely right.

When he was presented with the facts later, the President apologized to the police officer who made the arrest and even invited him to the White House to have "a beer with him."

Do you think that the President acted responsibly and learned all the facts of the case before he accused the police officers in wrongdoing?

    a)   Yes

    b)   No

    c)   Do not know

Which one is your answer?

Another story happened soon after this one. One Black American lady was making a speech and someone filmed her saying that while she was working for the US government, she received a request for help from a White farmer, but because he was White she didn't help him to the fullest extent.

This video was shown on TV and the President's staffers called her boss and demanded to fire her or to ask her to resign immediately. She resigned, but soon it was discovered that in her speech she was talking about her prejudice that she had twenty years ago and how she is now ashamed of it. She was sharing this experience with the listeners in order for them to not repeat her mistakes.

The President again began to apologize and called her on the phone to offer her another better job, than the one she was forced to resign from.

Do you think the President learned all the facts of the case before the White House forced this Black American lady to resign?

    a)   Yes

    b)   No

    c)   Do not know

Now tell me—do you want such president that acts before he learns the facts, do you want him to make decisions about nuclear submarines and attacking Russia or any other country?

a) Yes

b) No

c) Do not know

Do you want such a president to make decisions that may affect life of the United States of America and the world? Or you want him out of the White House as soon as possible?

Riddle #8 - the iPhone Question

A thief stole your iPhone. Is it good or bad, or you do not have an opinion?

It was yours, now he enjoys it. But let's say that he uses this iPhone only 50% of the time, and allows his handicapped friend to use it the rest of the time … does it make it OK to steal your phone?

How about if from time to time he allows an older neighbor to make a call when he needs to go to a hospital or see a doctor? Does it make it OK to steal your phone?

How about if the thief said to all his neighbors: "You also can use this phone … put your names on the list and each will have an opportunity to use it." Does it make it OK to steal your phone?

How about if he tells YOU that you can be on the list and from time to time use this phone … does it make it OK to steal your phone?

Thinking out loud:

Q1 - Is there such a thing as "good thief" and "bad thief?" A Bad thief probably would be a person who steals from you for himself, and a good thief would be the one who steals from you and will allow others to use the stolen property…Would you feel better about stolen computer or iPhone if it will be stolen by a good thief rather than by a bad thief?

a) Yes

b) No

c) Do not know

<u>Comment of a Progressive / Socialist</u>: It is a shame to spend hundreds of dollars and buy an iPhone when millions of people in Africa and India are hungry.

<u>Comment of a True Liberal / Capitalist</u>: Of course it doesn't matter who stole your belongings. Being in total control of your property is the first postulate of happiness.

<u>Author's opinion—Right answer is</u>: b

Riddle #9 - The Dream House

Jim and his wife Debby had a dream. They wanted to build a house that will be exactly as they envisioned. Two story, three bedrooms on the first floor, and a huge studio full of Sunlight on the second floor. Jim always wanted a great study for his collection of dolls and Debby felt that on weekends she wanted to paint. They had two small children, a boy and a girl and hoped that the kids will follow their hobbies. They worked hard and with the money they earned, they bought a parcel of land on an edge of their town bordering forest, near a beautiful creek. All four were very ecstatic about the place, especially the children, who imagined how they will play with their friends in the back yard and the forest. It took Jim and Debby another three years to build the house. This was a huge effort but the house was exactly what they dreamed of. They moved to the new house and felt happy beyond belief.

The town they lived in had some financial trouble. The mayor and the city council started many social programs they considered important. They fed the poor, organized a shelter for abused women, created re-educational schools where people who lost their jobs were learning new professions, gave subsidies to underprivileged families, paid rent for single mothers and created a series of musical concerts for under-employed. For all that they had to hire a lot of new employees, pay their salaries, medical insurance and other benefits. They also had to rent several additional buildings to conduct those programs and house employees who were involved in those initiatives. The town was also sending some money to starving children abroad and was subsidizing a cancer and aids research at a local college. The city councilmen were very proud of their achievements.

At a certain point, the mayor realized that there was not enough money to conduct those programs. The city council discussed cutting several programs, but they were unable to decide which ones are more impor-tant than others. All those programs were said to be important and necessary for the good of the community.

At that time, a real estate developing company was looking for a place to build a huge regional shopping center. The taxes received from such center would resolve the financial difficulties of the town. The town would get fees for the use of the land and taxes for the goods sold, and it would save the town's social programs.

The only problem was that the real estate people wanted the same land on which Jim and Debby's house was built. If not this parcel, they said, they also have a very good offer from a neighboring town and they would build their mall over there.

When Jim and Debby were approached with a proposition to move to a different place, they answered that they will not move out of their dream house even if they will be paid ten times what their property is worth.

Thinking out loud:

Q1 - What shall the people of the town do and why:

    a)   Apologize to Jim and Debby for disturbing their lives; tell the real estate developer to go to another town and start cutting some of the social programs that they do not have money for?

b) Move Jim & Debby by force out of their dream house disregarding their wants and desires and pay them its "market value"?

c) Burn Jim & Debby's house to the ground and run their family out of town?

d) Raise taxes on well-to-do citizens in order to pay for the programs for the poor

<u>Comment of a Progressive / Socialist</u>: Since many people would benefit from the shopping center taxes and payments, disregard what the owners of the house and the land want, kick them out of the property, pay them the fair price, and get the shopping center built in town. Then after the mall is built, hit those capitalists with as much taxes and fees as possible and initiate additional social programs for the poor.

<u>Comment of a True Liberal / Capitalist</u>: Try to offer Jim and Debby such a wonderful offer that they wouldn't be able to refuse ... if this doesn't work offer real estate developers another place, offer incentives to stay in town, cut taxes, offer free garbage removal, no electrical bills for the first year, participation in marketing ... and convince them to decorate shopping center's walls with Debby's paintings. Then invest the town's money into promotion of the center. Conduct competitions and festivals in the shopping center that would bring even more people into the town, subsidize opening of gift shops selling local handmade merchandise, additional restaurants and kid's theme park in the town, and create more jobs and a better life for its citizens. New jobs will bring much more joy and benefits to the town folks than all the social programs combined. The best unemployment benefit is a well-paid job.

If the deal with the RE developer is not working, move on and do not bother Jim and Debby again.

<u>Author's view—Right answer</u>: a

Did you ever hear about Lynch trials? How the mobs in American past killed (they called it lynched") people that they called "colored?" The mob was usually white, and the person whom they lynched was always Black American.

A band of white people would capture a black guy and vote to hang him or not. The majority (those that captured the guy) was for hanging him, and the minority (the guy who was captured) was against it. This was pure democracy in action. The question is—would you want to live under a rule when the majority can do whatever they want to the minority disregarding what the minority wants or likes?

Do you think it is OK to force the minority do what the majority wants? Would it make you happy if you were the minority?

You may recall us talking earlier about what each and every person wants. Each and every person wants to be happy. Each and every person can be happy if he or she is allowed to pursue the happiness of his choice without interference of others.

Does democracy (majority tells minority what to do) look like it is the way to allow <u>all the people</u> to pursue happiness they envisioned without others telling them what they can or can't do?

Do you know how those people who are told what to do, where to go, how to live their lives and how they will be compensated for their labor called? Yes, you guessed it, they were called slaves.

Hopefully now you understand why freedom is mentioned in the Declaration of Independence as a must have in order to be happy. Happiness without freedom is impossible.

Riddle #10 - Greed Builds Roads

Ronny lived in a small village on a South Side of a steep canyon with a fast and dangerous river on the bottom. On the North side of the canyon was the center of the valley with all the stores, post office, a barber shop and a movie theater, so lots of people from the South Side were going back and forth every day, making several miles detour to reach a place to make a safe passage.

Everyone was complaining about it but no one did anything. Ronny calculated how many times villagers cross the canyon every day and saw an opportunity to make a lot of money and to serve the village at the same time. He decided to build a bridge to shorten the way. He asked villagers what they would pay if he would build such a bridge. Everyone was very supportive of the idea and encouraged Ronny to build the bridge.

Ronny worked for two years, invested a lot of his own money, borrowed more and then even more. He worked hard, was in danger many times but finally he built the bridge. He began to charge for the passing exactly the amount he and the villagers agreed on. The bridge's cost was higher than he expected but he decided to honor his word and charge what he said he would charge.

From the beginning, all those who wanted to get to the North Side were happy to pay knowing well how much time and effort this bridge saved them. Ronny was happy too. He was becoming the richest man in the town and was looking into other projects he could do in order to better lives of the people and make money for himself.

In a little while, quite unexpectedly to Ronny, the villagers began to tell him that he is sucking their blood and getting paid for nothing.

Ronny offered villagers to use the bridge for free during weekends and holidays, offered not to charge children and seniors, but all that made people even angrier. During the next town hall, the villagers decided to make this bridge the people's property, charge money for passing themselves and make Ronny an employee of the village. When Ronny said that this is unfair and he will not agree to that the villagers asked him to leave the village.

The reasoning of the villagers was that since there is only one bridge that connects the two sides of the valley, there is no fair competition and that allows Ronny to charge as they said "exorbitant" prices. They called a business that has no competition a "monopoly" and argued that this is unacceptable.

<u>Thinking out loud</u>:

Did the bridge help people?—Yes. It was good.

Did the bridge produce profit for Ronny?—Yes. It was also good.

Did Ronny steal materials to build the bridge?—Looks like he paid for all labor and materials with his own money, and when he ran out of money he borrowed some more. No stealing here.

Did the property that Ronny built the bridge on belong to anyone, or was that a no man's land?—Looks like no one owned the property. Ronny discussed the building of the bridge with the only people that could possibly have a claim on this land, the South Side villagers. They wholeheartedly agreed for him to build the bridge.

Ronny didn't steal, cheat, rob anyone and he did something that was good for him and for others.

Now, we know that Ronny invested his time and effort, his own money and the borrowed money to build the bridge. Would it be possible for Ronny to miscalculate, spend all this time, effort and money and build a bad bridge that no one would want to use?—Yes of course. There are many instances when people invest money, time and effort but they fail to make a profit on their ventures.

Would anyone compensate Ronny for his time and pay him money he spent and borrowed if he would make a bad calculation?—Looks like the risk was his. If something bad would happen, he was the only one to suffer. When a businessman miscalculates and loses money, no one compensates him for that. It is his loss, his and only his. So if a businessman gains something from his projects, the gain (profit) shall be his and only his.

Now, do you think that if the bridge is making money—Ronny should be compensated for his time, efforts and the investment?

Do you think that if Ronny would be getting back his investment and profits it was bad for anyone? Did he cheat anyone in order to get profits?—Looks like he didn't.

Did Ronny force the people to cross the bridge?—No he didn't force anyone. They had a choice to pay and use bridge or not to pay and go the long way around.

Would people use Ronny's bridge if they would find an easier, simpler and cheaper way to cross the canyon?—No they wouldn't.

Whose bridge was it, Ronny's or the villagers?—Everything points to Ronny.

Do you think that the villagers would take the bridge from Ronny if the crossing would be free of charge?—No, they said it is because he is charging too much, not because it is unlawful or bad for the environment, or anything else. Just too expensive. The whole point is—they wanted the bridge in order to shorten the way to the West Side but they do not want to pay for it.

Q1 - Now to the big question—did they have a right to take Ronny's bridge from him? What do you really think?

   a) Yes?

   b) No?

   c) Do not know? I was not paying attention.

Comment of the Progressive / Socialist: No one person can own a bridge? It should always be communal property. If one person or one company can own it, one day they can decide to close it, or charge ten times more, or something else. Roads, bridges, lakes and oceans are not private property and can't be.

Comment of the True Liberal / Capitalist: First of all the bridge wouldn't even exist if not for Ronny. He created this bridge. Oceans and lakes are part of nature. Roads and bridges are built by people. If someone created something, it is his property, unless he cheated, bullied, stole it or part of it.

Author's view—Right answer is: b

Maybe, just maybe freedom is a right to do with your belongings (yourself, your thoughts and your things) whatever you want in order to pursue happiness the way you understand it without inflicting harm to other people and their properties. And the law in this case shall be—to stop others from interfering with your pursuits and you from interfering with theirs.

Simple? Yes, but very difficult to achieve

Chapter IV

Do you think people like to be free, or they prefer to be enslaved?

ARE YOU FOR slavery ... or against it ... or do you think that slavery is sometimes OK, and sometimes not? For example most of the people say they're against slavery ... but what do they mean by that? Is a slave a Jew who carries large stones to build a pyramid in Egypt, or is he a Black African man who works on the plantations of the American past? Is slavery a thing of the past or are there modern day slaves in America or other countries?

To determine that, we need to find out what is a "slave." You say that you are against slavery, but maybe you just do not exactly know what it is? Or maybe each of us is saying the same words while thinking about different things.

What is common among all slaves, disregarding when they lived, the country they were enslaved by or their race, gender, age? Are they all bold? Maybe they all very short? Maybe they all came from Bulgaria? Or they all lost something and this loss made them slaves? Yes, they all lost their freedom. Hopefully you answered that they had no freedom.

If a person can't change the place where he lives without getting permission from his master ... and he can't change his work place without permission, and he can't chose his food, his clothes and he can't say to his master what he wants to say without being punished … do you think he is in charge of his belongings and himself?

a) Yes

b) No

c) Maybe

No, he is not. He is not a free person.

If a person can be restricted in his movements at any moment, if a person can lose his freedom of movement, his freedom of speech, if the fruits of his labor can be taken from him without him being compensated, or his other belongings can be taken from him at any moment of his life, than indeed he is enslaved. And the person who forced him into slavery is his Slave Master.

What if that happened not because the Slave Master forced a person to serve him, but because the Slave Master tricked him into it? Would it still be called slavery if this was done without using brutal force?

Of course it is. How a person lost his freedom and his belongings is unimportant. The important thing is—is he in charge of his actions and belongings, or is someone else in charge? Either you're in total control of your actions and belongings, or another person is in control.

How about if a person worked for a period of time and was waiting for an agreed upon compensation, but when the payday came, he was told that he will not be paid? Was he in fact a slave of someone who used coercion to make him work without compensation?

How about if a person was told that he would receive a certain amount of money for his work and he worked hard for the money, but he was paid only one half? Was he in fact a slave for the half of the time he worked? Or maybe he was enslaved for the whole amount of time because he wouldn't agree to work for a half of the pay.

What if a person worked and got his money but someone stole this money from him? Where those robbers in fact enslaving him for the time he worked for the money?

If he would know that he will not get the benefits from his work, he wouldn't work, right? They stole his money which means they stole his time. They stole his freedom for this time and in fact made him a slave during that period.

Would you want to work for two days but get compensation for one? Would you feel that you were enslaved for the day you worked but wasn't paid for?

Would you feel happy about agreeing to perform a certain work for certain compensation, but after fulfilling your end of the bargain you do not get paid for the work? Would you feel happy being enslaved or would you prefer to make your own decisions and do only things that you yourself decided to do.

What if the person who took your money didn't have a car or had a small and old one and wanted to buy a new car ... but didn't have enough money and cheated (enslaved) you in order to buy a new car? Would you feel better knowing that he did it because he needed a new car or would you still feel that you do not want to be cheated?

What if the apartment he lived in was too small for his family (and situated in a bad neighborhood) and he badly needed a new apartment—and he cheated and enslaved you because he badly needed a larger apartment? Do you now feel better or you still wouldn't want to be cheated and enslaved? Would you want to decide whom to help and whom not to help by yourself?

Do you think it is OK to cheat and enslave people when someone wants larger apartments or new cars?

What if his daughter was sick and he cheated you because he needed money for the surgery? Would you now feel better being cheated and enslaved? Do you think it is OK to cheat people when someone's daughter is sick?

Riddle #11 - Island's Jewelry

On a beautiful island in the middle of the ocean lived a ten-year old girl by the name Shal'a. She lived with her mother who was sick and couldn't work and with a five-year old sister named Mona. Their father, who was a fisherman, died during one tropical storm. Shal'a's mom was making jewelry from the seashells and Shal'a was selling them to the tourists who were coming to the islands to spend their vacations bathing in the warm waters of the famous island's Laguna.

There were other children selling shells. Most of the kids were trying to make an extra buck, but for Shal'a selling jewelry to tourists was the only way to make a living.

The biggest dream Shal'a had, was to go to a beachfront restaurant and order a huge bowl of ice cream with lots and lots of whipped cream that children of the tourists were often having.

One day a cargo ship brought a dozen kiosks to the island and soon the kiosks were everywhere and filled with wonderful tourists attractions, such as factory made chains of shells, key chains with the island insignia, caps with printed palms and other wonders that the tourists loved to buy as a memory about the place they visited. From this day, the business of selling shells died. The children were trying to sell their homemade goods but one by one they dropped out and went to do something else. But not Shal'a; she simply couldn't quit. She knew that her family had no other means of survival. For a while she was the only child trying to sell shells and compete with the kiosks. People were buying from her from time to time, but mostly out of pity, not because they wanted her stuff.

"There are people who came to the island, fell in love with it and wanted to take home a small reminder. They are ready to spend money on it, but they are not buying from me. It means I am offering them the wrong product"—Shal'a thought. Maybe she thought this thought in a bit of a different way, but this was the essence of her conversation with herself. "I need to give them something they really want," she decided.

Shal'a looked around their house and didn't find anything that might have been of interest to the tourists. But she knew that she has no right to quit. Then she remembered that the tourists loved to make photos of themselves on a background of the ocean, mountains and palms. And an idea struck her. The next day, she and Mona all dressed up in the islanders' traditional costume, with jewelry and flowers in their hair, and were at the main islands promenade where hundreds of tourists were walking and enjoying magnificent views.

Shal'a put a sign "Photo with Little Mona—$1" and a display of exactly the same jewelry Mona had on herself. The first couple stopped even before she was ready. They would love to have their photos with Mona, they said. They paid a dollar and in addition bought two necklaces with shells. While they were photographing each other with the smiling and giggling Mona on their lap two more couples stopped by. Then two more and then some.

By the end of the day Mona was photographed by more than a hundred couples. Shal'a sold every piece of jewelry she brought from home and everything that other children brought from their homes. The next day Shal'a had several photos of Mona with tourists displayed all over the island and two kids were running around looking for clients. She struck a deal with a photographer and several cab drivers who would now offer photo tours to see Mona all around the island.

Shal'a has never made that much money before. She was helping other children by hiring them to do different jobs in her little enterprise. Once a week, Shal'a was taking all the kids who worked for her to the most expensive restaurant on the island and ordering them ice cream with as much whipped cream as they wanted.

Thinking out loud:

Q1 - Why did the tourists stop buying jewelry from kids and began to buy at kiosks?

    a)   Because the children didn't want to make money?

    b)   Because kiosks offered better quality products?

    c)   Because all tourists are racists?

Q2 - Why did the tourists come back to Shal'a and begin to buy jewelry from her?

    a)   Because they were forced by the Island's government

    b)   Because they suddenly felt bad about not buying from children

    c)   Because they learned her story

    d)   Because Shal'a offered them something attractive and affordable

Comment of a Progressive / Socialist: rich people shall be taxed more in order to give more money to the poor. The money shall be given to all people who do not work, to all women who had children without husbands, to all people who were sick and injured, and for all people who are of a retirement age. The money given to the poor shall be sufficient enough to let them live a good life … and if the rich of the island do not have enough money, or if there are no rich on the island, then Americans shall pay for everything.

Comment of a True Liberal / Capitalist: Shal'a is smart, shrewd and will soon become rich. Only rich people have money to invest in new businesses so it is good when someone becomes rich. They employ other people and improve the standard of living of everyone around them. If more people like Shal'a would live on the island, the islanders would have a good life much faster.

Author's opinion—Right answers are:

Q1 - b

Q2 - d

Riddle #12 - Share or Not to Share

There was an island not far from the shores of the United States of America where ten thousand people lived good lives by tropical farming. They grew coconuts and sold them to representatives of food factories, who used to come to the island during the fall and bid for the produce. The islanders were very nice and peaceful people and were governed by a circle of elders. From the sales of coconuts they were able to pay for the goods they wanted to buy, and services including medical assistance that they desired to have. Some islanders had farms, some organized businesses for tourists who loved quiet beaches and coral snorkeling, and yet some were intermediaries in the coconut trade and merchants for the goods the islanders wanted to bring from other islands

One day however a group of thieves stole coconuts that were prepared for shipping to one of the factories, and the islanders began to think how to protect themselves so such a thing will not happened to them again.

The unanimous decision was to hire guards and have them around the clock patrol the island and surrounding waters. Every islander agreed to pay one tenth of their earnings to those brave people in uniform who would day and night guard their borders and make sure that the streets of the island were safe as well. The elders found an experienced military leader to organize total protection of the island from any hoodlums, bandits, thieves and pirates.

From this moment on, the islanders began to pay a tenth of their earnings to the guards in order to protect themselves, their families and their belongings. They paid their share every month for several years, but one day the Leader came up with an idea to build a wall around the island to be able to protect the island even better. He came with this idea to the elders and they agreed that it is a very much needed project and decided that the islanders should pay a bit more money to build this wall. The islanders didn't vote and didn't agree to this increase in pay, but it was a very small increase and no one refused.

Then a little bit later the Leader came to the elders and said that they need to build an "Elders Hall" where they can meet and discuss important state issues. The elders liked the idea of an air conditioned hall with soft armchairs, rooms for every member of the council and young secretaries taking their calls and making coffee for them, and voted to take a bit more money from each islander to build this great hall ... and a bit more to build a "guard communication center"... and a bit more to organize a very important "financial stabilization fund"—the money that any islander would be able to use if he or she had bad luck with the business they were doing.

When some of the islanders began to protest, they were told that they are selfish and egotistic people who do not care about their neighbors, and they were hushed up again.

A bit later the Leader and the elders announced that they are planning to build a large medical facility very much needed for all those that have no money to pay for the medical services. And again since governments have no money and the only source of money governments have is what we the people give them, the elders and the Leader decided to take money that they need for the facility from the only people who have money—from those who earned them by making goods and providing services.

The Leader wasn't sure the islanders would give him the money he needed for this project. This is why he decided to announce it during a live TV broadcast from the Triangular Office in the Elders Hall. He sat down in a huge armchair surrounded by elders dressed in dark three-piece suits (some with ties and some with bow ties) in front of TV cameras and told the islanders that since it is very important to have this medical center, it is imperative from now on for everyone to send the government three times more money than before. Then he added that the Council entrusted him with the right to audit the accounting records of every islander and imprison those that didn't pay its share of the spendings. The Leader said that he is hiring hundreds of special agents knowledgeable in auditing financial records of businesses and individuals and that those agents will be paid from the money the islanders will now pay. All those islanders, he said, who work hard and earn money will have to pay not only the amount that was agreed upon, but also additional money they never agreed to pay. And the reason for that armed robbery, he said, because we the Government can do it and get away with it. We write laws, he said, and we write them the way we want.

The money will be taken from the islanders against their will. In other words, the Leader and his Circle of Elders took the islanders' belongings without their permission and in effect … robbed and enslaved them.

Do you think that the islanders are in charge of their bodies, ideas and things? Do you think they can pursue happiness any way they want? Do you think their properties were not harmed?

I am sure all the people who needed this medical facility on the Island would applaud the Leader taking money and property of others in order to help THEM. However, they are not parting with their money. They are getting something that doesn't belong to them. It is not theirs to decide what to do with it.

Also, most likely there will be nurses and doctors, and construction workers who would also cheer the Leader for robbing the "rich" islanders. But does it make it OK if they all would agree to rob you or your family from your belongings in order to build a hospital or to build a road or to create storage for old perishable films?

Thinking out loud:

Q1 - Do you want your government to receive only what your family agreed to give them and spend it on the projects you gave them permission to—or do you agree to give them any amount of money they decide to take from you for any project THEY want? Are you OK with the government taking whatever it thinks is needed for the good of the country as THEY understand this "good?" Do you think your family shall decide what to do with the money your family earns, or do you think that someone else shall decide what to do with the money you guys earned? Here are the multiple choices of a few different opinions:

a) My family is stupid and has no idea how to spend the money my parents earn. I want the government of the country to take from us as much money as they want, and spend it the way they want without ever consulting with any one of us

b) If my family is smart enough to earn money, it is smart enough to decide how to spend what we have earned. We ourselves are supposed to decide what to do with our belongings. No one has a right to rob us, steal from us or enslave us. America is the land of the free, or at least it was created this way.

c) Other _____ (what?)

Comment of a Progressive / Socialist: The larger the government is, the better it is for the country. The government will assure that everyone is equal and there is no one that suffers from the absence of medical and other care.

Comment of a True Liberal / Capitalist: Do not touch what I earned! I will share with others when I will decide to share. If you will convince me that the projects you want to do are good and necessary, I will give you what I can. If I will find them unnecessary and wasteful, I will not give you anything. Also, only people who keep their earnings are able to invest in new businesses. They hire new people; they create jobs and give work to other small and large businesses. If you will take this "additional" money from them, they will not be able to move the economy forward. That will be bad for everyone.

<u>Author's opinion—Right answer</u>: b

Is it important to you who is stealing from you? Would you prefer a tall blond guy to steal your belongings or you prefer a short red haired girl to steal your belongings? Would you prefer a dirty smelly robber to steal your money or do you prefer a good smelling guy in a three-piece suit smiling to the cameras to steal your money?

Or you do not care; you just do not want your belongings to be stolen?

Riddle #13 - Free in the Name Only

It happened many years ago in a huge and cold country called Russian Empire. Half of this Empire's population were slaves who worked the land and in small factories, served their masters, but didn't have a right to move from place to place or change their jobs and had no say in how they would be compensated for their labor.

Somewhere in this vast Empire, in a small village called Ivanovo, lived two peasants with the same common name Ivan. Ivan 1 was a slave. He worked at a farm owned by his master. He used to get up at six in the morning and work until sunset. He tried to not work hard, always took the longest road to work and back, and walked his slowest walk. His heart wasn't in anything he was ordered to do.

Doesn't matter if you work better or worse, you get nothing either way, was his philosophy.

When he was sick, the village doctor who was paid by his master visited him and prescribed him medicine. Ivan 1 was the property of his master and the master wanted him to function smoothly and therefore took good care of him like you would take good care of your horse or a truck.

Ivan 1 never left the valley he was born at. For that he needed a permit from his owner, and he knew that the owner wouldn't give him such a permit. Ivan 1 didn't have any ID papers and if he would escape, the police would stop him and return him back to his owner.

At the end of each season Ivan 1 was given enough food to survive until the next season, some clothing, and other "bare minimum" life necessities. Ivan 1 was allowed to have a cow and a small vegetable garden. He and his wife often went to the nearby forest to collect berries or mushrooms to add to their family diet.

Ivan 2 was a free man. He was once a slave, but was freed by a Tsar's decree because he served for twenty-five years in the Tsar's army. Ivan 2 was happy to be a free man, especially because he had some money that was paid him for his twenty-five years of service. He bought himself a parcel of farmland, a cow, built a house and settled very close to Ivan 1.

Before Ivan 2 started his small farm, he made all calculations of how much money he will need to invest, what are the costs and how much he will keep after selling the produce and paying all the expenses and taxes. The sum wasn't huge, but he planned for many years ahead and he liked the outcome. He foresaw his children going to college; saw his wife adding cows and starting her own dairy business; saw vacations in warm places and things that are not necessities, but life pleasures. He was a hard worker and he knew that he could achieve all he dreamed about.

He worked from six in the morning until sunset and then some. In the middle of the night he sometimes would wake up after a dream about a fire in his barn or foxes eating his chickens and would go check on his belongings. He was very proud of achievements. He loved his family and wanted them all to have a good life.

You work hard trying to achieve your goal and you will succeed, was his philosophy.

At the end of the year Ivan 2 sold his produce, paid mortgage and rent on the land he used for his small vegetable garden, interest on the financing of the cow, doctor's services and drugs, local stores for clothes he and his family purchased, sugar, salt and other food products they had to buy at a store and put aside a sum that his household was supposed to pay in taxes. The remnants were exactly as he calculated and that made him happy. This was his dream coming true. Until the Imperial tax collector came.

In addition to the previously agreed upon amount, the collector told Ivan 2, there is a war going on someplace and the soldiers need to be paid. The ammo is also very expensive these days. You will have to pay your fair share to contribute in this war effort.

We are thinking about starting another war and will take from you a bit more money to cover this new war expense as well. On another note, our beloved Tsar built his twenty-eighth palace and now has twenty-eight thousand servants to cater to his needs. I hope you understand that those servants have to be paid. You will have to help us with that as well. Now, a huge amount of guests will arrive for the soon-to-be Queen's birthday and she needs five-hundred hairdressers, and they are damn expensive. You shall pay for the hairdressers and do not forget to chip in for dentists for all of the Tsar's ballerinas. They have to have good teeth because they smile a lot.

After he left, Ivan 2 had only half of the money he thought he would have, but then the County Collector came.

Since you used the roads, went to forests to pick berries and mush-rooms, used the sun for tanning and growing your vegetables and wind to bring rain to the crops, and it all happened in our county, you shall pay the regional government as well.

The village elder took the rest of the money. Ivan 2 was so distressed that he even didn't ask why he has to pay him as well.

Ivan 1 came to visit Ivan 2.

"The Emperor has a right to tax you any time he needs money, and he doesn't even have to explain anything. He decides that he needs more and he taxes you. If you think that this is happening only in our country, look at the United States of America. They do not have the Tsar or Emperor, but they have a congress. The congress has a right to tax Americans and the congress constantly invents reasons to take as much money from people like you and I as they want. Russia has one emperor, but in America have five hundred emperors!" This is what Ivan 1 told Ivan 2 as they looked at what was left after all those tax collectors' visits.

"You worked hard day after day," continued Ivan 1: "You were worried sick about your crops and chickens, your mortgage and your bills, your ability to pay the doctor and all other things an owner of a small business worries about. I am called a slave. And I am a slave. I do not worry about anything and do not care about the results of my work. At the end of the day, you and I get exactly the same—we barely survive. They make me work and do not pay. They do not force you to work but take whatever you produce. You say that you are not a slave, that you are a free man? You are a free man in the name only. Truly, I think that you are more slave than I."

Ivan 2 didn't like it. He didn't like it a bit.

Q1 - Was Ivan 2 a free man or is he a slave?

  a) Of course he is a free man. He can move to another place, he can sell his house and buy another, or not buy one at all. He can work here or there, or not to work at all—and beg for money at a street corners. He can do whatever he wants.

  b) Ivan 2 is a slave exactly as Ivan 1.

  c) There are probably many different kinds of slavery and different degrees of enslavement. One is harsher, another is milder, but neither of the two Ivan's is free.

Comment of a Progressive / Socialist: The government (can be Tsars, Kings or socialists) are in charge of their countries and know what is good for the country and what effort or money they need to provide for the citizens. This is why they are entrusted with a right to collect as much money as the country needs. The story about two Ivans is not true. The good government will not touch workers or small business owners. They will get what is needed from the rich who can afford to part with the spare money they have.

<u>Comment of a True Liberal / Capitalist</u>: Let's recall what question we shall ask to resolve this question. Does Ivan 2 have in total (100%) charge of his belongings? His body is his. No one tells him where to go, where to work, or where to live. His thoughts are also his—no one steals his ideas. How about his belongings? He earned money in order to buy things he wanted to buy for himself and his family. He earned money in order to maybe invest in new business, or education or travel. Someone came and took his money. This someone didn't ask politely, they came and took, and said that it was done according to a decree by the government. They steal his money, his belongings, but attempted to cover their robbery by making it "legal." If Ivan 2 wouldn't pay what THEY decided he was supposed to pay he would be punished, and his property or his freedom would be taken from him. Is it freedom? Or it is slavery? Maybe a different slavery then the old South plantation days or the Egyptian variety of the Biblical times, but it still is slavery.

<u>Author's opinion—Right answer</u>: c

Can we now safely conclude that people do not like to be enslaved? Yes we can! This is the Third Postulate of the Volitional Science "<u>People do not want to be enslaved in any shape or form</u>."

Chapter V

Can you and I be wrong?

MAYBE YOU AND I are wrong? Maybe people like to be ordered around? Maybe they want to exchange their belongings including freedom for three hot meals a day plus an air conditioner during hot summer nights? Maybe for them, it is much more important to feel safe than to be free?

Is there a way to distinguish right from wrong? Is there an absolute right that is right for everyone?

Can smart people be wrong? Can your teacher be wrong? Can your school principal, senator or even the President be wrong? Can your dad be wrong? Can you as a dad be wrong? How can you, yourself, distinguish between wrong and right? How to make a scientific, like in math or physical science determination—what is right and what is wrong?

Did you ever hear about a guy by the name of Aristotle? I am sure you did. He was born three hundred years before Christ and was the teacher of Alexander the Great. He was also the most famous scientist in the world and for thousands of years people thought that he never made any mistakes, and that everything he ever said was an absolute truth.

Among other things he said, was that all celestial bodies (planets, stars) are of a perfect form. There was no one to dispute it, so people for more than two thousand years thought that the Moon for example was like a billiard ball, a perfect sphere.

Nineteen hundred years after this dude Aristotle dies comes a fellow by the name of Galileo Galilee who was an astronomer and worked at a university in Italy and some say was curious beyond normal human curiosity. It is a very excellent human quality and the one that led us to inventing wheels, taming animals, flying to the Moon, having agricultural crops and using computers instead of old papyrus scrolls.

Galileo heard that the Dutch created a tube that would enable people to see objects closer (this was the telescope of course) and immediately constructed one of his own ... and pointed it at the Moon. Remember, at that time everyone was sure that the Moon was like a billiard ball, perfectly shaped and bold. To his astonishment, Galileo saw mountains on the moon. The moon wasn't a perfect sphere after all.

WOW!—He said to himself and ran to his neighbors to show that there are mountains on the moon. One by one he showed everyone those mountains and everyone who saw them was saying "I see them; there are mountains on the moon! Aristotle was wrong!" Then Galileo brought his telescope to an astronomy department in the university where he worked.

The astronomers were all followers of Aristotle and they KNEW that the moon was bold and a perfect sphere. They KNEW that there were no mountains on the moon. Aristotle said that and he was the guy who never made any mistakes, right?

At first, they didn't even want to look into this stupid thing called telescope. Then the head of the astronomers, who knew the whole Aristotle writings by heart looked at the moon, saw the mountains and said "Yes, we all see the mountains on the Moon, and we know at the same time that there can't be mountains on the moon because the great Aristotle said that the moon is a perfect sphere. So the only explanation is that there is a thick layer of ice that is unseen to us but that covers all the mountains and makes the Moon a perfect sphere."

Interesting, right? The guy, a famous scientist as a matter of fact, looks in a telescope, sees mountains and says that there are absolutely no mountains on the Moon because so and so said that. Do you still think that if something is written in a book, or if something was said by a great man of the past or the present, it is a complete and absolute truth? Do you still think that the Moon is a bold and a perfect sphere, like a billiard ball ... or you know by now from the people who landed on the Moon that there is no ice covering it and there are pretty stiff mountains on the Moon's surface?

Let me tell you a bit about Galileo. He was a guy who was always testing everything; even if his teachers and colleagues would say that something is an absolute truth and no tests are required. His teachers were often upset with him because he would not believe what they would tell him unless he himself checked and verified it.

Same thing happened when Galileo decided to check another one of the Aristotle's statements that heavier objects fall to the ground faster than the light ones. "Do not waste your time," his colleagues in Pisa University told him. "Look how slow a piece of paper falls to the ground and how much faster a stone or a knife falls."

But Galileo took two stones of different weight, one large and another small, climbed to the top of the Pisa Tower, the world famous tilted tower, and released them at the same time. One stone was much heavier than another, but they hit the ground at the same time. Galileo repeated this exercise many times and every time the stones were reaching the ground at exactly the same time.

Galileo invited his students and the faculty of the university to witness the amazing discovery he made. They all came, saw that the stones of different weight were released at the same time and reached the ground at the same time and ... fired Galileo from the University.

Galileo left and the university continued to teach their students that heavier objects were falling to Earth faster than lighter objects.

Do you still believe everything written in the books?

For centuries people thought that the earth was flat ..."Otherwise" they argued, "all the water would escape from it." Try to pour water on a sphere, even on an imperfect one. Now try to pour water into a frying pan ... where the water will hold and from where it will not escape. Now tell me—based on this experiment, can the earth be a globe?

But it is a globe, and we have evidence that without doubt proves that the Earth doesn't look like a frying pan, rather like an egg-shaped ball used in the American football.

Should you believe what you hear and read, or not believe, is a very important question? Do you think that you have to believe everything your teacher says? What about your books—is there an absolute truth in the books that you read or study? How about if your dad says one thing and your teacher or even principal another? Who is right? Who is not? Is there anyone whom you shall believe unconditionally? Is there such an authority among us people whom you shall believe no matter what? Now, we are not talking about following your dad's instructions or orders. This you shall do unconditionally until you are eighteen ... and I would advise to listen to your Mom and Dad even after you are eighteen. We were talking about statements that different people make or write about on how to better live your life—some of them you can hear on TV, some read in books or newspapers, some hear from friends or relatives.

What if your best friend says that the heavier objects fall faster than the light ones—does it make this statement right? If your older brother says so—does it make it right? If your parents said when you were a child that the heavier objects fall faster, does it make it right? How about if the President of the country says that the moon is a perfect sphere and there are no mountains on it—does it make it right?

Do you think Pisa University made a wise decision in expelling Galileo?

Do you think that by expelling Galileo from the University they made heavier objects fall faster than the lighter ones?

Do you think that if two people think that something is true, that makes it true?

Do you think that if ten people think that something is true, that makes it true?

Do you think that if ten thousand people think that something is true, that makes it true?

Or you think that only hard scientific evidence can prove that it is true? Evidence that was tested scientifically and was proved beyond any doubt.

Do you think that if scientists were wrong for so long about heavy objects falling on earth and about the moon, is it possible that the science is wrong about anything else, or do you think that now everything scientists say is absolutely right?

Can the Mayor of the city you live in be wrong?

Is it possible that the Mayor says one thing today and another tomorrow? When is he right—yesterday, today or tomorrow?

What about if the next Mayor says something that contradicts what the previous one said? Who then is right—the first Mayor because he was the first, or the last one, because he is now in the office?

Many people say that God created the Sun, Earth and us men. They call it "Creation."

Many others say that men and everything on earth are the products of a slow development from primitive to complex. From an amoeba to dinosaurs and from pterodactyl to a very smart puppy you want so much to have as your friend, and finally to you. They call it "Evolution."

Now let me share with you another "absolute" truth—men were created by … creatures from another galaxy! Those visitors live on the planet that circles the Sun and appears in our skies every three thousand six hundred years. Those creatures came to earth millions of years ago and began to create men from the monkeys. They taught humans to build houses, to write songs, gave us laws and science. They lived through the deluge and were teachers of Moses, Aaron, Kings David & Solomon ... We will call this theory "Intervention."

Does the fact that this theory is printed in this book make it true? This is a good theory and some say that there is a lot of evidence to support it, but it is not yet proven. It is only a theory, not an absolute truth. The fact that it is printed in this or that book proves nothing.

How about another statement that for thousands of years was considered an absolute truth—the Sun is circling the Earth ... together with all the stars and planets?

Thousands of teachers, professors, scientists were absolutely sure that this is true. It was taught at schools and people who doubted this theory were sent to jails ... One famous scientist was burned at stake because he said that this theory is not true. Does the fact that scientists were burned at stakes make those theories true? Does the fact that everyone on Earth was absolutely sure that the Earth is flat make it flat?

Now I have a question—do you think that maybe (just maybe) something that we believe in today, just maybe ... is not true?

Is it possible or it is impossible that one day we will find out that we were mistaken in something that we believed today?

The question is—how to understand which statements are true and which are just wishful thinking or purposely misleading? How to distinguish ... how to sort the truths out?

We will try to attack this question further in the book when we will be talking about the scientific method of verification that helped to distinguish right from wrong in the physical science.

Riddle #14 - Charity

There were two great professors of social studies in this famous University both teaching their students about a need to donate time and money to charities. Both were saying that people shall help others who are in need, who are less fortunate or run into bad circumstances. One, whose name was Professor Indi, was telling his students that it is their moral duty to help when someone is in need. "When you see poverty or suffering, you first shall help, and then ask questions," he used to say. Students of Professor Indi sent money to cases dear to their hearts, volunteered to help sick and homeless and encouraged others to do the same. When they helped someone they felt pride.

Professor Publ told his students that in order to collect more money to help those in need they shall convince the government to adopt new laws forcing everyone to send money to the government. The government, in turn through a specially created department of charities, would find who needs help the most and distribute money among such people. He was saying that the government officials will know much better than simple people whom to give money and whom not to.

Professor Publ argued that there are many people in the country that lived just above the line of poverty and no one shall ask them to donate any money. They are supposed to be exempt from any request for charity or donations, he used to say. They are poor and underprivileged, we shall not forget that. The rich according to Publ were supposed to pay this involuntary donation in the quantities sufficient to help all the needy and sick.

Students of Professor Publ were constantly demonstrating on the streets of the capitol and organized poor and underprivileged to demand re-distribution of the money earned by others. They rarely sent any money to charities themselves.

Thinking out loud:

Q1 - Which one of the two professors is right?

Professor Publ. First, when people are obligated to give, they will have to give more than what they would give voluntarily and second because the government officials know better how to use the money than ordinary citizens. Government officials are trained in money distribution.

Professor Indi. People shall give not because they are obligated, but because they want to help. It is their money and they shall decide what to do with them. All the people, not only the rich shall help those who are in need. Helping others is their moral duty, not government enforced obligation.

Comment of a Progressive / Socialist: Every person shall work according to his abilities and get from the government according to his needs. It is not important if you are a general manager of a huge company or a street sweeper. Both shall work and do their jobs, and both shall live in apartments or houses that they will get from the state. Why does one person needs ten rooms and another lives with his family in one? Why is one person shall be seen by good doctors and another is not able to even get a medical drug?

If however, one has special needs, like a very expensive treatment or medication, the state shall decide to give this person this medication or not. If it is something that is too expensive and the state can't provide it for everyone, then no one will get it, even the President of the country...

Actually maybe the President will get it, and probably the congress people and senators and their families and staff also will get it ... and mayors and governors and their families and their staff ... and the heads of the government departments and agencies ... also famous scientists, sportsmen and entertainers will probably be able to get it as well ... and people who make decisions regarding who can get it and who can't and of course their families ... but no one else.

Others will not get this expensive medicine because it is too expensive. However the bosses of the unions that helped the President's party to get into power will get it. But this is it. No one else, except the President's cook and the First Lady's hairdresser. And their dog's groomer. But this is it.

Comment of a True Liberal / Capitalist: People who insist on establishing special tax to give money to a government entity to distribute among poor shall do just that—give money to the government because the government knows obviously better than THEY what to do with their money. They however can't force others to do the same. People who believe that it is their moral duty to help those in need disregarding how much money they have, shall do just that and teach their children to do the same.

<u>Author's opinion—Right answer</u>: Decide by yourself

Riddle #15 - Tolerance

On another planet intelligent beings eat each other. We can't and shall not do anything about it. We might try to convince them that this is not good from our point of view, but most probably they will tell us that in their opinion there are lots of things that we do that are not good from their point of view. And I am sure they will find plenty of such things.

In Saudi Arabia women are property of men, and men can do with them what they please. We do not like that, but this is their choice and we can't and shall not do anything about it, except telling them that we do not like it. They on the other hand, will probably tell us many things they do not like in what we are doing.

In San Francisco the majority of citizens believes in Global Warming and thinks that Ohioans and Iowans are causing this problem by driving huge trucks and using lots of electricity. In Ohio and Iowa people do not believe in global warming, but instead believe in Global Cooling.

In San Francisco they think that men are responsible. In Ohio they believe that God is responsible, and are quite certain that the Cooling is the God's punishment for the immorality of San Franciscans.

People from Ohio have no right and shouldn't force San Francisco residents to pray in Churches every day to ask God to stop the cooling that they fear. People from San Francisco have no right and shouldn't force people of Ohio to stop driving trucks or force them to pay more for electricity to stop the warming they are afraid of.

Thinking out loud:

Q1 - Both sides very strongly believe in their rightness, and are sure that the other side is causing the problem. What shall they do?

a) San Francisco shall conquer Ohio or otherwise impose their will and make them use less gas and less electricity, and change their cars to smaller ones. The ones that do not obey, shall be imprisoned or sent to concentration camps on remote islands.

b) Ohioans shall conquer San Francisco and make them pray to God to stop Global Cooling

c) Each shall do what they think is needed to be done. Ohioans shall pray to God and San Franciscans shall buy smaller cars and use less electricity. They shall talk to each other; convey their ideas and the reasoning behind them. They might establish mutual scientific or theological commissions to study weather problems and bible and watch respectfully the results of the research.

Comment of a Progressive / Socialist: There is no God, so he can't cause anything. People however cause a lot of problems, and if there is even a slight chance that Global Warming exists and we are the cause, then we need to modify our behavior even before we are certain that there is or there is not the Global Warming and that we are the cause of it.

Comment of a True Liberal / Capitalist: Study the subject. Study the subject. Study the subject. Do not make any drastic moves before you are one hundred percent certain. And then study again. As we all know scientists do make mistakes, and plenty of them. Don't force others to do what you want them to do. Do not allow others to force you to do what you do not want to do. Listen, consider and think. You are the only person who is responsible for your own life.

Author's opinion—Right answer: c

Riddle #16 - Joe, the Bike Lover

There was a boy by the name Joe who loved bikes. Joe loved everything about them—the speed, the beauty, the lightness and the sweat after a long fast run. Joe was good with his hands and he also knew how to fix bikes and make them run their best. Neighbors often brought bikes to him and he took care of them and was making good money fixing them. His father was an ambulance driver, his mom worked at a knitting factory and they were very happy for Joe. They often told him that a bike mechanic is a great profession and it is wonderful that he loved what he was doing. It is very important, his Dad would tell him, to get up in the morning looking forward to what you are about to do during the day.

His Dad loved his work and was very proud of his ambulance and the crew he worked with.

Joe was planning that when he would turn eighteen he would open a small repair shop out of his dad's garage, and gradually work his way up to a small bike store on one of the main streets of the town. Joe had a dream about making his own bikes—he knew exactly how he would do them, but he knew of course that it would take him a long time to get the kind of money he would need to create, test and build bikes.

But then something unexpected happened. When you wait and are ready, then opportunity knocks. It usually knocks only once and if you are not ready for hundred and ten per cent, it goes away.

A bike racing team was training not far from the town. A trailer with the bikes had an accident. It overturned on a freeway and several bikes got damaged. The team had an important competition in a short while and they needed their bikes as soon as possible, and even sooner. The only bike repairman in the vicinity they were told was Joe, and they came to him with an irresistible offer—repair and bring the eleven bikes back to a running condition during one night and we will pay you eleven thousand dollars.

Joe worked like crazy (having his Dad and Mom helping him as they could) and in the morning the eleven bikes were ready and waiting for the sportsmen to pick them up. They were in impeccable condition and the manager of the team shook Joe's hand and gave him an envelope with the eleven thousand dollars.

Joe never saw this much money in his life. His parents never saw so much money in their lives. Joe offered the envelope to them, but his parents told him that he shall decide by himself what to do with the money. If you were smart enough to earn it, you are smart enough to decide what to do with it, they said.

Everyone in town knew about Joe's fortune. This is why he began to get visitors who asked him to donate money to different charities. One asked him to give to an unemployment fund, another to help to abused women and children, still another to single mothers without jobs. Every time any of them began to describe to Joe why the people they represent need Joe's support, Joe would want to cry and was tempted to give all his money to this worthy cause. The only reason he hesitated is because he didn't know who to help first.

Then at night he began to think. If I will give money to the unemployed, they will get a good meal or two, would buy some clothes for their children and maybe will have an opportunity to go to movies once or twice. Then they will be back to poverty and would again need someone to donate in order to survive. Any relief I would provide them would only be temporary. How can I help them permanently?

And then he got it. If I will organize my bike building business, then I will be able to employ several people who otherwise would be unemployed. I will pay them a good salary and as long as my business works, they will have money to eat, pay medical bills and live a good life. And in the process, I will make a lot of money for myself by selling my great bikes, will be able to buy a new house for my parents and will pay my sister's college tuition.

This sounded like a plan to Joe, but all the people who were collecting money for charities and the people who were getting part of the collected money for themselves, told him that he is a dry, unappreciative and selfish person. A local newspaper wrote that Joe didn't want to share his fortune with anyone and showed a photograph of a small girl who would have been cured if people like Joe would share a little of their fortunes with her, but they didn't and she was about to die.

Every fifteen minutes, a local radio station ran a poem by a Korean War veteran who was condemning Joe for not helping people who defended his country, became invalids on service and the likes of Joe made them angry and sad. During the sermon a minister mentioned that he would want to buy new bibles for everyone, and he asked Joe to help, but got no response.

Joe gave some money to the unemployed, some to the minister, some to the veterans' affairs and some to mothers without support. He is repairing bikes from his dad's garage and does not dream anymore about designing and building new bikes.

Thinking out loud:

Q1 - What was better for everyone—if Joe would start a bike factory or to give the money he earned to struggling and suffering people?

    a)   The first priority of every human being is to help others especially if they are suffering

    b)   Joe did an honorable but stupid thing. The best help to an unemployed person is a permanent job

Comment of a Progressive / Socialist: Cheers to Joe. He overcame selfish interests and did the right thing.

Comment of a True Liberal / Capitalist: Joe missed an opportunity to do good to himself and by doing that to do as much good to others. Only rich people can invest in new businesses that will hire people. People with moderate means are usually unable to finance businesses and create new jobs. This is why in order to create new jobs we need as many rich people as possible. Taking from them the money that they can use for creating jobs and giving them to the poor will resolve problems only temporarily. The permanent solution is—new businesses and new jobs!

Author's opinion—Right answer: b

Riddle #17 - Change or no change?

A small village called ZhzuuBb was surrounded by a great farmland that was giving wonderful crops year after year. This is the best field with the best crop in the entire valley or maybe even the best in the entire country, everyone was saying. What a great luck those people from ZhzuuBb have, everyone was constantly saying to each other.

This crop was what fed the whole village, the source of their livelihood. Each villager had a small portion of the field and most of the villagers were happy with the results of their labor.

One day a farmer by the name Joe offered the villagers to fundamentally change the way they grew crops. He said that if ZhzuuBb'ians will follow his advice they will get much more crops with less effort and they will never ever have problems with hunger or sickness. Some cheered Joe's proposal, others said that they have a very good field that feeds them, that most of the time they have a very food life and they do not want to change anything.

Critical thinking:

Q.1 - What should the villagers do?

a) Let Joe change everything and risk their livelihood and their lives

b) Treat Joe as a dangerous crazy person and he should be imprisoned

c) Allow Joe to prove his ideas on a small portion of the land

Comment of a Progressive / Socialist: Joe represents the progress. Those that oppose him represent the conservative point of view but will not be able to stop the progress. The village shall be transformed into a communal ownership of land and means of production and Joe shall become the new leader of the commune. He is the one with the vision and he shall lead the people. The most important thing in life is "change." It is important for villages, town, regions and even countries. We the progressives offer to change the best countries in the world disregarding whether we know the result of the change or not. This is what we did to America!

Comment of a True Liberal / Capitalist: If something is not broken, do not try to fix it. Joe can turn his portion of the field into whatever he wants. If he succeeds, he can reap the benefits and if he fails, it is his choice. If Joe doesn't want to do it alone he shall try to find a group of villagers to do it together or he can convince the whole village that they need a small parcel of land to develop new methods and ways to work the land with more efficiency and better results without interruption of the work on the field. Either way, this will not endanger the livelihood of the villagers. Otherwise it will be as stupid as taking the best country in the world and starting to change the life of the people who live there without hard proof that the new way is better. This is exactly what progressives are doing in America.

Author's opinion—Right answer: c

Riddle #18 - Dog Sitting Business

Tony was a very smart and shrewd young entrepreneur. He saw that many people on the island need dog sitters and organized a dog-sitting agency. He made an agreement with several boys and girls from his school that he would look for jobs and they would share the earnings. He went to many apartment buildings and houses and left flyers everywhere.

People began to call him and asked to sit or walk a dog and Tony would send a boy or a girl to do the job. Tony paid two thirds to the worker and kept one third to himself for the services he was providing. Everyone was happy with such arrangement. More and more people were asking Tony for the services and he hired even more kids to help him. One day he was calculating how much money he made during the previous month and by accident calculated two thirds to him and one third to the dog sitters.

He saw that if he would split the earnings this way he would be getting much more money and he liked it. And he decided to change the rules. He told his dog sitters that from now on they will get one third and he will get two thirds of the money the customers paid for their services.

Next day not a single dog sitter came to work for Tony, they all quit. All the clients were outraged that Tony promised them help but didn't send it. Tony's reputation as a trustworthy businessman was ruined and he had to close his agency.

Critical thinking:

Q1 - Who is responsible for the destruction of a successful business?

    a)   Boys and girls that quit without notice

    b)   Clients who were angry with Tony

    c)   Tony that got greedy on an account of the people who worked for him

    d)   Other _____ (explain)

Comment of a Progressive / Socialist: Businesses belongs to the workers, because those are the people who really work. All Tony did was look for clients and get phone orders. The company shall belong to all workers, not to one person. Each shall be paid equally disregarding how much work they actually do … or at least per hour of work, walking dogs, sitting with dogs, answering phones … If Tony will not agree to this arrangement, force him out of the company and hire another person who will do the job for much less.

<u>Comment of a True Liberal / Capitalist</u>: Toni's company failed because he didn't take into consideration that people who work for him are the most important and valuable asset of his company. Tony was supposed to treat the workers with respect and compensate them according to the terms they agreed upon. Tony is not a smart businessman ... yet. Hopefully he will learn his lesson and in the future he will use his obvious talent in organizing people and starting up companies to achieve better results.

<u>Author's opinion—Right answer</u>: c

Riddle #19 - Best Friends

Bill, Ken and Bob were best friends. They grew in a farm country and dreamed about owning their own land. The three got married and had children and their wives and children became friends as well. One day they found a small uninhabited island and claimed it to themselves.

Upon landing, the three decided to divide the island into three parts and each got its own farm. They were happy to finally call something their own. Bill and Ken worked short hours, celebrated all holidays and planted the same crop they used to work with on the mainland. Bob investigated the earth on the island, decided which crop to plant, prepared irrigation and worked 24/7 for several long months.

Then the storm season came, then came the hot and dry season. The crops Bill and Ken planted dried, but Bob's farm produced great results.

Bob was a good friend and he shared what he got with his friends, told them what they did wrong and helped them with some starting capital to re-start their farms anew.

Bill and Ken blamed their problems on the weather, on condition of earth, on the suppliers, and during the next year they did the same things they were doing the previous year. Not surprisingly they got the very same results.

When they came to Bob for help he told them that he can't help them anymore. Bill and Ken were outraged. They told Bob that money made him a bad person that he has no compassion, and they will not speak to him ever again.

Critical thinking:

Q1 - What shall Bob do?

a) Give Bill & Ken money and food again … and again

b) Tell them to get lost

c) Buy their farms and hire them as workers.

d) Other_____ (explain)

Comment of a Progressive / Socialist: Bill & Ken shall form a democratic government on the island. Under the democracy the majority rules, and they can lawfully force Bob to pay most of his profits to the government and this amount will be divided between the poor (Bill and Ken). If Bob (in the progressive language people like him are called "rich fat cats") will not agree to pay, vote two against one to arrest him, and confiscate his farm. Divide everything he had between them and make Bob-the-prisoner to work for the state. If this will not work, run his farm into the ground and sell everything they can. When nothing valuable will be left, convince Bob to take his farm back, wait until he will rebuild it and confiscate it again. Repeat the cycle as many times as possible.

Comment of a True Liberal / Capitalist: It is very normal that some people are better as business owners then others. They are better organized, able to think several steps ahead (it is called planning), can manage their time and are ready to work hard to achieve their goals. Bob who is by far a better business owner than his friends shall purchase Bill & Ken's farms, hire them to work the land, pay them salary and benefits that they shall negotiate before they start working together.

Probably Bob will soon become a well to do man and by paying Bill and Ken their salaries and providing benefits he will help them, the people who are not able to manage their own businesses, to build a good life. They will not be equal in terms of compensation, but all of them will have bread on their tables and adequate means to survive.

Author's opinion—Right answer: c

Chapter VI

Can what's good for one person be bad for another?
Is there an absolute good that is good for everyone?

WE WERE TOLD as children that "this is good" or "this is bad." We naturally assumed that there are GOOOD things and there are BAAAD things. Is that really so? Or maybe Albert Einstein was right and everything is relative at least in our galaxy?

Riddle #20: Positive Impact of Civilization

An island (I do not want to name it in order not to stir unnecessary emotions) lived a primitive life of no modern medicine, no clean water, hunting, a bit of agriculture ... Out of every five children four were dying at birth or in early childhood. People in general were dying early, in their forties. They had no TV, no philharmonic, no cars, no freeways; their houses were built from mud bricks, not one single high-rise. The tribes on the island were constantly at war and were killing each other and using captured enemies as slaves. There were about two hundred thousand people on the island. Maybe less, maybe more, no one knew for sure.

One day, there came a bunch of "industrialized and educated" White men and said that this situation is unacceptable. First we will help you to clean the water. You will now drink good water. Second we will build a hospital and you will not be losing so many children at birth and they will live much longer lives. Also you will have democracy on the island. We will explain to you how it works later and you will not be fighting each other with spears and knives any more.

And the good men of the progress succeeded beyond belief. Because of the modern medicine, clean water, vitamins, no wars, the island-ers began to live much longer—and the population of the island grew to seven million people. There is not enough food for everyone. There is nothing that the islanders produce that can be sold abroad or exchanged for food. The educated and civilized outsiders built tall apartment houses and office buildings all over the island, and the guys who are in power are corrupt like their colleagues in the Western world or even more.

The islanders can't live without outside help and when help comes, the strongmen and gangs take everything valuable to themselves. They enslave people to work for them and kill them at will. There is no effective justice on the island, and most of the population is starving even more then during the good old days of tribal wars.

The only thing that unites all islanders is their hate for the civilized White people who have so many things the islanders do not have and never knew about, but now desire with all their hearts. The islanders dream about killing all the White men in the world to claim those wonderful things the White men have to themselves.

<u>Critical thinking</u>:

Q1 - Did civilization have a positive impact on the Islanders' lives?

   a) Yes

   b) No

   c) Other _____

<u>Comment of a Progressive / Socialist</u>: It is our obligation and moral duty to help any person who is in need. White people, especially White

males are guilty so much that they have to pay for centuries to remedy their sins and damages they inflicted on the environment and primitive nations.

<u>Comment of a True Liberal / Capitalist</u>: If you want to help people, educate them fist. They will figure out what they want. The goal is not to build their lives instead of them, but to tell them that they have a choice.

<u>Author's opinion—Right answer</u>: your choice

A boy sits at a river bank and eats an apple—is that good?

a) Yes

b) No

c) I need more information

He stole this apple from his friend—does it change anything?

Of course it does.

The part that is not good was in taking someone else's property (belongings) without this person permission … Eating an apple was good for the boy, but it was on account of others … who suffered because he wanted to get this good tasting apple.

A famous runner won a gold medal—is it good that he got the medal?

a) Yes

b) No

c) I need more information

At the beginning of the race he kicked a better runner in the leg so hard that the other guy wasn't able to run. Do you now think it is good and he got his medal fair and square?

The runner did good for himself (he is happy to get a medal), but the good wasn't "absolute" good. It was done on account of others. He achieved it by cheating and depriving someone from a fair victory. The medal and the satisfaction wasn't his, he stole them from a fair winner.

Would you like someone to cheat YOU out of the winning a contest or a competition?

Two boys enjoy a watermelon … is that good?

Yes, it is good for them. However what other question we need to ask if this is good for them only or it is really and absolutely good thing? What do you think—which of the below written questions we need to ask?

Is it a tasty watermelon?

Is it a hot day?

How did they get it? Did they get the watermelon by stealing another person's belongings?

Of course we need to ask, "How did they get it?" … We need to find out if they did badly to someone else in order to get this good to themselves …

Let's assume that the mother of one of them gave it to them. Now it is really gooood! Not only they enjoy the watermelon, they also didn't cause any damage or suffering to others in order to enjoy it.

Wishing, working toward something you want and enjoying what you like and want (it is called "pursuing happiness") without causing any damage or suffering to other people called "absolute good."

John wants to be a conductor of an orchestra and he works hard … is it good?—Yes, it is. His dream is to do good to himself and other people. He is not planning to steal, damage, and make other people suffer. Very possible that when he will conduct the National Orchestra there will be several unhappy conductors that wanted the job but didn't get it. However John didn't harm them or didn't do anything to their belongings. He won this right to conduct the orchestra fair and square. Let the best conductor win!

Elisa wants to heal people in a hospital and study medicine … is it good?—Yes, if she is not planning to steal money to pay for her education, it is a great goal. It is definitely good.

Bobby said to his friends that he wants to become a very good killer and be hired by the Mafia to kill people—is that good? Not so good … he is planning to make people suffer, damage their lives and the lives of their families. I hope he's just kidding.

Mathew wants a large sandwich with a lot of lettuce and mayo. He is planning to do it himself from the things his older sister bought at a store and put there. Is that good?

a) Yes

b) No

c) I do not know

Monica dreams about a new mountain bike. She loves sports, but outdoor sports she loves the most. Is that good?

a) Yes

b) No

c) I do not know, I have no idea how she is planning to get it.

What is better—to dream about a large sandwich or about a small sandwich? … To dream about being a bus driver or a teacher? … To dream about a skirt or about a dress? … What is better—to dream about a bike, about being a conductor or about a sandwich?

It doesn't matter. It is your life, it is your dream—if you do not damage another person or his belongings, if you do not steal or cheat then all dreams are equal. The only difference between good or bad is—are you going to take something without owner's permission or damage someone else's belongings?

Riddle #21 - Lemonade Stand

Gary and Molly decided to make and sell lemonade. Gary lived on one side on their island, and Molly on another. Their parents had same lemon trees in the backyards, but Gary said to Molly "I will sell more lemonade then you because I have my great grandmother's secret recipe."

"Oh yah?" said Molly who a minute ago had no idea that they are in competition "I will sell more lemonade then you because … because I have blue eyes!"

Molly understood that she was at disadvantage. Gary had the secret recipe and her blue eyes she knew had nothing to do with the taste of lemonade. How to beat Gary she thought?

Next morning on every street corner of the island were signs posted by Molly that read "Best Lemonade on the Island. Original taste. Molly's 'Blue Eye' lemonade. Delivery available."

Similar flyers were distributed to every school and kindergarten on the island and put under wind shields of every car parked at the shopping mall.

On the same morning Gary opened a small stand at the corner of the street he lived on with a sign "The grandmother's secret recipe lemonade." During the first day, Gary sold two pitchers of his lemonade.

Molly sold twenty-two and had to enlist help three neighboring children to make the drink and deliver it to all clients who called to order the cold drink. On the third day Molly stopped making lemonade by herself and concentrated on taking orders, organizing deliveries and telling her new workers what to do. A local radio station interviewed her as a successful young entrepreneur. While on the air Molly came up with an idea of bottling her lemonade and selling it at the local gas stations and convenience markets.

Soon she had to move her production out of her parents' garage to a small warehouse nearby. She began to think about other types of drinks and other products she would promote as a part of her "Molly blue eyes" line of tasty goods. The very first product she added was "The grandmother's secret recipe lemonade" the rights for which she purchased from Gary.

<u>Critical thinking</u>:

Q1 - Was Molly's good an absolute good or only her good?

    a) Molly didn't cheat Gary and didn't steal his belongings. She was just better than him and won the competition fair and square.

    b) Molly infringed on Gary's happiness and therefore it is not an absolute good.

<u>Comment of a Progressive / Socialist</u>: Children shall not be allowed to work. They suppose to have a happy childhood and that means playing, relaxing, and studying at school. Studying at school shall not be hard as well. Children shall be happy and free of any thought of money, profits, business, or responsibilities beyond cleaning their rooms and helping older people to cross streets.

<u>Comment of a True Liberal / Capitalist</u>: Molly's parents shall be proud of her. But Molly's success most probably came because they encouraged her, allowed her to do what she wanted to do and supported her initiatives. Way to go girl!

<u>Author's opinion—Right answer</u>: a

Maybe something that is good for you is not that good for a family that lives in rural Russia? Maybe a boy from Mexico will perceive good differently from the same age girl from Mexico? Maybe an Indian scientist thinks differently about what is good and what is not than a Scandinavian farm worker? How about 14th Century farmer and 21st Century farmer? Do they perceive good and bad the same way or they will have a disagreement about this issue?

Do you think eating an apple and watching a sunset will be perceived differently depending on the gender, age, historical period—or it is good for everyone?

Is there any person or any time period in which a person likes when his apple was stolen from him? Is it different for a person who lived two thousand years ago and for a person who lives today?

Do you think that seven hundred seventy-seven years ago people loved to be conned, bullied, lied to, enslaved and imprisoned? Personally I do not think so.

Tibetan monks love to be left alone in the caves. They pray, think and fast. This is how they perceive good. They do not steal anyone's property by doing so. What they are doing is an absolute good.

Stamp collectors across the globe to collect stamps and exchange them between themselves. They form philatelist societies, read books about stamps, talk with each other and cherish their collections. They do not steal anyone's property. They feel good, no one suffers. This is an absolute good.

Socialists want to help the poor and those who suffer. This is good. They want to do it by taking belongings of someone else and dividing it among those in need. They do their good by stealing someone else's belongings (stealing as you recall is taking someone's belongings without this person's permission). Do you think what socialists are doing is absolutely good? Or you think that it is called theft, bullying, robbery and enslaving?

Would you prefer to be enslaved by Marxists, progressives, liberals, socialists or by Tsars, Khans, Kings and Ayatollahs? Or you do not want to be enslaved at all?

Personally I prefer to be a free man. How about you?

Riddle #22 - Guatemalan Boy

A boy lives in Guatemala, in a small village near the top of a mountain. He is sick. He needs medicine that was just invented in Germany and his parents can't buy it. It is much too expensive for them. The government of Guatemala either has no money or doesn't want to spend it on such an unimportant person. Actually there are seven thousand four-hundred twenty seven boys and girls who live in the mountain villages of Guatemala, all of them sick and in urgent need of this medicine. They can't buy it.

Your parents work hard to earn a living and have very little money left for movies, a new dress or for once in a while taking the family to a restaurant. You also baby sit and do domestic chores to earn a little money for things you want and like. Do you think that instead of going on a family vacation and buying yourself this little present you were saving money for, you and your parents shall send all your money to Guatemala?

a) Yes

b) No

c) Do not know

How about four-hundred seventeen million people, including small children in India that do not have enough food to feed them through the day? Do you think your mom shall stop putting money aside for her retirement send it to India?

a) Yes

b) No

c) Do not know

What if seven thousand four-hundred twenty seven boys and girls from Guatemala would come down from the mountains and live in the biggest Guatemalan city—shall you and your parents send them money and food instead of buying you and your siblings a new book, a pair of shoes and an ice cream?

a) Yes

b) No

What if those seven thousand four-hundred twenty seven boys and girls moved from Guatemala to Mexico and now live close to the US border—will you and your parents feel obligated to pay their medical bills?

a) Yes

b) No

Now what if those seven thousand four-hundred twenty seven boys and girls illegally crossed the US border? Do you now have to pay for their medical needs? Do you want your parents to pay for their doctors and their food instead of spending money on you and themselves?

a) Yes

b) No

And if you will start paying for food, schooling and health of those seven thousand four-hundred twenty seven boys and girls from Guatemala, what do you think the four-hundred seventeen million people, including small children from India will do? Will they say "good for Guatemalans" or they will say "We are moving to America and since legally we can't do it, we will cross their borders illegally and we will get exactly the same treatment the Guatemalans got?"

Shall your parents pay for their food, education and medicine when they are in India, when they are on the way to the US or after they illegally crossed the US borders and live in the US?

a) Yes

b) No

And if your parents would pay for children from Guatemala but will not pay for children from India, do you think all those millions of Indians will say "Good for Guatemalans" and will go home, or they will be very upset with your parents?

a) Yes, they will be upset

b) No , they will be happy for Guatemalans, will take their belongings and will go back to India

I personally think that they will take Indian flags and will demonstrate on the American streets demanding their rights to get part of the money your parents, you and I are earning. I think that they would feel that you and your parents owe them something for not shooting them when they crossed the US borders. They would feel that the money you and your parents earn belongs to them and not to you;

because they need the money and you might decide to spend it on unimportant things like ice cream or electronic gadgets, or on family vacations.

I am sure many people say that the "universal good" (another name for taking yours and giving it to others) demand that you would share with those sick and hungry people. I am not sure that the people who say that will share their belongings with others. What they usually mean is that it is YOU who shall share. They love to give away someone else's belongings.

It's very possible that if Guatemalans or Indians would come to your mom and dad, and to you, and explain their situation, you guys will decide to help them and will send some of the money you earned to them. Very possible that your mom would say to you and your sister—kids, what do you think, can we live with an old dress and without a new electronic game? And you will say "yes" and will send some of the money to the struggling Guatemalans and Indians. And then it will be an absolute good. You did with your belongings what you wanted to do and you helped other people. Otherwise it would be theft and enslaving all over again.

Q1 - Tell me, is it good when the government decides to send your money to people who are struggling in our country and around the world?

   a)   Good, because people around the world need our help and this is an obligation of America to help everyone

   b)   When government steals our money it maybe good for the US government and for the people who receive our belongings, but definitely not good for us. It is not an absolute good. Only people who earn the money can decide what to do with it. I the person who earned money decide to send it to anyone, then it is an absolute good. Otherwise it is robbery and theft.

<u>Comment of a Progressive / Socialist</u>: It is all good in theory. Practically speaking no one would help if not for government programs.

<u>Comment of a True Liberal / Capitalist</u>: There are plenty of private charity organizations that ask for donations for foreign help. The best way to help is to teach people to grow food, to make things, to earn money. This way they soon will not need any help. If you bring them food, they will need you forever. The more you bring them what they need, the more dependent on your help they become.

<u>Author's opinion—Right answer</u>: b

In the physical science "good" and "bad" equal to "right answer" and "wrong answer." Maybe we shall take a look on the physical science and learn how they distinguish right from wrong. Maybe they have a method we can use in our life, to determine what is good (right) and what is bad (wrong)?

Man has inhabited the planet for at least 100,000 years according to one source and about 6,500 years according to another, and yet virtually all progress has occurred in the last 300 years. Why?

First, let's see if there were other civilizations prior to ours and if yes, what might happened to them and why?

Three of the earliest Giza pyramids in Egypt were built in a totally different way from all others and by technologies the later Egyptians were unable to duplicate or understand. According to some scientists they were built before the Biblical deluge. There are also many scientists that now say that the Sphinx was carved before the deluge, because its wear and tear shows that it was under water for quite some time.

There is a place in Lebanon, in the high mountains, that is constructed from the cut of stone panels that weigh a thousand tons each. Even today we can't imagine how to move them up and put them together. A giant floor of about a square mile was built using those panels and is hidden between the mountains. It is absolutely flat and can withstand the pressure of a rocket ship landing or being launched from it.

There are the same type stone panels of enormous weight that were used by someone as building blocks for mountain constructions in Guatemala and Mexico ... who built them? When did it happen? Why do we know nothing about those people? Why did such powerful civilizations perish? What happened to them?

On many of the clay tablets of Sumer, papyruses of Egypt, on the walls of deep caves all around the world, in legends and religions of many nations of the past and present there are stories and images of people flying in rocket like ships, or creatures wearing helmets or flying gear. Who were those people?

Who built the stone calendar in Great Britain? Who created the Moon calendar of the Mayans with precise knowledge of how planets move around the Sun? If they knew how to fly, if they knew how to build huge structures using thousand ton brick panels, if they knew intergalactic travel and astronomy, then why during several thousand years' men were using the horse as the only means of travel? Why were there no energy sources to heat and to light houses? Why was there no medicine, prevention of diseases, understanding of how planets move and no answer to an intriguing question of why there are waves in the oceans?

There were civilizations on earth we know nothing about. They were long before the deluge or after it, they were during the sixty-five hundred years of the recorded history of our civilization (maybe we do not have full records) or it was long before, we do not know.

The first fact is—it looks like there were civilizations on Earth and maybe even more powerful than ours. They are no longer here. Why?

Another fact is that in the last two thousand years we didn't have any technological progress and suddenly in the last three hundred years there was an enormous progress in everything having to do with the science and technology. Three hundred years ago people were not driving cars, not watching TV, not discussing intergalactic travel, not treating most of the diseases and living very short lives.

The huge problem is that three hundred years ago people were shooting each other with spears, a hundred years ago they learned how to do it with rifles, fifty years ago they began to understand how nucleolus works, and now there are several countries that can easily blow up the world if this crazy idea will come to their heads. It took us a very short period of scientific development to come to this point where we can blow the world up by pushing one button.

People now can kill each other on a much larger scale and if we will not find out how to coexist, we will eventually kill each other. Here is one of the versions of what happened to all previous civilizations on earth. There was ONE revolutionary fanatic who had an access to the button and he pushed it. End of story, end of several thousand years of a powerful civilization.

If we do not want to go the same way they went, we need to learn how to resolve our differences and we need to learn it soon. Otherwise there is no future for the humankind. We might perish like all previous civilizations, much faster than the mammoths did.

Is it possible you might ask? First we need to establish what is good for all and each of us, define right and wrong and see how we can exist on one globe, each being in command of our own belongings and with no one touching or stealing the belongings of other people.

Physical science made so much progress that we shall try and learn from it. About three hundred years ago, coinciding with the beginning of the scientific revolution of our civilization, humankind came up with a scientific method of distinguishing right from wrong. Here is this method that is responsible for huge advances in technologies that changed the lives of almost everyone on earth:

The Scientific Method

Observation (gather data): First you observe the facts. You observed that the level of water in your pool goes down in summer much faster than in the winter. You checked—water itself was the same during summers and winters, no apparent change. It didn't look like it was condensing. There were no leaks on the bottom of the pool or on the sides. The only way water can disappear you said to yourself is up. You spent a day sitting at the side of the pool and didn't see any water going up, but the water level was down.

Hypothesis Formulation (generalize): You came up with an idea that it has something to do with air or water temperature. You remembered what is happening with water in a teapot when it heats. At this point you said to yourself—it is changing when it heats up and then it is going up in this changed form ... maybe I just do not see when it goes up? So your hypothesis was that water is changing under the sun's influence and goes up in this invisible state that you decided to call "vapor."

Extrapolation (predict): You predicted that if we will put a cover over the pool the water that went up during the day will be captured by the cover and will go down during the cooler part of the day.

Observation (corroborate work): You checked a hundred times. When there was a cover, water levels were back in the mornings. When there was no cover on the pool, water went down and stayed down.

It looks like a very difficult task to understand this scientific method, but actually when you get used to that it is easy.

Does right and wrong in physical science depend on the time of history? Will water evaporate from a pool or any other vessel during a hot day if the observer will be a woman? How about if the observer will be an Indian? Will it stop evaporating if the observer would be a monk? Will it evaporate faster if there would be two people observing? How about a different speed of evaporation depends on the age of the observer?

It definitely can evaporate faster or slower depending on the amount of moisture in the air and other meteorological conditions, but all that can be calculated and put into an equation. The scientific method can help to create a hypothesis, help to evaluate it and provide a clear explanation of what can be called right conclusion and wrong conclusion.

For example if ten times water evaporated from the pool and then one hot day it would not, then something would be wrong with the hypothesis. If however, you checked many times and it always gave you the same result, than you hypotheses is right and now can be called truth.

The history of men is filled with wrong conclusions that people reached before the scientific method was discovered. Many people make the very same mistake even now, but this is because they refuse to use the scientific method to confirm or deny their hypothesis.

Let me tell you about a couple of wrong conclusions that brought our ancestors to disastrous results. I will start with the ocean waves.

People were wondering about those waves for centuries. Sometimes they were small and nice, other times they were huge and threatening. The ocean was sending them toward the shore and then they were coming back with regularity, like a breath. So people came to believe that there is a demon, or a sea god called Poseidon, that is sitting in the ocean and breathing in and out. And this demon or Poseidon was sometimes in a good mood and sometimes in a bad mood. When he was in a bad mood, many sailors and fisherman died and many villages and towns on the shore suffered. It was very important for many people to pacify the guy who sits in the middle of the ocean and can take their livelihood and even their lives away.

How about you—do you think, was it a valid hypothesis that in the middle of the ocean was a creature that was starting storms based on its mood?

a) Yes

b) No

c) Maybe

The question that people of course asked was—how can we make this guy feel good and not send storms that are bad for us? Someone then came up with an idea to send to this all-mighty guy presents like silver and gold, cows and sheep. For hundreds of years people were sailing with their boats and ships into the ocean and throwing their presents into the ocean asking the demon to be merciful to them.

But the demon or Poseidon wasn't always ready to stop his anger just because he would get a piece of gold or a cow. So people decided to give him the most important thing in their lives—their sons and daughters. They made sacrifices of beautiful girls and boys by throwing them into the ocean and asking Poseidon to stop storms and give them enough fish to feed the rest of their families. And when Poseidon wouldn't stop, they gave him more and more.

Do you think that throwing young boys and girls into the ocean stopped many storms?

a) Yes

b) No

c) Maybe

It was only three hundred years ago when Sir Isaac Newton found out that all celestial bodies attract each other and that the ocean waves are a direct result of the moon and earth's mutual attraction.

Do you think those people who sacrificed girls and boys for hundreds of years said to themselves "Oops! We are sorry!" But even if they did, did it change anything in the lives of thirteen-year old girls eaten by sharks?

a) Yes

b) No

c) Maybe

In your opinion, did those people who sacrificed precious metals, cattle and humans in order to get favorable weather from Poseidon use the scientific method of creation and verification of their hypothesis?

a) Yes

b) No

c) Maybe

Another story is even worse.

You may recall from the history books you studied at school that there was a catastrophic Bubonic plague (they called it The Black Plague) in Europe in the Middle Ages. About a quarter of the population of Europe died. People were scared and were asking themselves—what happened, why is this terrible disease killing us, what is the reason? And the official explanation was—the devil is spreading this illness in attempt to wipe the humankind of the face of the earth through witches.

Since they couldn't burn the devil, they began to do the next best thing—burn witches. Thousands of innocent people, including men, women and children were burned alive if someone would suspect that they were spreading the plague. In Milan for example two old women saw a men walking on their street in the dark, touching the walls of some of the houses with his left hand. They immediately called the authorities and the man was arrested and tortured. He happened to be a local scribe who got some sticky ink on his left hand fingers and was trying to get rid of it while coming home from work by scraping his hand on the walls of the houses he was passing.

Of course no one believed him. Under extreme torture, he was forced to name all the people he knew and they were arrested and tortured, after which he was burned alive at a stake. The arrested people were tortured, named all the people they knew and themselves were burned at stakes alive. Those other people were arrested, tortured ... and that went on and on and on ... until the death toll was enormous.

One of the arrested was a pharmacist and he was forced to confess that it was he who created the plague in his pharmacy. He was burned alive, his house was burned, his family driven away from the city and on the place of his house the city built an obelisk to let all others know what will happen to them and their families, if they decide to create a plague.

Now you tell me, what do you think, was the plague spread by witches, or were the authorities a bit wrong about this issue?

a) Yes

b) No

c) Maybe

In about 264 years from the death of the pharmacist, he was completely vindicated and was proclaimed innocent, as well as thousands of others. The reason for this happy ending was that it was found that the cause of the plague was a little microscopic size bacterium called Pasteurella pestis.

The authorities wrongly identified the cause of the plague and this led to the torturing and killing of thousands of innocent people.

But this is not the end of the story ... or I would say, there was a beginning to the story that led to Bubonic plague and to deaths of hundreds of thousands of Europeans.

Some years before the burst of the Bubonic plague, the same people who later burned witches on stakes decided that cats are evil agents of the devil. They started crusade against cats and obliterated them from the face of Europe. When the cats disappeared the rats came to play. Rats began to multiply by millions and took over Europe. The rats carried a small flea that carried bacilli called Pasteurella pestis which is the cause for the plague.

The rest is history. One bite of a flea and the bacteria is introduced into a human body. The killing of cats that were at the time considered the devil's agents (this was the prevailing hypothesis behind the crusade) was in fact the cause of an enormous disaster, one of the most terrible disasters in European history.

Now you can appreciate what can happen if we do not understand which is the right assumption (hypothesis) and which is a wrong one. You are now knowledgeable enough to see how important it is to think and check before acting, and to think and check using the scientific method.

It is important in all sciences—physical, biological and the science of people's co-existence called social science or volitional science. It is in this science we are all doing very poorly.

There are wars everywhere; there is poverty everywhere. There is an attempt to steal and enslave each other in almost every country on the globe. Are we doing well on co-existence?

   a) Yes

   b) No

   c) Do not know

Libre is Latin for freedom. You are either for freedom, or you are for slavery. If you are for a little bit of slavery … or for slavery of others … that means that you are for slavery. If you are a bully, or a thief and a liar that means that you want to enslave others. If you want to enslave others then beware—you have the soul of a slave and you can be easily enslaved yourself.

The goal of this book is to show you that it is better for you, for me, for everybody else to be liberated, to be free … not to be a slave or to enslave other people.

A Bully just doesn't know it, but it would be much better for him not to try to enslave other people.

It is better for everything in our lives, and I will try to prove it to you throughout this book.

If someone controls your thoughts, you are a slave. If someone restricts your movements, you are a slave. If someone controls your property— you are a slave. Your body, your ideas, your thoughts, your house and things—they're supposed to be yours and controlled by you.

If you control absolutely everything that is yours ... and do not control and do not try to control anything that belongs to other people, then you are a FREE MAN!

And if everyone in your country does the same, then this is really a FREE COUNTRY!

The Fourth Postulate of the Volitional Science is: "Absolute good is when a person's good was achieved without causing damage or suffering to other human beings or their belongings."

The Fifth Postulate of the Volitional Science is: "Free Man is a human being that controls 100% of his belongings and controls 0% of other people's belongings." The only exception is when a person takes care of another person who can't take care of himself and has to control his belongings in order to provide him such care.

Chapter VII

Is this the same—good of a group of individuals and good of an individual?

YOUR COUNTRY'S BASKETBALL team won, but at the same moment you are having terrible tooth pain. Are you happy at this moment or not? Please be honest.

   a) Yes?

   b) No?

I for example can't be happy while having tooth pain. Sorry, my dear beloved team. I can't celebrate your victory.

You won first prize in a sailboat championship and you are getting a trophy while the hymn of your country is played out loud. At the same time three thousand children on the Himalayan Mountains are simultaneously having terrible tooth pain. Are you happy at this moment or not?

   a) Yes?

   b) No?

I would be happy. I care about children anywhere in the world, but I am happy.

Your city got money from the federal government to build more roads, but you lost your valet with all the money you got for your birthday. Are you happy at this moment or not?

   a) Yes

   b) No

I would be devastated, not happy.

You will have to paint the house you live in and three other houses from top to bottom, and your street will receive an award for the cleanest street in the world ... Or you will have to paint all those houses, but this time your award will be a car of your choice ... which option excites you more? Please honestly decide:

I want my street to win an award for the cleanest street and am ready to spend two weeks of my life paintings houses in order to achieve this wordy goal, or I prefer to get my own car, especially if I can chose whichever car I want

Hmmm ... this is a tough one, right? Let me think. I would prefer a Corvette ... how about you?

We can continue with similar questions, but the result will probably be the same—you seek your own happiness rather than happiness of the groups to which you are belong by chance (the city you were born at, your ethnicity, your age group) or by your own choice (the team you play with, club you signed in, political party you joined).

I am not telling you what is good, what is not. I am just establishing what I know most of the people feel. There are probably some exceptions. I personally never met one.

There is an instinct deep down in every one of us that triggers people to think about themselves first. There is one exception however—parents. Parents are often ready to sacrifice their own good for the well being of their children, but here is another instinct at work.

Only after thinking about themselves and their families people start thinking about their teams, schools, cities, social, political or religious groups, their country, and the entire human race. People do enjoy when their city's sports club wins, and they feel proud when their country sends space ships to the Moon and beyond. But again they are happy because it is "THEIR city" and "THEIR country."

"Volitional" beings (creatures that are able to make decisions) often do things seemingly against this "me first" tendency. People often decide to do things they do not enjoy because they have to do them. Some do not enjoy their jobs, but they need to pay for food and shelter and to buy shoes and electronic games for their children. They go and work at those jobs they do not like. Others will sacrifice their lives because they feel that their religion or social responsibility calls for that. For example a person can go to the jungle to look for Indians to teach them Christian faith because he thinks it is more important than anything else he can do in the world. Or another person would blow himself up in the middle of the crowd because he thinks that blowing people up is very important for his faith in Allah.

Many of us will voluntarily give parts of what we earn to people in need whom we never met and have no relations with, or animals in need, or even to save forests and rivers on distant continents. Those who give to the causes they believe in tremendously enjoy (derive happiness from) helping other people or helping a good (in their opinion) cause.

But I need to point out here that they give money and lives to causes THEY feel are good and important. Those cases in many instances are not "absolutely good." There are many people for example who give money to fanatics who make bombs. Some of them blow up Israeli children, some American airliners, some Christian nuns, and some blow up Muslims in Mosques, on streets and bazaars. They think that their cause is so important that they are ready to part with their belongings and sometimes with their lives in order to blow up a bus full of travelers or a bunch of coffee shop goers.

How to learn which cause is good and which is not so good?

Do you remember that earlier we were discussing a simple but important question—will what I do interfere with someone's belongings? If yes, then this is probably not a good cause.

But maybe it is not good to seek happiness for yourself? Maybe this "instinct" is wrong. Maybe we need to try to get rid of this instinct? Maybe we have to think first about the group we belong to, about the city or state we live at? Let us try to solve a couple of riddles and decide what is absolutely good and what is not.

Riddle #23 - Whose Good is Better?

Once upon a time a tribe of travelers came upon a great valley that was split in the middle by a beautiful river. The travelers decided to stay in the valley and make it their home. They however weren't able to decide how to govern their new home place and since they had two very different views on the subject, they decided to form two villages. Half of the people wanted everything in their lives to be governed by a Central Committee. They thought that whatever they produce should be given to the Committee, and the Committee would divide it between the villagers. Those people went to live on the Left side of the valley.

The other half wanted each to harvest land the way each of them wanted to do it, to grow what each of them wanted to grow and each wanted to keep to themselves whatever they produce. Those people went to live on the Right side of the valley.

For ten years the Left side people were growing food and giving it to the Committee, and the Committee was distributing it among the villagers. The Left Side villagers were very proud that they do everything for the good of the village, not for the selfish good of each of them. We are collective, they were saying to their Right Side neighbors. And you are self-serving selfish individuals who will not give water for free to a dying person. Very soon most of you would want to join our collective ... but we might not accept you.

However people on the Left who worked hard soon found out that they are getting the same amount of everything, exactly as people who didn't work hard or exactly what people who didn't work at all were getting. Those who worked hard gradually stopped working hard and began to produce less of everything. Less bread and less apple juice, less shoes and less toys for their kids, less cars and less apartment buildings. And soon what they produced was not enough for everyone.

Some people realized that if they are in good relations with the Committee members, they can get more and a better share of everything. They began to give small presents to the Committee members and did favors to them waiting for favors from them in return. Money that the Left Village people earned was distributed almost equally and no one had to buy more necessities. Because no one had excess money no new businesses were started. You see, starting a new business requires not only a good idea and fast legs, but also an investment. If you want to start making hats, you need to buy a sewing machine, fabric, and rent a space where you can make your merchandise. After you make your products you need to find a store that will sell it and wait until they will sell it and give you your share of the money.

Everyone on the Left Side except the Committee members lived the same life. The members however built a wall surrounding their houses and no one knew exactly what was going on there. The Committee members hired a couple of bodyguards that were guarding their houses from the "regular" folks' intrusion. Life in the village was dull and eventless, and the only thing that was good in the opinion of the Left Side villagers was the "equality" of almost all villagers, except of course the Committee members, their families and close friends. They were (quoting Orwell) a bit more equal than others.

The life of the Right Side went a completely different way. Whoever worked hard was getting rewards in the form of products and money. Some of the more successful ones began to hire other villagers who didn't know how to manage their businesses or they brought in outside people to help.

A couple of villagers began to make good money. They had enough to feed their families and more. They took this "more" and invested in a restaurant and a small factory. They offered other villagers to invest in a casino and soon a new casino was built on their side of the river.

People from all over began to come to the Right Side. They enjoyed shopping, gambling in the casino and loved to eat at the restaurant. Many of the visitors wanted to stay overnight. Soon a couple of outside investors built a hotel and a salon with a show. Several stores were opened in no time and the village's Main Street became the place to spend weekends and "cruise" during hot summer nights.

Some of the Right Side villagers became rich, some got hired by new businesses that were opened in the village, some less fortunate ones become poor and cursed the system, but most of the people were happy. They had an interesting life, they were getting more if they worked hard and less if they didn't. But what was strange was that practically all young people from the Left Village crossed the river and came to live in the Right Village.

How weird it is, mused the Right Villagers, each of us over here was trying to build good life for himself, and see what it led to—it came out to benefit all of us, everyone enjoys the life we built. And the other side, they wanted to do good for the collective, and ended up in a dull and poor world.

They thought and thought and thought about it but couldn't understand it, and decided that they don't care for the reason. Most of them lived their good life and were happy that their kids would inherit a little bit better world than the one they inherited. This is exactly what they wanted and exactly what they achieved.

Thinking out loud:

Q1 - Which village would you prefer to live—Right or Left?

You can choose between these answers:

   a) Right

b) Left

c) Do not care

Q2 - If you work hard, would you be ready to give half of it to a person who didn't work at all?

a) Yes

b) No

c) Do not care

Q3 - If you didn't work at all would you like to get nothing, or would you want to get a half of the money earned by a person who did the work?

a) Yes, I would like to get half of the money the other person earned

b) Of course I would want to get something for nothing. It is a dream. I understand however that this is not a good system. If I will start taking from those that work, one day someone will start taking from me what I earn.

Comment of a Progressive / Socialist: The picture in this example is not exactly right. The Left Side people enjoy equal healthcare. It is not as good as on the Right Side, but it is for everyone. Also, the standard of living is lower on the Left Side but it is not because of the system. The system is good, but the managers were bad. If different managers would be in charge, the system would work better. On the Right Side there are some very poor people who are barely mentioned in the story. Those poor people are not happy with the system. Also not all young people crossed the river and now live on the Right Side. Some of the young people stayed on the Left Side.

Comment of a True Liberal / Capitalist: Please count how many people escaped from the Left side and came to live on the Right side. Plenty. And count how many of the Right Side people left for the Left

Side. None. Even poor people didn't want to go to the place where the Good of the Group was obviously more important that the good of a person. Even "bad" at the Right Side is better than the "good" of the Left Side.

<u>Author's opinion—Right answers</u>:

    Q1 - a

    Q2 - b

    Q3 - b

Riddle #24 - Good of the Class

One day a principal came to a graduating class and said that from now on the class will be graded based on a collective effort. In other words, each student will get an average class grade. If for example two students were taking a test, one got "C" and another "A", then the average would be "B" and each of them would go home with the "B" for the test.

You should start learning to fight for the good of the group, not only for your own good, he said.

He was a very enthusiastic principal and he thought that the good of a collective shall be much more important to people that the good of each individual person, and that students would start learning much better if they would know that grades of others depends on their knowledge. He also thought that the good students would start helping poor students in order to raise the average grade of the class.

On the test this day the average grade was C+. The better students were disappointed fearing that this grade will reduce their previous excellent or good average. The poor students were happy. They never got such high grades.

One week later another test gave an average of "C-" and one week later the average plummeted to "D." When the puzzled principal began to investigate, he found out that the good students decided not to study because they knew that they will not get the grades they deserve. The bad students were not studying as well. They knew that the good ones will pass the test and they will not need to worry about a failure.

In two weeks the average grade was already "D-." Two of the best students were quickly transferred by their parents to other schools, but at the same time a couple of really bad ones from other schools asked for a transfer to this class. Soon the class was filled with bad students and became the worst graduating class in the history of the school district, or even maybe the whole state if not the country.

Thinking out loud:

Q1 - Why did the students stop studying when they understood that they will be graded as a class, not each one personally?

   a)   Because they didn't want to get good grades?

   b)   Because they hated good students and wanted them to fail

   c)   Because they didn't have motivation

Q2 - What is producing better results, the good of a group or the good of a person?

   a)   You shall always think about the group. This way those who work suffer a bit, but it always helps the weak ones. It brings equality to the group.

   b)   It is always better to build on an individual responsibility. It turns out to be good for everyone.

Comment of a Progressive / Socialist: There are many ways to make people work or study. One of them is called punishment. If such moral incentive as "good of your classmates" is not exciting enough for the student body, the principal had to start punishing those that had an ability to study but didn't. There is no sense in punishing bad students.

<u>Comment of a True Liberal / Capitalist</u>: Volitional beings prefer to make their own choices. If you feel it is beneficial for you to study, you will. If you do not see any benefit in it for you, you wouldn't. It's that simple. Yes, it is possible to force people to do things. Usually when socialists see that "good of the group" is not working well and people stop producing, they start forcing them into submission. This is called enslaving. It usually does not bring happiness into people's lives.

<u>Authors opinion—Right answers</u>:

> Q1 - a
>
> Q2 - b

A Tomato Story

Once not so long ago in a not so distant country the weather conditions were unusually bad and a lot of tomatoes died. Growing the remaining tomatoes took much more effort and money than usual. Because of the high cost and unusually large demand the sellers began to offer tomatoes at high prices, and poor people were unable to buy them.

At that time the country had a progressive (socialist) compassionate government which said "we will not tolerate that some people are able to buy and enjoy tomatoes, and some not," and they issued a decree setting a very low price for tomatoes. The tomato sellers were forced to sell tomatoes at such price so even the poorest person would be able to afford them.

The government said to the producers that if they will not sell for the prices set by the government, they will be severely punished.

The price set by the government was so low that in some instances it was even less than the cost of growing tomatoes. I hope you understand that "the cost" is how much the farmers spent to grow tomatoes and "the price" is what they were selling them for. For example if he spent for water, electricity, cars, tractors, boxes and other stuff to 90 cents per pound of tomatoes, and sold them for 80 cents a pound, they lost on each pound 10 cents, right?

Do you think the tomato growers liked to lose money or they would prefer to make money?

I think tomato growers do not care if they lose or make money. They grew tomatoes to make other people happy

I think people work in order to make products, sell them, make money and with this money buy other things they need or want. If tomato growers are not making profits or even losing money on tomatoes they will stop growing tomatoes.

Poor people all over the country became very happy and praised their government for defending their interests. They voted for the members of the government to continue being in charge of the country in order to pass more of such wonderful and just laws. They liked to be able to buy tomatoes for less money than what the farmers spent to grow them.

Next year, however, there were no tomatoes on the market, for neither rich nor poor. The price limit made growing them not profitable, or not as profitable as growing other vegetables. Most of the farmers knowing they will not make much money selling tomatoes stopped growing them.

Very few farmers continued but were selling them secretly to a small number of expensive restaurants and to some very rich people at ten times the price they sold tomatoes last year.

Do you think the government achieved what they said they intended to achieve—namely allow poor people to enjoy tomatoes?

   a) Yes

   b) No

Of course not—there were any tomatoes on the market anymore!

Do you think that dictating to tomato growers at what prices to sell their products was a good idea?

a) Yes

b) No

c) Do not know

Based on this logical approach, do you think that dictating to car manufacturers at what price they shall sell their cars would be a good idea

a) Yes

b) No

c) Do not know

OK, let's try to understand if dictating prices to car manufacturers would be a good or a bad idea.

Car Price Calculation

The government calculated how much money a car cost and said to the manufacturer that he can't sell his cars for more than one thousand dollars above the cost of the car. We are doing it because we want more people to be able to afford cars, the government was saying.

Again, let me repeat that "the cost" is the total amount of money a manufacturer (producer) spent on everything to build a car, or a TV set, or a toy. Producers call it "cost of the product."

Sounds like a fair idea to restrict prices. Many people who were unable to buy a car now would be able to afford it, right? Good for them, good for the business, right?

Not so fast! Let's assume that the government said to Mr. Manufacturer that he can't make more than ten per cent profit. The government says—twenty percent is like a windfall, five percent is what many banks pay for just keeping the money on the savings account. So ten percent sounds fair, right?

Poor folks praised their government again for taking care of the "regular" folks. They went to elections and gave their votes to the government people to stay in power even longer and pass even more laws like this one.

You probably are waiting to see what happened in the meantime to car manufacturers? Every so often comes a very important moment in the life of every car manufacturer—they need to construct new models, and they need a lot of money for design, preparation, testing, and marketing. Where would they find the money? They go to people called investors.

Investors are the people who do not spend all the money they earn. Instead they put some aside and are using it to finance businesses. They do it not because they have good hearts (maybe they do, maybe not—it is irrelevant for this discussion), they simply want to earn money by investing, or to put it in plain English they want to get back more money then they spent. It is their business to invest money and get back more. If investors get back more than what they invested, they are "successful investors." If they do not get more they are "unsuccessful investors." Some investors give money to producers that are unable to fulfill their promises and the investors lose part or all of their money. To invest is a risky business.

Many of the investors are regular folks like myself, maybe your mom and dad, who have savings and who want to use those savings to make a bit more money. They give money to mutual funds and those funds are looking for investment opportunities for them. "Money makes money"—you may heard this saying before. This is how money makes money. You invest and you anticipate to be paid back what you invested plus "some." The more you are getting back, the more successful your investment is.

What about you—are you spending all the money you earn or do you put aside for the future and for making investments? Below is a choice of two simple answers to this question:

I spend any spare dollar I have on electronic gadgets, cars, clothes and partying. I do not need more money than what I earn on my job. I do not want to be rich and do not want to have secure future. All I care about is today and now.

I am putting some money aside and will invest. Investing is very interesting and allows making much more money than what people get from just working.

The investors always look for a good opportunity. What is good opportunity, you might ask? The good opportunity is the one that give you a good return on your investment. If you for example would invest in an Apple computer company one hundred dollars, and got a year later a hundred and twenty dollars, it is a very good investment. If however you gave someone hundred dollars and received a hundred and twenty in ten years, it is not a very good investment.

Now, what if you would invest one hundred dollars and get back ten dollars, how you would call this investment? Good, bad or terrible?

Businesses that need money compete with each other for investors. How do they compete you might ask? The businesses offer investors to pay them back as much money as they can. They offer them high "return on the investment."

So the car manufacturer that was restricted by the government goes to investors and says—we need money to build a new car. How much you will pay to me in one year if I will give you a million, asking the head of the investment group.

The government restricted our profits, answers the car manufacturer, so in one year I can pay you not more than two dollars for every hundred you would give me.

Sorry, says the investor, but a watch manufacturer offers me twenty dollars on one hundred of my investment. I will not be able to help you to build a new car.

The car manufacturer now can't find money to build new cars. He is stuck with the old ones. His competition from around the world is not restricted. They can charge prices that allow them to pay investors high return and they are getting a lot of investors who are interested in investing in their factories. The restricted car manufacturer soon loses his customers. The customers go to manufacturers who can sell them new and exciting cars, not the old ones this manufacturer offers them.

The government's decision by restricting the price that the manufacturer can charge for his cars made the manufacturer unable to compete. People do not buy his cars, he has no money to pay the workers and has to fire them, close the factories and end the business.

Do you think the government achieved what it said it wanted to achieve—namely help poor people to buy cars?

    a) Yes

    b) No

Hmmm, in my book they didn't.

Do you think government people didn't know what they are doing? Here are two possible answers:

    They do not know what they are doing

    They know what they are doing

Let's examine both options.

If the government doesn't know what they are doing, why do we need such government? Do you want school teachers that do not know what they are doing? If your teachers were not knowing what they were doing you probably discovered that you can't compete for better jobs and pay with the ones that had teachers who knew what they were doing.

If the government however knows what they are doing, knows that their regulations will bring terrible results (companies firing workers, closing factories) than why they do it anyhow? Maybe they are just wanting to appear good for poor people so the poor will vote for them?

Maybe they care only about themselves? Maybe they are even greedier than the bankers they call fat and greedy cats? At least those bankers were not sworn to defend our interests.

The governments are hired by people to serve The People. They receive salaries in order to serve us, meaning to do good things for The People. This is why we hired them. And it looks like they do bad to the people who are paying their salaries. It looks like they are trying to do good for themselves only ...

If an employee who works for your company receives salary but does nothing or does bad things to your enterprise, should you continue paying him his salary or maybe this worker should be fired? What do you think? There are two options:

>This worker shall receive a raise

>This worker shall be fired

Which one is yours?

But if the government doesn't do good things (intentionally or unintentionally) then maybe, maybe should you stop paying them their salaries? Do you want such a government to work for you or you would want to fire them all?

I want such government that thinks about themselves only and I will cast my vote for them every time there is an election.

I do not want such government, and will vote against them. I want government that thinks about the good for us, the people.

What is your decision? What would (will) you do?

Salary Regulation

The progressives like to say that producers pay too little to the workers and that they take too much home to themselves. The progressive governments always start pushing producers to pay more to their employees.

Maybe they are right? Maybe the government should regulate salaries and help workers to get more money from the producers?

Let's talk about dictating to car manufacturers how much to pay their workers ... simply because the government decided that the workers are getting less than what the government officials think is fair. The progressive government orders car manufacturers to raise their pay from $20 per hour to $30 per hour.

The workers shall be able to enjoy life more, says the government. They are also people like you! You, bad capitalistic sharks do not care about anyone except yourselves!

The workers are happy—the government is fighting for them, and they vote for this progressive socialist government again and again. They are ready to defend this government to the last drop of their blood!

What about you—do you think it is good for workers?

a) Yes

b) No

c) Do not have enough information

I hope you answered "c" because you really do not have enough information. I will try to provide you with some important facts.

As we were already discussing, the cost of a car is everything you spent to build it. Let's say that for making a car a manufacturer spent $5,000 on parts, $3,000 on marketing and sales, plus various workers labored 200 hours to make it up and running.

If a manufacturer pays $20 an hour to the worker, he will spend $4,000 for labor (200 hours times $20), and the total cost of the car will be $5,000 (parts) + $3,000 (marketing) + $4,000 (labor) = $12,000.

The manufacturer that has to abide by the government order and pay $30 per hour to his worker will have a higher cost of labor and higher cost of building cars. His labor will cost him $30 x 200 hours

= $6,000. Cost of the car he manufactured is $5,000 (parts) + $3,000 (marketing) + $6,000 (labor) = $14,000.

If there is no competition and no other car manufacturers selling cars, then the customer (you and I) will pay $2,000 more for a car. In other words, the government did good for one group of people but did it by robbing our money, forcing us to pay more for the car. Is it an absolute good? Don't think so. In my opinion it is theft and robbery.

If there is competition on the market and other companies sell similar cars to the consumer, then when you come to a car lot to buy a car and see there are two similar cars, but one is cheaper by $2,000 ... and everything else is the same ... which car would you buy? You have two choices:

a) More expensive

b) Less expensive

Most of the people will buy the less expensive car and the manufacturer who has to pay more to the workers will not be able to sell cars. As a result of the government intervention his car is not selling well. Actually no one buys his cars and he has to fire the workers and close down the factories. For several months they were receiving a higher salary but then they were fired.

Now do you think it is good for the workers—to receive more for several months and then lose their jobs?

a) Yes

b) No

You see how important it is to find out if the good you are promoting is a partial (one-sided) good or it is an absolute good? Are you stealing someone else's property while doing your partial good? Are you robbing anyone by doing good to yourself or to your preferred group of people?

The cars were not selling and the manufacturer lost all his factories and money. The workers lost their jobs. The consumers lost a once good product. The only winners are—the government, who pretended to fight for the "simple" people and got their votes during the elections.

Would they regulate prices and salaries if they would really care about people?

a) Yes

b) No

So, why do they do it?

Why do you think American jobs went overseas?

Chapter VIII
Life and thoughts of Douglas F. Jr.
(as he shared them with the author of this book)

The Flower Story

EVERYONE CALLED HIM Junior. His family lived in a small house with a small backyard, lined up with many other small houses that differed from each other by the color of the fences and by the type of the flowers planted around the fences. At that ancient time we are talking about there were not many cars on the streets and boys and girls freely rode their bikes back and forth and weren't afraid of any strangers because frankly there were no strangers in the neighborhood at all.

Junior was quite small but very smart and very fast. When he was five, he found out that when people went to birthday parties, weddings or holy day celebrations they brought presents to the hosts. One of the preferred presents as he noticed was flowers.

Junior also learned another very interesting information—people exchanged those presents and flowers for money. And Junior liked money. His loved sweets and his mom was telling him from time to time—today we do not have money so we can't get you anything, you little sweet tooth. Or, today we got some money to spend, let's go and celebrate! In his head he formed an opinion about money—to have it was good, not to have it, bad!

One day when his neighbors were dressing for a party, Junior knocked at their door and offered them a bouquet of white roses for a staggering amount of twenty-five cents. The bouquet was accurately tied with by a blue ribbon that Junior found at his older sister's "jewelry" box.

The neighbors were happy to get such a wonderful bouquet for such a small price and even gave Junior an extra twenty-five cents. Only when they came home they found out that the flowers were cut from the rose bushes in their own garden. They didn't like it.

Junior's parents didn't like it either. They apologized to the neighbors, returned them the fifty cents and offered to pay to restore bushes.

Junior thought hard and long about why everyone was upset. First he thought about the neighbors. They definitely were happy to get beautiful flowers for such a small price. He thought about people whom the neighbors gave those flowers and came to a conclusion that they were probably happy as well. The flowers were beautiful and smelled good. He thought about himself and again felt the joy of getting paid for a job well done. Everyone was happy he thought and suddenly everyone was upset. This was strange. The last thing he remembered about this episode before falling asleep was his conclusion that adults are not logical and very emotional.

Question—Why were the grownups upset and angry with Junior?

(Answer—he took other people's property without their permission)

The Newspaper Story

During Junior's elementary school years all the boys in their town wanted to make money by delivering newspapers prior to going to school. The job however was given only to the kids from the second grade and up. Junior waited for years to the moment he officially was able to make money. The day before school he went to one of the newspaper delivery centers, showed them his student ID, his bike (means of transportation) and signed up to deliver newspapers on one of the neighboring streets.

Next day he came to the center and the men in charge of distribution gave him a stack of newspapers to deliver. Then came the next day and the next. Then came rain.

Junior didn't like distributing newspapers in the rain, but he wanted the money. He thought hard about this dilemma and found a perfect solution. He knew a boy in the first grade who would do anything to be able to deliver newspapers and like himself couldn't wait for the next year to be the second grade student and be able to do it.

Junior made a deal with him and the boy began to pick up and distribute the papers at a half price.

Two days later Junior came up with another brilliant idea. He signed up for newspaper distribution at all four newspapers in the area, and made agreements with several first grade students to distribute the papers instead of him for the half price. Now he didn't care if it was raining or hot outside. His sub-contractors were picking up and distributing newspapers and he went once a week to each of the four newspapers and collected money.

Two weeks later the story blew up and Junior was severely reprimanded. This was another of the grownups unexplainable outbursts he decided. He even tried to talk about it with his mom, but she was furious and didn't want to hear anything about this "episode" as she called it.

But what, he was asking himself again and again, what did he do wrong? The newspapers were delivered on time, no complaints. The boys were happy. He was happy as well. What went wrong?

Question—What did Junior do wrong, if anything?

(Answer—he cheated newspaper people)

The Earrings Story

When Junior was in the third grade he was invited to a birthday party of a next door girl. One of the presents she received got his attention. It was a small oven called "kiln" for making ceramics. The next day Junior knocked at the girl's door and asked her point blank if she intends to use the kiln.

When he got a "no" answer he offered to exchange the kiln for anything he had among his possessions. Soon Junior went home with the kiln and the work started. Junior baked two small ceramic balls with a piece of wire in each and painted them in bright colors.

After the earrings were ready he took off and went to a neighboring street, away from his mother's eyes. He knocked at a first door and when a nice woman opened the door he told her that he was a neighboring kid, that he dreamed about buying a good bike, and he decided to earn money by making jewelry and selling it to the neighbors.

When a nice and very sympathetic woman asked him for how much he is selling his earrings he answered "ten cents each, but I really would prefer to sell them as a pair." The woman asked him to wait, went into the room and came back with about forty cents in change. She refused to take the earrings and wished Junior to soon make enough money to buy the bike of his dream.

Junior thanked her from the bottom of his heart and went to the next door.

Every day Junior was making between three to five dollars, a huge sum at that time, and soon he became the richest kid in the school. He always had enough money to buy everyone an ice cream or a chocolate bar. He never told anyone the source of his riches, but one day he knocked at the door of the school's principal and the project came to the end. The parents made a thorough search of his room and found nine hundred seventy five dollars in small bills and change.

The money was confiscated, but deposited into Junior's college account. The parents then had a talk with Junior. They told him that he has to worry about the grades, not about making money.

I am getting good grades, said Junior.

You always can try to get better grades, said his mom.

There are no better grades, said Junior.

It is a shame to go to neighbors and ask for money, they told him.

I didn't ask for anything, said Junior, I offered them jewelry I made by myself and they paid for it.

Don't argue with your parent's young man, said Junior's mom. She was already visibly upset. Junior decided not to argue with anyone and be as silent as possible.

Why are you not saying anything, are we talking to a wall, asked Junior's dad. He thought that he himself was calm, but he also was already pacing the room and yelling. He thought that this is OK since he was the father and Junior was his son. Grownups often think they can yell at their children, but become angry when children yell back.

Never do it again, he said to Junior and the kiln went into the garbage can. End of story.

Question—Did Junior as always do anything wrong?

(Answer—this time Junior didn't lie, didn't cheat, didn't steal and earned his money fair and square. There was however one small thing that was not very good in what he did. His earrings were not good and he knew that the people would not buy them, but give him money nevertheless ... But he didn't steal anything, didn't cheat anyone and didn't lie to anyone. They gave him money voluntarily without any coercion on his part.)

The Stamps Business Story

Junior went to the fifth grade when he discovered that stamps for most people are just glue to envelopes, but they have value, and sometimes very high value. His dad read an article about a guy who found an old stamp on an envelope that belonged to his grandparents, then went to a store where they sell collectibles items and found out it was worth a cool million.

Junior collected all envelopes he found in the neighbor's garbage, went to a store that was called "Philatelist Paradise," and was told that only very specific stamps have value. The store made a huge impression on Junior. Thousands of stamps, leather covers, light music playing, a lot of bronze and other seemingly expensive things.

The owner was very kind to Junior and even showed him a book called "Rare and Unique Stamps" with thousands of illustrations of stamps that were worth looking for.

Junior spent all his birthday money and bought this book that weighed about six pounds. It took him two months to read, and another two to memorize. By the end of this period Junior knew every single image of every single stamp that had value to serious collectors. He could look at a stamp and say immediately its value, origin and why it was valuable, but also the page number where it was in this wonderful and insightful book of stamps.

Junior learned that every Saturday the stamp collectors and sellers were gathering at a swap meet downtown and selling and exchanging stamps. This is where Junior went to get his first field education. He was sure that every person at the Swap Meet knew this and other philatelic books by heart. He soon learned that most of the people knew very little or sometimes they knew close to nothing.

He was standing near one of the kiosks looking at stamps, and overheard a conversation between the seller and the buyer. The buyer was asking how he could be sure that the stamp he wanted to buy really was worth three hundred dollars. Junior looked at the stamp and immediately recognized it. The actual worth of the stamp according to the catalogue was six hundred dollars, but the seller obviously had no idea about it and was trying desperately to sell it for half of the price.

"It's worth six hundred" he said out loud. Both the seller and the buyer turned to him in silence. Then the seller said "Get lost." Junior began to walk away, but the buyer stopped him: "How do you know?"

"It is on the page 226 of this book" said Junior and pointed to the book standing on the shelf behind the seller. The book was open on the page 226 and the image of the stamp was found. "Thank you" said the seller, and gave Junior a dollar.

Soon a rumor started about a wonder boy who knew everything about stamps was all over the Swap Meet. Every Saturday Junior would come to the place and was asked to give his opinion about different stamps. He was paid his standard fee of one dollar. The money went to buy additional books and a subscription of two philately magazines.

One day Junior saw a stamp that was offered for sale for twenty dollars. He knew exactly that this stamp was worth at least twenty thousand. This was his first major purchase, and from this moment on he added buying and selling stamps to his business endeavors.

When he was graduating from the high school his bank account had over two hundred thousand dollars and his first move at the day he turned eighteen was to purchase the "Philatelist Paradise." The second was to enroll himself into a business and administration program at a local college.

Question—What did the buyers and sellers at the Swap Meet pay Junior for?

(Answer—he gave them knowledge, his thoughts and ideas. They are his and he can do with them whatever he wants—give as a gift, just share or sell.)

Now let's talk about whose good Junior was seeking in all those stories. He obviously was seeking his own good, and in the episode with flowers he overstepped and in order to sell flowers he stole them. Such business will not last for long. At one point the stealing will be revealed and he will be punished.

In the newspaper story Junior did everything smart, but he cheated the newspaper people. Such business will not survive for long. It is not a good business when every moment what you are doing can be revealed and stopped. You can't build on such a foundation. It is not practical. You will be punished for doing it and your business will be ruined.

The third business with earrings was straight, but it was also not for long. The business wasn't built on a good product or service, but on an image of a "nice boy" coming to the doorsteps and asking for so little … and he had a worthy goal to buy a bike, so people gave money to him out of sympathy. It was like begging, but nicely. It is not OK for a long term, and actually is a bit of a "con artist" type business. It is on the border of lying and conning people.

The stamp business is good. It is solidly based on Junior's knowledge that he possesses and others do not. He exchanged his knowledge for money. It is called "consulting" and this is how many people make their living. Some people go to colleges and universities in order to know more than others and give them advice in exchange for money. There are political consultants, engineering consultants, medical consultants and antique goods consultants. This is an honorable and a long-term business.

When Junior was twenty-five he got his MBA from a major university, bought a new house for his parents, helped his sister to start her own business and acquired three more stores selling antiques, stamps, coins and other collectable things. He became one of the most knowledgeable antique experts in the world and was constantly invited by major auction houses and estate sales to evaluate furniture, vases, stamps, coins and even paintings. He also began to help several different charities collect money for the poor and sick people around the world.

The Fundraising Story

After a terrible natural disaster in a state of Louisiana, a local charity decided to ask members of the community to donate money to help Louisiana families that lost their homes and had to relocate. It was a very honorable task and three well-known people in the community said that they would spear head the effort.

The principal of the local school brought together a group of people and told them horror stories about the ordeal the people they are trying to help went through. She also told them how important for those who are suffering to receive help as soon as possible. The good people she assembled immediately understood the importance of the task and began to call their friends and acquaintances.

A pastor in a local church brought in his usual group of volunteers. He told them that as an incentive the group will get a percent of what they together will collect. The incentive money will be evenly distributed among all the members of the group.

Junior called on several good salespeople. He explained to them the importance of the task and a need for an immediate action and offered each of them a percentage of the money they would collect. You can help many people who lost their belongings, he said, and also you will at the same time make money for yourselves. The more you get for the cause, the more you will earn yourselves.

Junior's group raised twice as much as the pastor's group and three times more than the principal's group.

Do you know why?

In Junior's group everyone knew that each person's award was based on each person's own performance. No performance, no award. Good performance, hefty award. This added merits to their efforts to collect money for the important cause. They won and the cause won.

Riddle #25 - Coconut world

There were two neighboring islands both engaged in production of coconut based products. They made coconut soup in cans, coconut milk in bottles, coconut strudel and coconut sauce. The demand for coconut products was really high and two factories on each island were working day and night to supply the demand.

The workers on the island called UBBA decided that they shall receive more money for their work. They threatened a strike and the owners of the factory agreed to pay them twice as much, including a month vacation, reimbursement for all their medical expenses, full salary for eighteen months if they fire a person for any reason, salary for two years for new mothers and many other important benefits.

Islanders on the island called BODU didn't make such demands and worked for less and their factory produced cheaper products than the UBBA factory.

Then one day the demand went down. The supermarket chains were not buying as much coconut as they used to. Since BODU products were cheaper all of the remaining buyers switched to buying from them.

The UBBA people didn't like it. They sent community organizers to the BODU Island, who convinced workers on BODU to join the Inter-island workers union, had bloody demonstrations, stopped work all together, beat up several non complying workers … and all the entire island went on strike. The factory agreed to pay whatever the union demanded, and the salaries and benefits on both islands were equalized.

The supermarket buyers soon found out that on both islands the coconut products are expensive and they all left. They found another island that was producing those products much cheaper. Now there is no work, no payment for unemployment and no maternity leave on either of the two islands. Actually there are no salaries, no factories, not even medical facilities anywhere. They have no money to pay for any of that. The only thing remaining from the good old days was the paved in gold headquarters of the coconut workers union.

Thinking out loud:

Question—How to bring buyers of coconut products back to the islands?

Below are a number of ideas you can choose from:

a) Send community organizers to every coconut producing island in the world, unite all workers into unions and demand equal pay for all coconut workers of the Universe. If those workers will not agree to join the union inflict as much damage as possible, organize demonstrations, interrupt work, burn factories and their production and force owners of factories to retaliate. Then use the worker's anger to unite them in the union.

b) Let workers alone and have the market determine what to pay for a good worker and for a not so good worker. This will stabilize the prices for the coconut products and the best producer with the best prices will win. The consumers will be happy because they will be getting good prices and buying good products. The better workers will be rewarded. The better producer will get more profits. The only people who will not be happy are the coconut union leaders.

c) Contact unions at the supermarkets and convince them to go on strike if the supermarkets will continue buying inexpensive coconut products from other islands. Pay their leaders under the table to convince them to join the strike. Promise them when they will go on strike to join it and fight for their goals.

Comment of a Progressive / Socialist: Unions play a big and important role in protecting the rights of the workers. Without them the workers would receive a very small salary and will not get any benefits. Unions are the only real defender of working people.

Comment of a True Liberal / Capitalist: Nothing killed more businesses than unions. When union organizers are in town, cars burn, windows are smashed and people killed. Unions always are trying to get what they want by forcing others into accepting their point of view. More is paid to the union workers, we the consumers pay more at the cash register or American jobs go overseas.

Author's opinion:

Can you guess what is my opinion?

Chapter IX

Profits - are they good or bad?

THE IDEA OF socialists is to control every aspect of people's lives and distribute earned money and goods between the population disregarding who worked and who did not. They call it social justice, equality and 'freedom from property'.

They fight viciously against profits, calling profits the biggest evil of them all. They call bankers "fat cats." If people who work hard are rewarded for their good work by high profits they call it "windfall profits" and are trying to take away as much as they can.

If socialists say something is terrible, than this thing shall be awesome. Let's together try to understand how bad (or maybe not bad) those profits are.

Profit is the difference between what you received for your product or service and what you spend to make and sell your product or service. For example, if the total cost of making and selling a toy was $100 and you sold it for $120, your profit is $20. If you found someone who is willing to pay $130 for the toy, your profit is $30.

As a producer you want to make as high a profit as possible. As a consumer you want to pay as little as possible. How do those two opposing tendencies work you might ask?

We already discussed what happens when government is trying to regulate prices and tell producers how much they shall pay to workers and how much they can charge for their products. The only way to establish a right price for your product is to test it on the market and see how much you can get for it.

What is "market"? How it can determine prices? This sounds crazy but actually it is quite simple. You made an arrow with spears and offered it to a toy store. If they sell well, you can raise the price a bit. If they continue to sell well, you can continue raising prices … but then customers can decide that your arrows are not worth such a high price and can start buying arrows made by someone else and are sold for less. They were buying yours because you had good prices and high quality, but if someone offered them better products for the same price, or the same product but for better price, they will vote with their money for his product.

Riddle 26 - Friends of Why

In a small village called O lived a young boy whom everyone called WHY. They called him WHY because he was always asking questions. Why the Sun is shining during the daytime and Moon is only at night? Why horses do not speak? Why men have beards and women don't?

The O people were mostly working the land, but also fishing, hunting and picking mushrooms, berries and medicine flowers in the vast forests surrounding the village. They were bringing all they picked or grew to the barn in the middle of the village, and when the barn was full, three or four of the villagers would put the goods on a horse wagon and ride to the nearest town to sell them and buy necessary products for the village things. The food and everything the village had was distributed by village elders equally to everyone or when needed.

O was a poor village. One year they had a good harvest and were able to buy new clothes, kitchenware and from time to time pay for doctor's visits. During the next year they would not be able even to afford a pain medicine or change a broken plow.

Why we can't buy candies, WHY was asking his parents? Why other villages have cars and television and ours do not, he was asking the village Elders. Why one person works hard and another doesn't work at all, but everyone receives from the Elders the same, he was asking his friends.

We can't buy candies because we do not have money, his parents were telling him.

Why we do not have money, WHY was continuing.

We do not have money because we have nothing to sell.

Why wouldn't we fish more, get more mushrooms and berries, sell them to the town folks and get more money, WHY was asking.

In our village, his parents were telling him, we all work and bring what we did to the village Elders and they then sell and distribute money and food to everyone. Even if you will work hard and bring more mushrooms that will not affect by much what you will receive at the end.

Other villages have cars and television, the village elders were telling WHY, because they are luckier than us. Their villages are in the better woods with more mushrooms and more fish. They have better fields. Also they are very selfish and we do not like them. Several times we approached them to build a barn in the middle of our valley and have everyone bring to this barn everything they pick, produce or make, and from this central barn the central committee of elders would distribute everything to each and every village. This way the inequality in land and amount of fish in the river would be fixed. But those cruel and self-centered people refused.

The Elders are taking what we make and giving it to others who do not work because those others also need food, and clothes and medicine, the friends were telling WHY.

OK, said WHY one day while talking to a group of his five best friends he hanged around since his childhood. For eighteen years I was trying to understand why someone has to tell me what I shall do with the goods I make or grow, where to bring them, and most of all how much of it I can take to myself. I want to go to the other side of the valley and start a new village. We will do everything differently. Are you with me?

Six of them left O and began to build a new small village that had no central barn. The new village became known as the "Friends of WHY" village. They worked extra hours, made a lot of extra-efforts and by the end of the summer each one received more money than what they needed for their necessities. They sat down to think what to do with this additional money. Each one can do whatever he wanted with his money—to buy things they were dreaming about all their life, to take a long vacation, or to invest. They decided to invest together in a new food processing business.

Since they had profits that they didn't spend they purchased equipment and instead of selling mushrooms, berries and fruits began to make and sell pies with mushrooms and berries, make and sell jams, jellies and marmalades. They worked hard, each receiving only what they needed to buy food and clothes and putting profits aside. The factory began sell well almost from the beginning and the gang decided not to spend all the profits but built a fishing and hunting lodge. The lodge became well known and many city folks started coming with their families to spend time in the magnificent woods, and fish, hunt and pick mushrooms and berries.

The friends of WHY began to buy products from O, and they also hired many villagers from O to work at the factory and at the lodge. Those who worked at WHY were able to buy themselves new clothes, go to dentists, repair their houses. They saw movies for the first time in their lives and even took vacations abroad.

All six of the friends of WHY built large houses on the riverbank, bought good automobiles and had television sets all over their homes.

One of them decided to live in a capital. He sold his share in the company and moved away. Another one went to study pharmacology in a college in order to open a new factory himself to produce drugs based on healing flowers their valley was famous for. He now had enough profits to do it alone.

Those villagers of O that continued bringing their products to the central barn still live without cars or TV sets. When they need medical help they go to the friends of WHY and beg them for money. Actually when they do not have enough food they also go to WHY but WHY instead of giving away food hires them to do odd jobs and pays them so they can buy food for themselves.

The elders in O are still telling each other that the reason they are poor is because the land is bad, the woods are dry and if all the villages would build a central barn and everything in the valley would be distributed by a central committee the life would be much much better, almost good as in The Friends of WHY village.

Thinking out loud:

Q1 - Why the friend of WHY were able to built good life and villagers of O were unable to do it?

   a) The woods near O not as good as near the village of WHY

   b) People in O are lazy

   c) The friends of WHY were keeping their profits, not giving them to the government (elders) to distribute, and invested them in new businesses that allowed them to build good lives for themselves and many others.

Comment of a Progressive / Socialist: Profits create inequality. Maybe some people would live better if they would keep their profits. But what about sick, injured and unemployed people? One day you yourself can become sick, old and unemployed. Then you will cry "help me, help me" and would be happy to receive a share of someone else's profits!

<u>Comment of a True Liberal / Capitalist</u>: If profits are distributed among many non-productive citizens, they create equality. They do not create good life, just "the same life for everyone." When profits are kept and re-invested, that creates new businesses and new jobs. Profits enable producers to create better life for most of the people. One thing it doesn't create—equality. But why would a person who works hard and a person who does nothing be equally rewarded?

What to do if a person who had his own small business didn't save any money for his retirement years? He is now old, sick, has no income and needs to pay his rent, his electrical bills, buy food and pay doctors. Who shall take care of him?

What to do if a person who worked all his life but didn't save anything because he was dining in good restaurants, vacationing on fashionable beaches, buying great cars and electronic gadgets, now needs a surgery that he can't afford? Who shall take care of him?

What to do if a person, who was robbing and stealing all his life, spent years in prison, never worked or did anything good for anyone, now requires a 24 hour a day nurse, money for drugs and special food? Who shall take care of him?

What to do if a person gambled away all his belongings and now is in need of everything including clothes, toothpaste and toilet paper? Who shall take care of him?

The government has one answer to all problems—to rob producers from their belongings. If there is a sick person who needs help, rob the producers. If the government decides that there is a need for a new park in the capitol, rob the producers. If the government decides to have another dinner for thousand people at the White House, rob the producers. Steal from them, rob them, dine on their dime and at the same time curse THEM for being selfish.

Riddle #27 - Subsidy

This island was famous for their artichokes. Everyone was coming there to buy artichokes that two companies produced, packaged and made great products with them. One company was called "GUM" and another "BUM." The GUM Company was very innovative. They used sophisticated irrigation, always checked out new technology and established temperature control in their storages and trucks. They had superior artichoke and artichoke products and sold them at competitive prices.

The BUM Company was sloppy, slow, used old technology, had poor storages and the artichokes were often rotting, and offered buyers only a narrow variety of products. On top of that the packaging wasn't as attractive and their brand not as promoted as the GUM Company's brand.

At the end of the year the GUM Company calculated their sales figures and found out that they made a good profit of two million dollars. They were happy and gave their employees additional bonuses for the excellent year of work. They were planning to use their profits to start a new company "Solar and Wind Energy Corporation" that would provide cheap electricity to the islanders, would allow them to reduce the cost of their artichoke products and would employ many islanders.

The BUM Company found out that they spent a million but had only half a million dollars in sales. In other words, they found out that they lost a lot of money, and now have to close their factory and fire all their employees.

The government of the island announced that they are very concerned about a possibility of firing so many people. They said that the BUM Company is too large to fail (meaning that it is bad if so many people will be fired) and decided to do something to not let the BUM Company fail.

The only thing they can do to help BUM, they decided, was to give them money to cover their loss and to continue paying salaries to their employees. And the only place they could find money at was the GUM Company.

The island's government passed a law that GUM has to pay the government half of the profits they made. After receiving a cool million the government gave this money to the BUM Company.

Now BUM had enough money to continue paying their employees, and to do what they did before—produce bad and unattractive products.

Another year passed. The GUM Company sold even more products. They planned to use them to open a chain of stores throughout the archipelago and employ many of the archipelago citizens.

The profits were good, more than three million dollars and the government immediately seized half ... and gave it to the BUM Company that again had a lousy year.

Year after year the GUM Company was working hard, doing a great job and getting better and better profits. Year after year the government took half of their profits and gave it to a bad company that did a lousy job, had bad policies and terrible management.

And one day the BUM Company's management suddenly realized that they do not have to work at all. The only thing they had to do is to wait for the money from the GUM Company, take some to themselves and distribute the rest among the workers. This was great, they decided. From this moment on this is exactly what they did. They even didn't pretend to work, didn't do anything for the whole year and waited for the money the government was stealing from a good company to give them in order not to fire the employees and not to close the bad factory.

Thinking out loud:

Q1 - Is it a fair system to take profits from good companies and give them to bad companies?

a) Yes, this is a good system. Good companies still have some profits left and bad companies will not fire people. This is good for the morale of the people.

b) No, this is not a good system. The government punishes good companies and awards bad ones.

c) The government in some cases can take money from good companies and give it to bad companies, but only if they promise to do things differently. Or if they would promise to vote for the government at the next elections.

Comment of a Progressive / Socialist: The subsidy is a very valuable way to help producers who are temporarily out of luck. Yes, you take money from good producers and give to "temporarily ill" ones, but it is like to help to cure and nurture a sick person. He needs time and help to recover and re-group. It is very humanitarian to help the weak.

Comment of a True Liberal / Capitalist: By not allowing failing companies to fail and go out of business we are not helping people and the economy. The GUM Company had enough profits to invest in a new business. They know how to run businesses and they would have a good chance to succeed in a new one. The government took large part of their profits and didn't allow them to grow. Why did the government keep alive a bad company? Is it possible that the head of the company and the head of the government are relatives? Or maybe the liberal government took from producers and gave to non-producers in exchange for their votes? Liberal governments usually pay for the votes with the money they stole from one group of people and gave to another group of people.

Author's opinion—Right answer is: b

If you are a producer, you shall be able to sell above your cost, above the amount you spent to buy or make the product. If you are unable to sell above your cost, your business will collapse.

A friend of mine had a popcorn business in Russia. He told me that he kept receiving conflicting reports. The sales go great, many popcorn stands are in movie theaters, but there are no profits coming from this company. I was going over there and he asked me to help him understand what the problem is.

The problem was very simple. The cost of one small portion of popcorn after adding up the cost of corn, transportation, electricity, salaries of the sale people and other expenses was 37 cents. They were selling such a portion in theaters for 35 cents. They were losing 2 cents every time someone would buy a small portion of corn. They were losing 5 cents every time someone would buy a large portion of corn. Do you think it is a good business to spend 37 cents on a portion of corn and sell it for 35 cents?

a) Yes

b) No

This is how a middle school student Nik determined the fair and right price of his product, and this is how his profits were determined:

Riddle #28 - Nik's Candies

Nik was a student at a junior high school. He loved electronic games and always wanted the newest ones. His parents however didn't share his interest in playing games and thought that he has to study more and play less. Because of that Nik came to a conclusion that he has to find a way how to find money to purchase games without nagging his parents.

One day he was with his mom at a wholesale food store and saw a box of candies that he knew every child would love. He asked his mom to buy the box, promising to pay her from his weekly allowance. There were 42 candies in the box and Nik got them for ten bucks. Nick ate two of them and quickly calculated that the cost of the remaining ones was a quarter a piece.

Next day at school he offered candies to his fellow students at one dollar for a candy. He sold two candies and the business stopped. No one wanted to spend a dollar for a candy. His profit from each candy was 75 cents, but no one was buying them anymore.

Next day Nik offered the candies at fifty cents each. He sold two here, three there. In a week the box was still half full. Nik's profit from each candy was now 25 cents, but he wasn't selling fast enough and every day he sold less and less.

After much consideration, Nik made an announcement—buy two candies for 99 cents and you will get one for free. And suddenly the sales picked up. The students felt that this was a good price for a candy. Three students would group together and get candies for 33 cents apiece.

Nik made eight cents profit on each, but he sold the remaining candies in one day. Nik said—it wasn't me who determined the price. I would love to sell for more, but there were no sales at higher prices. So the right price of the candy at my school is about 33 cents.

Thinking out loud:

Q1 - How you can determine the right price for the product you want to sell?

Here are several ideas about who can help you with this decision:

a) Ask the government worker who is in charge of this segment of the economy

b) Ask your senator or congressman

c) Ask your wife

d) Check for how much similar products are selling, evaluate the differences between your product and the others, offer it at a comparable price (or less) and look how it sells. If it doesn't sell, either improve the product or lower prices. If it sells fast, either make a lot of it or raise the price a bit and see how it sells now. Repeat either option as many times as needed.

Comment of a Progressive / Socialist: First of all when no one supervises what is going on at school, children might be getting products that are not so good for them. Second the government workers in charge of public education can purchase any products they feel are good for the kids for much lower prices than an individual student, and the price for children will be much lower. Also the money for such products will come from government programs, not from the kids' pockets. Some of those children are underprivileged and poor and can't afford candies sold by an individual seller. They will feel hurt and unfairly treated if other children would be able to buy candies and they wouldn't. If the government will distribute products they will be given for free to everyone, or given for free to selected kids whose parents can't afford to buy them candies.

Comment of a True Liberal / Capitalist: Again and again progressives want to take money from producers and distribute them among other groups of people. Their solution for every problem is to steal as much as they can and quickly give it away.

We were however talking right now about profits, not about social justice. Nik found the "market way" how to price his products, or in another words what profit he can make on them.

When children will stop being interested in the candies they will stop buying. If there will be a huge demand for such candies, Nik can try to raise prices again. I am quite sure however that there will be other students who will pick up the trend and will start offering the same or better products for less. Either you offer something very unique and people pay you practically any price, or you play by ear. This is called "Market."

Author's opinion—Right answer is: d

Timely questions:

I have a question to you—would bad producers and people who do not work vote for progressive (socialist) government that takes money from good producers and gives them, or they will vote for the True Liberal pro-capitalist government that doesn't interfere with what producers do?

Bad producers would vote for progressive government that takes (steals) money from good producers and gives them

Bad producers would vote for pro-capitalist government that doesn't give bad producers anything

Personally I think that many of the bad producers will vote for the guy who will take money from elsewhere and give it to them. They will even scream and cry that good producers are selfish people who do not want to share with those in need. They would even believe that they themselves are altruistic and noble.

Another question is—would good producers vote for progressive (socialist) government that punishes them for their good work by stealing money from them, or they would vote for the government that doesn't interfere in their business?

Good producers would vote for conservative (socialist) government

Good producers would vote for True Liberal pro-capitalist government

Most of the good producers, at least the ones that have time to think, would vote for the True Liberal pro-capitalist government. Why? Because capitalism is the only system that is fair to those that produce.

And still another question—since we have a democracy and the majority decides which government will be in charge of the country, who was a majority when progressive government is elected, good producers or bad producers?

Good producers were in majority and they elected a progressive (socialist) government that punishes them by robbing profits from them, calls them "fat cats" and "capitalistic pigs" and with the money taken from them awards those people and companies that produce either nothing or bad products.

Bad producers were in majority. They want the government to give them money and they do not care from where the money comes from.

I do not know who was in majority. I was watching reruns of "Friends."

Let's see if you will agree with me on this one—I think that politicians especially socialists/progressives are very generous people ... because what they distribute is not their money. It is our money that was stolen from us. They first are robbing us, then having a field day by throwing our money around. They call themselves Robin Hoods, but actually they are thieves and robbers who got together and legitimized their great ideas of expropriating money from those whom they call "deep pockets"—you and me. They smell better and have better clothes than the street thugs, but that doesn't change who they are.

Riddle #29 - Zelda's Designs

Zelda was a very good knitter. She worked at home and had many happy clients who told their friends about her and they in turn told their friends. For many years Zelda was dreaming about her own store where she would employ several knitters and tailors who would implement her own designs. Thinking about the future she registered her own company and came up with a very nice and catchy name "Zelda's Designs" that would be written above the front entrance to her store.

Meantime, her little company was making profits. Zelda could have moved to a larger apartment, or went on a vacation, or got herself a new car. But all she wanted was to fulfill her dream and open her own store. She knew that without an investment it would be impossible and was saving for this worthy goal.

When economy in the country began to decline, many stores closed their doors and prices for rent went down. Zelda thought that with prices for rent and supplies dropping she can afford to start her own business. She found a great place for a fashion design store, negotiated a good rent (half of what they were asking just a year ago), and visited several of her friends who were good knitters and tailors that were laid off their jobs.

She told them that she is finally opening her own place and she would want them to work with her. She also told them that she can pay them only five dollars an hour. She said that otherwise with all the other expenses and costs she will not be able to sell her designs. When and if I will be able to pay more, I will pay more she said.

Every one of her friends agreed to receive the five dollar an hour pay. It is better than nothing that we get now they all told Zelda.

Everyone was happy. Zelda was about to open her dream store. Her friends wanted to work and receive compensation for their work. The clients who Zelda knew would be happy to wear her designs were happy. But then enters the government.

You can't pay employees less than the minimum wage, Zelda was told. And the minimum wage is two times what you intended to pay your workers. If you will pay less, we will punish you, make you pay a fine and if you will not comply with our regulations we will close your business down and might even arrest you and put in jail.

All of the workers agreed to work for this pay; said Zelda and all her future employees confirmed that they did. We do not want to sit home and do nothing, they all said.

No, said the government, we will not allow you to work for half of the minimum wages. We the government prohibit employers to pay less than this amount. We feel that if the employers pay workers less, the workers will not be able to afford the good life in our country.

But we want to work, said Zelda's friends.

It is not important what you want, said the government. What is important is the good of the workers as we understand it, not an opinion of the workers. Since you obviously do not understand what is good for you, we will not even listen to what you are saying. We- the-government knows what is better for you because we are smarter than you.

But we can't live without earnings. We need to pay rent and feed our families, pleaded Zelda's friends.

Do not worry, the government told them, we will pay you enough money for the rent and other important expenses, give you food stamps to buy food and provide you with medical services for free. You do not have to do anything to receive all that.

But where will you would take this money from to cover our expenses, asked Zelda's friends. Governments do not have money of their own; they have to take it from somewhere.

We will borrow a bit of the money from the Chinese and will take the rest from Zelda and other working and producing people, the government said. We will create new laws and regulations and make her pay from the profits she made in the past or will be making in the future.

And they did as they said.

Zelda didn't open her store. She is working from her small apartment and still has many of her clients who love her work. The government every month takes part of the money she earns and pays unemployed workers, the same people who otherwise would be working at her store and making money.

Since Zelda and producers like her are unable to hire workers for less, there is no more knitting factories in the United States and all knitted dresses and sweaters are imported from China. The Chinese are making profits and then loaning us the money we then pay them back with interest.

Actually Americans are not producing almost anything that people need for their day-to-day life because the government dictates what to pay to the American workers, and American companies can't compete with other countries that pay their workers less.

The only way to compete with other countries is to hire illegal emigrants, but this is another story and we will talk about it separately.

Thinking out loud:

Q1 - Do you think government and union leaders do not understand what they are doing by forcing employers to pay minimal wages or you think they understand it?

I came up with two possible answers. Here they are:

a)   I think government people do not understand what forced
     wages do to our economy and the people in this country. They
     are not well educated, have no experience in economy and do
     not think.

b)   I think government people and union leaders are smart and
     they understand what they are doing. However then comes
     another question—if they understand what they are doing,
     what is their reason for continuing doing it?

What do you think? Are they stupid, or they are (simply put it) crooks,
thieves, liars and robbers?

Comment of a Progressive / Socialist: If government will not interfere
and will not regulate minimum wages, the capitalists will pay workers
so little they will not be able to survive, less have good life.

Comment of a True Liberal / Capitalist: When government wants to
regulate businesses the result is usually just opposite of what they say
they intended to achieve.

Author's opinion—make up your own mind.

We discussed this so much in this book that it is about time you shall
rely on your own logic.

Chapter X
Cause and effect

REMEMBER THE STORY about Poseidon whom people wrongly attributed storms and winds, and in order to pacify him killed many young boys and girls? Did they correctly identify the <u>cause</u> of storms and based on that did they find the right solution to the problem?

a) Yes

b) No

Remember the story about the Bubonic Plague, when Europeans killed all the cats thinking that they are agents of evil, which allowed rats to multiply and bring the plague on Europe? And how people responded—they thought that witches bring plague to them and they began to kill innocent women, men and children whom they suspected to be witches. They wrongly identified the <u>cause</u>, found a wrong cure (solution) and it brought devastating <u>effects.</u>

Our humanity faces a very urgent task now. If we will not find out why we the people are constantly at war with each other, we will not be able to find a solution to this problem. In the past one person was able to kill very few. The wars and fights were local, not threatening the whole civilization, and were fought with a sword and a spear. Now we have biological, chemical and nuclear weapons, and not finding a solution to the problem of co-existence might bring devastating effects on the entire population of the planet. What do you think might happen if terrorist groups will get biological and nuclear weapons and will trigger the third World War? Below are some of the possible answers:

We have more nuclear and other weapons than anyone else and no one will even think about fighting with us.

Most of the humans on Earth will be dead but small groups like some of the Amazon natives or Bushman in Australia will survive

Terrorist groups would never use any of the weapons because they are just joking that they want to kill all the people who do not believe in their God.

For sixty-five hundred years of its recorded history most of the humankind lived in poverty. More than three quarters of people lived in what we would call today "inhuman conditions." Kings and Leaders, Khans and Strongman were unable and maybe unwilling to create good lives to the citizens of their countries. Then two hundred years ago the United States of America was created. And in a short period of time three quarters of its population began to live good lives, unheard of in any country or any period of the existence of our civilization. It wasn't easy life especially at the beginning, but the people were owners of their own destiny and they began to build this destiny in an unprecedented speed. Why? What happened? What was the cause of it? If this happened in America, maybe the same recipe can be applied to the rest of the world?

We need to learn how to identify causes of good things and learn how to apply them in other places and situations.

We need to identify causes of bad things and learn how to cure them thinking through all possible effects of the cure. The killing of innocent boys and girls didn't stop storms. The burning of innocent women and children didn't stop plague.

Let's take a look on some other cause and effect stories to start learning how to search for the right cures for our problems.

End of the Roman Empire

This is one of the theories of why the Roman Empire fell. The empire was standing for a thousand years. Romans built much better and civilized lives for the citizens than any other country contemporary to them. Romans had plenty of slaves and for them they didn't build a good life. The whole world was dreaming about having what they had (much like our contemporary world is dreaming to have what Americans have) and every barbarian Ruler, King or Chieftain dreamed about robbing their riches.

Rome however had a good army that was constantly engaged in wars with barbarians who were attacking Roman's borders. The Roman army was much better equipped than the barbarians, much better trained and much more disciplined. Most of the Roman men were trained in case of a large scale war and they were helping the army when needed. Rome was always winning.

When one day several barbarian armies attacked at the same time, many of the Roman's men had to be recruited into the army to fight them. Because of the burden of many simultaneous wars the country produced fewer goods and they went up in price. The government of Rome decided to stop food prices from rising and in order to help the poor to buy affordable food issued a price control decree. At that time usual punishment for disobeying government decrees was very simple—death.

The decree said "If you sell food over such-and-such price you will be hanged" and "If you do not sell food that you grew you will be hanged" and "If you have a farm and do not produce food you will be hanged." This was a very simple and easy to understand decree.

And the farmers understood it very well. They understood that the progressive government of Rome decided to give something to another group of people (the poor) what they would steal from them, the producers of food.

The cost of growing and producing food was higher than the sales prices listed in the decree. The farmers were unable to sell their farm products at the prices the government mandated them to sell, but if they would sell for more the penalty was death. They couldn't produce food and not sell it, the decree prohibited it as well—and the penalty for that was death. They couldn't live on a farm and not to grow food. The decree said that the penalty for that was death.

Hundreds of thousands of farmers ran away from their own farms. They sent letters to their sons who served in the army and were fighting barbarians on the borders. Their sons deserted the army and ran away to meet with their families who didn't know where to go, what to do and how to survive. The deserting was so massive that the barbarians entered the empire and since no one stopped them they destroyed all the major cities and killed many thousands of Romans. The slaves joined them and helped to kill and burn the houses of their former masters.

The single price control decree destroyed an empire that was standing for thousands of years and didn't show any signs of dying. Progressives did what millions of barbarians were unable to do. They destroyed one of the greatest empires in the history of humankind.

The progressive government of the Roman Empire decided that the reason for high food prices was farmers' greed. Actually it was the absence of workers, absence of many needed supplies and difficulty in production that was the direct result of wars the country was fighting at that time. The government wrongly identified the <u>cause</u> and offered a <u>solution</u> based on the wrong assumption.

Did they in your opinion think through the effects of this solution? Did they observe the effects and confirmed that the solution is resolving the problem?

The only people who were happy about that decree were the barbarians.

Maybe you are thinking that what happened in Rome will not apply to the great country of ours, The United States of America? Hmmm… let's me show you how our own American government's order can inflict harm to hundreds of the great American cities. One "ordinance" (this is how laws enacted by local governments are called) is single-handedly responsible for the destruction of thousands of great buildings and turning them into slums. Here is the story.

Destruction of Housing in America

When you make your store beautiful, better than other stores, when you play nice music inside, when there is parking near the store, people come to your place instead of going to other stores that smell bad and have no parking attached.

If you are an owner of a building you can make it attractive to your clients that are called tenants. You want people to rent apartments at your place instead of going to other places. In order to attract them you plant trees, paint buildings in nice colors, have soft music playing at the entrance of the building, repair it when something happened and take care of your property in order not to lose tenants who are already renting from you.

When you, your neighbors, everyone in the area are taking good care of their buildings, the area becomes attractive, many people want to live there, and tenants are ready to pay higher prices in order to live in such a great area.

The owners of the buildings are obviously trying to get as much money from tenants as possible, but they know that if they will ask for too much, no one will rent apartments in their houses and even the existing tenets will leave. They try to charge "as much as possible" but not more than that.

The agreements between owners of the houses and their tenants are usually made for one year. Most of those agreements say that the tenants can leave the apartments at the end of the year and the owners can raise prices at the end of the year. If the tenants do not like new prices they can leave the apartments and rent where prices are lower. Since prices in really good areas are rising, people who are not able to afford them are moving to more affordable areas.

American progressives didn't like it. They decided to stop this "terrible discrimination" against tenants and decided to impose something called "rent control" to stop this discrimination once and for all.

Rent control in real estate (housing) business is like price control in commerce. The government tells you if you will charge more than so-and-so we will punish you. They say that the purpose of rent control is to allow a poor person to pay less for his apartment. The government again is trying to show how good they are to one group of people by stealing money from another group. One American citizen, (owner of a house, can receive high rent for his apartment, but is forced to receive low rent. The government did good to one person by taking from another. For example a landlord can charge a thousand dollars a month, but is forced to charge seven hundred dollars a month. The difference of three hundred dollars is stolen from him by the government and given to the tenant.

The house belongs to the owner ... but he is not in control. Do you think he is happy?

As you may recall that in the first chapters of this book we discussed exactly the same situation—you own a car, but someone is driving it. Who is in control? Or you worked hard, put money aside, invested it in purchasing a house for rent and ... can't get a fair market price because someone decided that you can't use your property the way you want to use it. Does it look like you are 100% in control of your belongings? Does it look like freedom to you? How you would call a person who is not 100% free? Maybe he is enslaved in one of the many forms of slavery?

The poor people think they won. They do not understand that they actually lost. They say—this government is thinking about us, poor people. They are fighting for us and we will vote for them to continue to be our government. They are truly our representatives.

But you and I are already a bit smarter than that. We already know what question we need to ask to find out if this good they are doing is an absolute good. And the first question is—when you do good to one person, do you harm another person's belongings? We already know that they do. But there are more—the harm the government inflicted on the landlords will eventually harm the tenets. Here is why and how.

If I have an apartment and have someone who is ready to pay me a rent of $1,000 per month, why would I rent it to another person who will pay me only $700 a month? Does it make sense to you? If one person is ready to pay ten dollars for your baseball card and another offers you one dollar ... whom would you would sell your card to? Do not bother to answer, we both know whom you would like to buy the card.

How would you like it if a large bully comes to you and says—you will sell this card for one dollar to my friend, or else. Would you be happy with that? This is what government does with the homeowners who are in the "rent control areas."

It is my property, my apartment. I bought it with the money I earned. I wanted to rent it because I want to use this money to pay for my college tuition. Or because I want to buy bread and milk for my children. Or because I want to rent an apartment in another city using the money I am getting from this apartment.

I can rent it for $1,000 ... but here comes a socialist who says "You can't do with your own apartment what you want because I want a poor person to be able to live in your apartment."

Do you think it is OK for the government to tell me what to do with my own apartment that the government didn't build and didn't pay for?

Do you think it makes any difference if this person who tells me what to do with my apartment was a quarterback of a local football team? Can he tell me what to do with my apartment and whom to rent it if he is a good public speaker?

How about this person who issued the order to rent my apartment to a poor person for less money and is stealing three hundred dollars every month from my pocket is the Mayor of the city? Don't you think that the Mayor is acting as a bully who is forcing me to do things I do not want to do?

And what if two socialists and one progressive got together and tell you that it is your dad's house, but they will control it nevertheless? Do you think it makes it OK to control your dad's house if not one but three of them decided to take over? In some other countries they were coming to peoples' apartments and houses and telling them that they have to accept tenants even if they didn't want to.

They steal our money outright and probably think we will be happy about it. Are you happy when someone steals your belongings? I think we discussed it already. I am definitely not happy.

You can't really argue with the government. You can try to sue them, but it is a costly and lengthy process. You have however once in four years an opportunity to vote for the different group of guys and gals, and throw the ones that imposed this rent control on us out of their offices.

When most of the population in the area is poor and is accustomed to receive money stolen from others, the socialists and progressives will stay in power. When there are more well-to-do and hard working producers in the area, than the conservatives will be in power.

One of the reasons that conservative politicians want people to be rich is because most of the good producers, who work hard, open new businesses and create new and exciting things are voting for them.

Now I have a question to you. If well-to-do people are voting against socialists and progressives, do you think the socialists and progressive politicians want the people to be well-to-do?

a) Yes

b) No

c) I do not know

Now to the problem of the devastation of the real estate in America caused by rent control.

The landlords invested money into building of apartment complexes and were counting on a certain amount of rent to cover their debt, expenses and to receive profits. Because of the rent control the landlords can't receive profits they were counting on when they built those apartment houses.

They see that profits are higher in other areas of business. The only reason you build a new apartment building is to rent apartments and receive profit from it. Why would people invest money in building more houses if they can't charge rents that will bring good solid profits to them? Of course they will not build new houses. Instead they will invest either in a different industry or in a different country.

They will build houses for people in other countries so the lives of people in those countries will become better. Can you blame them for that? This is their job—to invest money, start new businesses, and create more jobs and all of that to get profits. When profits in America were high, many people from around the world invested in American businesses and houses and it made our life better. With rent control and similar laws passed, foreigners are looking for other countries to invest and even American investors started looking for good investment opportunities abroad.

So as a result of rent control (price control) there will be less good new houses in America. Do you think it is good for us the people or not?

a) Yes, I think it is good not to build new houses

b) I think it is very bad

Now let's see if this rent control is good for tenants or not. Imagine that your family lives in one of those houses that are under rent control. Your parents enjoy it. They stay in this place already for many years and rent didn't change. Their salaries had risen, the prices for everything had risen, but their rent stays almost the same.

One day however your little sister is born. And your grandma becomes old and moves with you and helps your mom with a new child. You live in a one-bedroom apartment and you desperately need more rooms. But there are no new buildings in the area. Investors do not build new houses simply because they can't get good profits from them.

Also people are not moving out of the rent control houses—they are paying so little that they do not want to move out, and there are no available apartments in the old buildings as well. When someone dies or moves out the managers of the buildings offer those apartments to the people who give them larger bribes. There is usually a line of people who are waiting for such apartment to become available and they give bribes to managers in order to get it. When something is in great demand but in low supply, someone makes money from it.

As a direct result of the rent control your family of five now lives in a one-bedroom apartment.

Want to hear more? The owner doesn't get enough profits, so he doesn't have enough money to repair the buildings when things begin to break.

When the owners were competing with each other for tenants, they were planting trees, playing music in lobbies, building fountains and pools in the backyards, and doing many other things to keep the tenants happy. With the rent control in place, the landlords know that whatever they do, the tenants will not move out. They are paying a really low price if they stay in apartments for a long time. They will not be able to get such price in any other place, and they are stuck.

If your tenants will not leave you whatever you do, why bother making improvements? They are your customers for life.

The buildings are getting worse and worse. The garbage stinks. The bulbs are broken. Such great results of the rent control are evident everywhere it was implemented.

Q1 - Do you think that rent control is good for the tenants it was suppose to defend?

a) Yes, rent control is good for tenants.

b) No, rent control is bad for everyone, but the government.

c) Progressives know that but enact it nevertheless ... What do you think is the reason for them doing it

d) They never read any history book or books about economy

e) They think that all those economists are wrong and they, progressive politicians, know better ... even if they are not economists

f) They want to stay in power and they trick poor people into believing that they defend their interests.

Personally I think it is "c" but you can have your own opinion.

It is still a country where our thoughts belong to us ... but possibly progressives are working on a new law that will allow them to control our thoughts and ideas as they control the rent I can charge for my own property.

Massive brainwashing and mind control is not unprecedented in the history of the humankind. It was done by their socialist comrades in Vietnam, Cambodia, Czechoslovakia, the Soviet Union, Poland, East Germany and many other countries.

They can try. Will we allow them or not is another question.

Now, progressives are saying that they invented rent control to fight against the greed of the landlords. They witnessed movement of poor people from good neighborhoods and began to show the poor that they fight against it. They decided that the greed was the source of the raising rents. If the greed was the problem, than to curb the greed by the rent control was the remedy they designed.

Did they accurately identify the cause of the problem?

Did they think through the consequences (effects) of the solution they implemented?

Did they observed the effects and confirmed that the solution is resolving the problem?

I will leave you to answer to those questions by yourself and will go to the next story.

You have a right for a job ... or don't you?

I think Vladimir Lenin said it first—every citizen of our country has a right for a job! Several decades later Mussolini repeated it. Right after him FDR (who thought that Mussolini is a "distinguish gentleman" and a great economist) attempted to bring this idea to America as a part of his "Second Bill of Rights."

FDR's dream was to build an all-powerful state in the US much like Duce did in Italy. He called it "the third way." This is how fascists called it as well—not socialism, not capitalism, but the Third Way.

During his radio address on January 11, 1944 FDR promised to implement in America an economic bill of rights which would guarantee every citizen an employment with a living wage, freedom from unfair competition and monopolies, housing for everyone, free medical care, free education, and guaranteed social security. He didn't mentioned how the country will pay for all those wonderful goods.

On the surface this was a great program. Who wouldn't want to guarantee to every citizen in our country and even beyond it that he will have free medical care, a home to live in, education, large enough pension, and all that he will be able to afford by doing work that the government would guarantee so he will not need to worry about tomorrow.

Wonderful, wonderful, wonderful! But let's ask our usual magical question—will this good be bad for anyone else? Will it be necessary to steal someone else's property in order to fulfill this goal?

FDR told America that the "political rights" guaranteed by the constitution and the Bill of Rights were not enough to assure equality in the pursuit of happiness. So the problem in his opinion was that many people were unable to pursue happiness because they were unable to find well paying and stable jobs.

And the solution to this problem was to guarantee each and every American well paying jobs ... without a possibility to kick any of them out for anything they might do. Oh, you can kick a worker out but he doesn't really care. He has another job waiting for him around the corner, and it is guaranteed by the government.

Well, let's try to see where this proposal if implemented would lead America.

Let's speculate a bit. For example a person comes to an auto company and says "I am here and ready for a well paying job. Where it is and how much I will get?"

The car manufacturer says "We do not need anyone."

"But" says the job seeker, "The government guaranteed me a job and someone has to provide me with one."

"Go to the government and ask them"—answers the manufacturer and thinks that the case is closed. Not so fast!

The job seeker goes to the government and says "I want a job and a well paying one. It would be really convenient for me to work at a car manufacturer, but I can entertain other offers. Go ahead, tell me the options."

Now the government really has two options. First one is to obligate the car manufacturer to take a person that they do not need and pay him a salary. Most probably there will be many such people who would have to be hired by the car manufacturers, whom the manufacturers do not want or need.

If a manufacturer is forced to pay salaries to people whom he doesn't need, then the cost of making cars or any other products he produces is rising. His foreign competitors do not have this problem. They hire only people they need. They do not pay unnecessary salaries. The cost of their cars is now lower than the cost of the US cars. People around the world stop buying US cars and switch to less expensive foreign cars.

The US car manufacturers then will start losing money. They want to let go some of their workers, but can't because of the new laws that stated that every American has a right for a well paying job and this right is guaranteed for life disregarding his own performance or stability of the company he works for.

The company goes belly up (files bankruptcy) and all the workers they employed lose their jobs. Is this what FDR intended?

Another scenario is if the government says to the job seeker—yes, you have a right for a job and since the car manufacturers or anyone else is not hiring you, you will be employed by the government.

The job seeker comes to the government office and is given a chair, a desk, a computer and tons of office supplies. Someone has to pay for all that. Then the government goes to the car manufacturer and says—we have a new government employee now, but we do not have money of our own. So from now on you will pay a salary of an additional employee and also you will pay for his car's expenses, electricity he uses at work, his medical bills and his vacations and sick leaves.

But I do not have enough funds, says the manufacturer!

However, he can't do anything. The new law says that every American has a right for a job and the government begins to tax (steal money from) producers to pay for the unnecessary workers the government hired.

The US cars are becoming costly because of all those additional expenses of paying government workers' salaries, the US cars can't compete on the market and the US car manufacturers go bankrupt. All the people employed by the manufacturers lose their jobs...

That is not all! Imagine that every person is employed and you can't lose your job. Would you really work that hard or you will work only when you feel like working? Would you come every day on time or you will sleep as much as you want? Would you listen to your nagging boss or you would tell him to shut up and go to hell? Remember they can't fire you. You are guaranteed your well paying job by law.

FDR's solution would have a devastating effect on the US economy. It would be destroyed beyond repair.

Do you think FDR accurately identified the cause of the problem?

Did he in your opinion think through the consequences (effects) of the solution he proposed?

Did he observe the effects of similar solutions in other countries and confirmed that the solution he proposed is resolving the problem?

Or maybe he knew exactly what this solution would do? Maybe he never intended to implement any of the "economic bill rights"?

So why would FDR go on radio and proclaim that he wants to give all those goodies to Americans if he knew what kind of devastation such a bill would bring to America?

Maybe he just wanted people to vote for him? What do you think why FDR promised America to implement this Second Bill of Rights? Which of those answers rings true to you?

FDR intended to destroy America

FDR thought that he is so clever that under his guidance this bill would bring results different from the ones such policies brought in all other countries

FDR never intended to implement the bill. He just wanted Americans to think that he cares about them and he fights for them with bad people in other political parties.

Equal Housing Disaster

Do you know what the "American dream" is? People who came from all over the world were dreaming about owning a piece of land, having their own house built on this land, and an opportunity to live without anyone telling them what to do while honestly earning their bread. All those people who came to America to seek this American dream wanted to leave their children a little bit better world than the one they inherited from their parents.

But in order to own a piece of land one should buy it. And in order to live in your own house one should build it. And the tools needed to work the land or make products that other people will buy—all cost money.

First you need to work hard, save money and then purchase tools and build ... or hire people who have tools to build, and pursue your dreams. This is what many emigrants did. They worked hard, saved, worked more, saved more—and either they themselves or their children were able to get good education, well paying jobs, apartments, houses or other things they wanted. Many of them bought land. Some decided to be farmers; some built houses for their families, and some decided to conduct their businesses from their homes.

There were also many people who were less fortunate. Some of them because they didn't want to work hard. Some because they didn't know how or didn't want to save. Some because they didn't have parents who would help them—in explaining to them the importance of education and in passing their savings to the next generation.

Some drunk or gambled their money away. Some lost their money due to a business or a stock market crash. Some just came to this country and yet didn't begin to amass property to start implementing their American or simply human dreams.

People are equal in the eyes of God, and in the opportunities that lay ahead. They are not equal otherwise. Some are better sportsman. Others are better in math. Some can make money by playing piano, others can't. Some can teach chemistry to middle school students, others can't even understand chemistry. Some people can build their own businesses and others are not able to organize even their own time and totally incapable of supervising others.

Some are lazy and some are not. Some are ready to put endless hours to resolve a problem, and others prefer surfing. These unequal people can't receive equal rewards from life. First they do not want equal rewards, each one wants what he or she wants. Second, some deserve more and some deserve less. It is not for you and I to decide who deserves what and when. But life separates them and this is a good thing. We are different, and there is nothing bad in it.

However progressives and socialists are always trying to take from those that work and distribute to the ones that do not have or have less. It doesn't really matter for a progressive why this person doesn't have money. Their idea is to punish those that have and reward those that do not have.

They do not quite put it in those words. What they say is that we are all human beings and we all shall help each other. Great! Wonderful! But doesn't work in reality.

In order to fulfill the socialists' and progressives' dreams you should force people to do what they do not want to do. Does that make people happy?

   a) Yes, that makes people happy

   b) No, that doesn't make people happy.

Except for several unique individuals, most of the people on the planet will work much harder if they and their families will get the benefits from their work.

This story is about a terrible market crash when millions of people lost their money, our country was plunged into a deep recession and tens of millions of people around the globe lost their jobs, their belongings and in many instances their livelihoods. It all started with a wrongly identified <u>cause</u> and wrong remedy offered to resolve it (<u>solution</u>) ... without thinking through the <u>effects</u> this solution might bring.

Almost like killing cats enabling rats to multiply and by that enabling bacillus of Bubonic plague to reach millions of people in Europe.

"People would love to have their own apartments and houses," said socialists and progressives. "They want but they can't. The problem (cause) of them not able to buy their own houses," again were thinking progressives, "is because they didn't have rich parents who would give them money to put as a 'down payment' to buy houses."

"We need to help those Americans that have no money to live in their own houses"—proclaimed progressives when they once again got the majority of votes in the congress and began to be in charge of the country. "The solution to this problem is to pressure someone to give money to those unemployed and underprivileged people to buy houses," they were saying to each other. We will find how to get money for those poor people.

And they did as they said.

In order to buy a house or an apartment you need money to pay for it. In America you have only part of the money, let's say a fifth of the money that the house is selling for and you can find a bank that will loan you the rest.

For example if the house is selling for $100,000, you can pay $20,000 and ask a bank to give you a loan (they call such loans "mortgages") for the rest, which is $80,000.

The bank will give you money if you will agree to pay them back not only the money they gave you, but also an additional sum that is their profit. For example you took $80,000 from them and you will pay back $10,000 a year for ten years. You took $80,000 from them but shall pay them $100,000. They got $20,000 profit.

They got their profit and they are happy. The seller of the house got $100,000 he asked for—$20,000 from you and $80,000 from the bank and he is happy. You start living in your own house not when you saved all $100,000 but when you have only $20,000.

You live in your own house but you owe $80,000 plus what you agreed to pay to the bank as their profit.

The bank before he gives you the money checks if you can really pay them back. If you have a good salary, if you already paid back for previous loans, if you are using your credit cards wisely, they will give you a loan. They might however tell you that you are a good guy (or gal), but your salary is too small to pay for a loan of $80,000. They would probably advise you to start with a smaller house that will cost you less.

If they agree to loan you the money, you give your word to the bank (and confirm it by your signature) that if you will not pay them back what you owe them they can take your house from you and sell it in order to get their money back.

The bank will give you the loan only if you put some of the money to buy your house from your own pocket. They know that if you put your own money, you will fight not to lose the house and your money. If you didn't pay anything by yourself, than you might not care, not pay them and leave the house without any remorse. It is not yours, you didn't invest anything into the house so why you would care?

Since socialists and progressives thought that the problem of people not buying houses is their poor parents and the injustice of a capitalistic system, they came up with a solution to loan or just give them money to put as a down payment. The progressives pressured banks to give loans to people who didn't have permanent jobs or high salaries. They pressured banks to start giving loans to people who had no money at all.

This is what happened—the government told millions of people that they can go and "get a house" without paying for it, but asked them to promise to pay later. The government will give a (loan) the down payment for them and the banks will loan them the rest. The new owners didn't have to pay a single cent to get into the house.

Millions of people said "sure" and took the houses. When banks asked them to pay back their loans, those people said "we do not have money, sorry," and continued to live in the houses without paying anything. Would you want to "buy" toys, electronic games and everything else this way? I hope however that you are an honorable person and when you give your word, you fulfill your obligations.

So millions of people bought houses, moved in but many of them were unable or didn't want to pay back what they received from the banks. Financial institutions gave money to millions of people, and were not receiving back anything from them. Not only profits, but actually they lost billions of dollars on those "bad" mortgages.

Since banks lost so much money, they didn't have enough money to finance businesses. Businesses can't work without financing (I can't now start explaining why and how, just believe me that businesses need short term loans to operate and when they do not have those loans they die).

Many businesses began to collapse and fire employees … who now didn't receive salaries and also like many others were unable to pay their rent … and now additional banks were not getting money from the loans they made.

Many banks collapsed and many additional people were out of jobs. Since they were out of jobs, they were not buying things that they wanted and needed to buy.

Now companies that were not selling the usual amount of products were unable to pay salaries to their workers and began to fire their employees.

This was the result of not-rightly identified <u>cause</u> and not thought through <u>effect</u> of the wrong <u>solution</u>.

The government saw that many people are unemployed and since they didn't want to admit that they made a mistake, they blamed "bad capitalists" accusing them of firing employees without reason and not caring about working America.

They issued a new law about paying more money to those unemployed people. The money that government promises to one group of people always comes from another group of people. The bankers, the producers, the service providers always pay for government mistakes.

No one apologized. Progressives and socialists usually do not apologize. They say that everybody else is to blame for the problems, and they are always right. Do you know such people, who never blame ourselves, but always someone else? Those are usually progressives and Marxists, even if they do not admit or even do not know that. They never say "I am sorry" whatever they do. Real honest producers and capitalists usually say "I am guilty. I apologize. What can I do to remedy the situation?"

Millions of people are out of jobs. Millions can't pay for their houses and had to move out. Millions of homes are for sale and since many people do not have jobs no one buys them. Millions of people abroad who were preparing products for America, or who invested in America, or who loaned Americans money lost everything or a big part of what they had.

Now let's start asking questions.

a) Do you think socialists and progressives rightly identified the cause of the problem?

b) Did they think through the consequences (effects) of the solution they proposed?

c) Did they observe the effects of similar solutions implemented in other countries and confirmed that the solution they proposed can resolve the problem?

d) Or maybe they knew exactly what this solution would do? Maybe they never intended to make people happy? So why would they implement this solution that brought no happiness to anyone? Why would they implement a plan that will bring such devastation to America?

Possible answers:

a) Progressives and socialists intended to fundamentally change America. The hymn of socialists says "we will destroy the country in order to built it anew from the ruins left of it."

b) Progressives and socialists wanted to steal a lot of money from producers and get part of it to themselves.

c) Progressives and socialists never intended to help anyone. They just wanted Americans to think that they care about them and that they fight for them with the "bad people" in another political party. They just wanted to stay in power and didn't care what it takes. "Results justify the means" socialists often say.

d) All of the above

I do not know the answer. Probably one of those four.

Chapter XI

Competition - is it good or bad?

PHONE COVERS—A math exercise for a middle school student:

You made a great cover for his cell phone and every one at your school is raving about it. Then you came up with this great idea of making and selling hundreds of those covers (each one will be unique and different from others) and becoming rich beyond imagination. You already calculated that the materials will cost you about two dollars, and that your friends and their friends would pay five dollars for such a fashionable item. If you would sell your phone cover for five dollars, how much profit you will make on one phone cover?

a) Twenty dollars

b) Fifty cents

c) Two dollars

d) Five dollars

During one week you made two dozen of such covers and on the weekend you went to a Mall, set down on the ground not far from the movie theaters and put your covers for everyone to see and buy. You sold six during the very first day and there were several people who said that they will come with their friends next week.

Next Saturday you came back to the same place and were enraged to see two girls sitting near the theaters with a blanket on the ground offering cell phone covers. They smiled at you but you wanted to kill them. This was YOUR place, YOUR idea, YOUR money to make. And they were now interfering with YOUR business, this is what you thought. It was however impossible to do anything. Your head was spinning, heart pumping blood fast, and you were almost in tears.

You sold three covers during this day and those ugly and terrible girls sold two. They sold two covers that otherwise people would buy from you, you thought! You hated them, hated them, hated them!

On Sunday there was another surprise! A new guy with a pony tail who sat down nearby with HIS phone covers. This was now impossible to bear. Now, you thought, you will not be able to sell even one cover. The business was dead. The idea was dead. You decided to give away the remaining covers but something strange began to happen.

There suddenly were much more people coming to check your merchandise than in any of the previous days. And they already knew that you are selling phone covers with rhinestones on them. They had friends who told them that there is a place near the movie theaters on the plaza where MANY DIFFERENT phone covers were sold. People were telling each other—if you want a fancy-trendy original phone cover why to go to places where you can find only one design. Go to the plaza, where there is a variety of covers sold.

And people came to see and buy.

OK, you said to yourself, the competition sells for the same amount I began to sell two weeks ago. My designs are better than theirs and if I will offer my covers for less they all will come to me and buy from me.

You offered your better designs for less and became unbeatable—you sold all the covers you had, and took some orders. The competition is not that bad, you said to yourself. It can be good, very good.

So, do you think this thing called competition is good or bad for the buyers? And maybe, just maybe it also good for the sellers?

Shoe Store

When I was young, I lived in a country called The Union of the Soviet Socialist Republics (USSR). It was a socialist country and while living there I learned to dislike socialism very much. My family and I were lucky and were able to leave this unfriendly place and came to a country called Israel where we encountered freedom and capitalism for the first time in our lives.

We came out of the USSR with one hundred dollars each and if not for the help of the Israeli people we wouldn't survive even a week. We were provided shelter and food, and were helped in learning the language of the land called Hebrew.

We however had to purchase our own clothes, items of personal hygiene, newspapers and shoes. We were hoping to find good jobs and start earning money, but in the meantime having so little money made us think five times before buying anything. But eventually we had to purchase some things that were a real necessity. The very first thing I needed badly was a pair of summer shoes. I had a pair of boots good for the Russian winters, but when an average daily temperature in Israel reached 110F I realized I need something different. And I knew exactly what I wanted.

For the whole two weeks we already had been in Israel, I was eying a pair of sandals that were my "impossible dream." After consulting with our parents how much we can spend on my shoes, my brother and I went to the store that I knew had the sandals. I was afraid they are out of my reach and I was right. After trying them on, enjoying their beauty and the feel they gave me, I have heard that they cost "forty lira" (lira was at the time Israeli currency). My heart was broken. This was twice as much as we all decided what I can spend for a pair of shoes.

I didn't want to see anything else in this store and despite my brother's offers to find me something that would be as good as, I left the place of my shattered dreams.

On the other side of the store I saw a small shoe store with an old guy standing in the door frame waiting for customers. I didn't want to go into any other shoe stores. I knew that the shoes I wanted so much would cost me two times what I can afford, but the guy smiled at us, motioned friendly with both hands and somehow we ended up in this small and a bit dark store.

There was no comparison with the palace we just left. There was only one salesperson compared to four sellers and three helpers that were constantly running in the big store. There actually were not a lot of shoes on display. "So, my young friend, what is it you want?"—the old salesman asked me.

"I liked one pair of sandals" I said, "But they are way over what I can pay" I told him.

The salesperson was very sympathetic to my problem. "Tell me which one, maybe I can find you something like that?" he suggested.

Despite my assurances that I can't afford the shoes he with the help of my brother found and brought to me the exact copy of what I wanted so much. I knew that I can't afford them, but put them on nevertheless. The shoes were magnificent.

"How much money do you have?" asked the salesperson. I answered and began to take the shoes off. "OK, you got them, do not take them off, they are yours," he said.

I was happy of course but at the same time I felt guilty. I was definitely taking advantage of the old guy who didn't know that those shoes cost twice as much. I wanted to grab the shoes and run, but instead I told the old and poor guy that I do not want him to find out about his mistake when it is too late.

You should check with the people across the street, I said, and they will tell you that the shoes are much more expensive than what I paid you for them.

The old guy shook my hand, and informed me that he is the owner of the store and he knows what he is doing.

At the door I made one more attempt. Before I leave, I said, I want to clear my conscience. I want to tell you that the shoes you sold for twenty are sold in the store across the street for forty.

I know, said the guy.

You do, I asked puzzled.

Of course I do, he said, I own that store as well. Competition is such a good thing he said, that I decided to compete with myself.

Every time I was on this street I saw him standing at the doors of the small and inexpensively looking store watching for customers that were coming out of his other store empty handed. He would smile to them and invite them into his small store and ask "what exactly did you want to buy but were unable to afford?" and would find them the exact pair they were looking for but for less. If they didn't buy for forty at the large store, they might buy for twenty at the small one.

Fruit Juice Stand

On the Island called Bo there were ten hotels always filed with tourists. The main street was busy and the tourists and the islanders were offered everything they could even imagine. One thing they didn't have—cold fruit juice blends. Actually they didn't know that they do not have it until a company called "FruJu" built a pavilion offering customers a variety of such juice blends with ice.

Everyone instantly loved it. There were huge lines to the pavilion and despite the fact the FruJu charged eight dollars for a glass; they always had plenty of people ordering the drinks.

Two weeks later on the other side of the street popped a small stand called "FruJoe" offering exactly the same blends but for five dollars. The smiling owner by the name Joe was always near the stand and handed samples of his drinks to the passerby. "The only difference between us and them," he was saying to everyone who would care to listen, "is that we are three dollars less. Everything else is the same."

So what do you think happened? Joe now has long lines of customers and FruJu had only occasional people who didn't know better.

FruJu thought for a week, brought in nice chairs, tables and umbrellas and began to offer waffles, exotic teas, decaffeinated coffee from Sumatra and brought a local band to play at the sunsets and evenings. They started selling FruJu for five dollars and were handing a coconut cookie to each customer.

Joe answered by putting small kiosks everywhere on the island. The FruJoe's were on every corner and every street. Joe made a deal with each and every hotel on the island and had kiosks in every lobby and near every pool. He lowered prices to three dollars a drink and still was making fortune selling them day and night. When Joe started his empire he wasn't even eighteen. He was at that time a student in a local high school but already employed more than eighty people who were unemployed for some time and didn't know how to feed their families.

Do you think the customers suffered because of the competition? Why do you think prices went down? Why do you think the competitors began to invent new services and new products? Do you think those new services and new products made life for the tourists and the islanders worse more or better?

What do I think? I think that the competition made life on the Island better.

Potatoes

The villagers on a village called Grruum loved potatoes. They loved potatoes so much they were ready to pay anything to get them. There was only one farmer in the area (his name was Trum-Brum) who knew how to grow potatoes. Every Saturday he would open his barn and would sell potatoes to the villagers who were waiting for this moment since dawn.

Sometimes he would open the barn at seven in the morning, sometimes at noon. Sometimes he sold potatoes for five dollars a pound, sometimes for three dollars a pound. Sometimes he would say that he is tired and is closing his doors, and would close the doors even if there were many people still waiting in line.

The potatoes Trum-Brum was selling were dirty, even rotten, but Trum-Brum was saying that he will sell fresh potatoes only when he will finish with the rotten ones.

Villagers however were afraid to say anything fearing that he can single someone out and stop selling potatoes to this person.

One day a passerby from a nearby town saw the line and asked what they are waiting for. After witnessing how Trum-Brum insulted his buyers, the passerby went back home and in a couple of days appeared with a wagon of potatoes.

The potatoes were fresh, kept in nice wooden boxes, and clean. The price was dollar a pound and the merchant told the villagers that if they would guarantee him buying all the potatoes, he would half the price.

Trum-Brum went out of his barn and saw that there was no line waiting for him. He ran to the village and saw that everyone was having potatoes for lunch. The next day he offered to deliver potatoes to each villagers home, guaranteed that they would be clean and fresh, and that the price including delivery would be a quarter a pound. He was smiling to everyone, well shaved and wearing a clean shirt.

Do you think Trum-Brum was well shaved and offered potatoes to the villagers because he suddenly became a nice guy? Or there was another reason why he decided to deliver potatoes to villagers' homes and for small portion of the price he charged them earlier?

What was the reason Trum-Brum suddenly turned into the nicest person in the world? What do you think?

He was enchanted during all those years and suddenly a great magician came to town and took a spell off him

He was afraid that he will lose his income because the villagers might stop buying potatoes from him. Because of that he shaved, changed clothes, threw away rotten potatoes, began to deliver potatoes to their houses and reduced prices. All that happened because he got competition.

He received a secret order from the government instructing him to shave, reduce prices and start behaving like a human being.

<u>Author's opinion</u>—Trum-Brum is not smart. He offended so many people that they might not want to buy from him even if he would offer them the very best prices. If he would behave well and provide good service and great prices from the beginning, he would have loyal customers for life.

Food Story

Chaco was really scared when he learned that a big supermarket right across the street from his small lunch restaurant was planning to open a food court. He was telling himself that people will not go to eat there, trying to convince his dog and his parrot that the tacos and burritos he makes are much better than what those supermarket people would be able to serve their customers. But deep down inside he knew that this is the end of his small joint.

He was not making any money in the cantina, as he called it and for the last several months he was sleeping at the cantina's small room behind the kitchen. The room was supposed to be used as storage, but Chaco brought his belongings there, his two best animal friends and felt that this was his home. He didn't have money to rent even a small room. The cantina was barely feeding the three amigos, and now even this small income would disappear.

Chaco knew many people who lost their businesses due to competition from large chains. Some of them went to work for the same chains, some moved out to open businesses in other areas and waited until the competition would squeeze them out of there as well. Chaco didn't want to leave. He liked the area, he had friends who loved to play guitar and sing, and from time to time he would bring them into his hangout and they would close doors and sing Guatemalan songs.

Chaco always had tequila and some remnants of food to serve them, and they all had a wonderful time together.

It all would come to the end soon, thought Chaco.

And the day of opening of the supermarket food court finally came. Instead of the usual dozen lunch customers there was only one lunch special sold at Chaco's.

A week after the "bad day" as Chaco called it he knew the exact damage done to his business. He lost half of his customers. He now didn't have enough money to pay the lease, to buy food supplies and pay his two helpers even minimum wages. This was the end. Chaco cleaned the restaurant, cooked his last tacos, opened his remaining tequila and told all his friends that he is having a going away party. He had no idea where exactly he was going away.

The night party started and the very best guitar players from Guatemala, best dancers of the Latino quarter and even a priest from a local church all came to say good-bys to Chaco's restaurant. "Everything on me" said Chaco, but his friends didn't agree. You are going away Chaco, they told him, and you need a bit of the money to take with you. You sell, we buy.

At ten Chaco ran out of beer and sent one of the helpers to get three dozen bottles at the supermarket. At eleven he ran out of tequila, and everything else. Two cooks from the supermarket came to Chaco after their shift ended and brought everything to make great burritos, tacos and enchiladas.

At midnight half of the block was at Chaco's listening to music and dancing their heads off. People didn't want to leave until three in the morning. Chaco paid the helpers; they cried a little and went home. Chaco himself cleaned everything squeaky clean and went to sleep his last night at the restaurant. He didn't open the restaurant for the breakfast or lunch. He woke up in the late afternoon because someone was knocking at the door and his dog was barking. The guy at the door asked him if there will be a show tonight and reserved eight seats "close to the stage" he said.

Chaco didn't hesitate even a second. At six he had all the food bought and delivered to him. Two of his helpers were told to come back to work and bring additional help. Two guitar players and one singer were hired by eight. At nine the party started again. And again the next night. And again the next. Then Chaco shifted his schedule from morning to night.

The supermarket people loved to come to him after work and dance and sing together with the crowd. Chaco even hired out from the supermarket the best cook they had. Actually it was their only good cook. If not for the competition, says Chaco, I would be sleeping all my life on the back room of this joint, and getting nowhere.

Chaco is opening his third restaurant and plans to have a chain all over the state. He says that Chicano culture will dominate the night life just because it is the friendliest culture in the entire world. He takes guitar lessons and is thinking about buying a private jet. Otherwise, he says, without good and fast transportation I will not be able to manage the chain.

What if there will be laws such as:

"A person who plays tennis better than others and wins all school competitions shall have his right hand tied up to his body at any time"—would you like such "fair" law?

Or "If you are a better basketball player than others you shall have a twenty pound weight tied to your neck and you shall keep it always on?"

Or if you come to school and see a poster that says—"The teachers should single out boys and girls that are taller than others and punish them by making them walk on their knees"—would you be happy? If you are tall, probably not. If you are short you might like it.

How about—"Better students shall answer first two questions of any test in the worst possible way or they will be punished?"

Do not laugh. This is exactly what our government is doing to the business people. Look at the laws they enact. The politicians vote for those laws because they say it is "for the good of the country!"

Take for example the anti-trust anti-monopoly law.

Anti-Monopoly Law

The competition is good, right? It lowers prices, pushes producers to create new innovative and better products, provide better services and make stores beautiful. Everyone knows that. The government saw it as well and said "If it so good, we must create a new law that will assure that our fellow countryman always have this wonderful thing."

Let's together see one more time what happens when the government makes it their business to interfere with our business. In all previous stories we saw that the government involvement makes things worse. There is a law of bureaucracy formulated by professor Alvin Lowi of the Free Enterprise Institute that says "Legislation <u>always</u> has the opposite, or reverse, effect on its ostensible purpose."

In plain English it means that the results of the government intervention always leads to the exact opposite effect of what they intended to achieve.

But maybe this law is not universal; maybe this time they finally would succeed (for a change) to do something good for the people. Let's examine what government did to preserve competition and what are the effects of this "smart" law.

Riddle #30 - The Aluminum Story

In 1988 in Pittsburgh a half-dozen men started production of aluminum in a shed with a dirt floor. Aluminum was then selling at $8.00 a pound. The Aluminum Company of America (Alcoa) produced its first specimens in the fall. Output averaged less than ten pounds a day at the start. The hard-working founders locked up the product each night for safety in the office safe.

Alcoa was built on an idea to develop something new and keep it always cheap, desirable, and ahead of competitive products. All those ideas were typically American; and still are. Alcoa succeeded to lower the price of Aluminum from eight dollars to … twenty cents a pound (forty times less than their competitors) and raised its production to over 300,000,000 pounds a year. They had developed new markets for it in novelties, in bicycles, saucepans, high-voltage wires, production of steel and airplanes.

They worked so hard that Alcoa became the only maker of aluminum in the United States. They kept lowering the prices and making their products better and cheaper. They knew that the moment they will sell aluminum for more, they are opening doors for competitors. If they sell really inexpensive, there is not a lot of profit to be made and no one would want to start producing aluminum and compete with them. Great strategy—the company wins, the users of aluminum win and the people who buy their products win.

And here comes the government that wanted to make sure that everyone shall have competitors and that to have the only one producer of aluminum is not good.

The government took Alcoa to court demanding to stop being a monopoly.

But what can we do, asked Alcoa? We make good product and we sell it cheap. Others sold it not as cheap and no one wants to buy from them.

You are guilty, said the government, of creating a great organization, of making your product better, of training your workers better and of selling your product so inexpensive that no one else is able to compete with you. For that you shall be punished!

The government told Alcoa and several other companies that were in the same situation (Du Pont is another example) that they have to train the employees of their competitors, give them all the innovative technologies Alcoa, Du Pont or others invented, and give those companies money to start making the same products the good producers made.

The great result of this law was that Alcoa stopped making innovations and making their products better. They are not lowering prices any more. They are afraid that if they do that, they will become a monopoly again and will be punished again, this time even harder.

As a result products made with aluminum are more expensive for you and everybody else. Isn't it just the opposite of what the government said they wanted to achieve?

Thinking out loud:

Q1 - Do you think Alcoa shall be punished for making good product and selling it very inexpensively?

    a) Yes, they shall be punished. They are supposed to make inferior product and sell it for more money

    b) No, it is good for everyone if you can buy a good product and for as small amount of money as possible

    c) I do not care if I buy good products for less or bad products for more

What do you think?

Comment of a Progressive / Socialist: When knowledge concentrated in the hand of one person or a company, this person or company can blackmail the whole society. We are already depending on this product and can't lose it. It doesn't matter who owns the product or who created it and has the rights for the product. Here we are talking about the good of the society and it is much more important than the good of a person or even a group of people.

<u>Comment of a True Liberal / Capitalist</u>: No one has a right to steal my belongings. If I invented something, it belongs to me. If I produced something, I can do with it what I want. Even if you want it very much, it is not yours. Do not touch my belongings and I will promise not to touch yours. But if you need something, come to me and I will either give it to you or exchange for something yours I might need or want.

<u>Authors opinion—Right answer</u>: b

Riddle #31 - The Tungsten Story

The General Electric Company began to produce a synthetic cutting material called tungsten carbide. This material was cemented on the tip of machine-tool cutting arms to cut steel. It was the next hardest thing to a diamond. But it was difficult to make and difficult to cement on to the tool. In other words, it was a great invention but not practical.

General Electric invested a lot of time and money into research and development. They worked hard for eleven years and finally made it a success! Finally Americans had very important tool that proved invaluable in World War II.

Now everyone wanted this new material and General Electric was working hard to meet the demand. Everyone was happy—the users of the material, the consumers buying products that were made with this material and the General Electric who put so much time, effort and money into it and finally began to see some profits.

But here comes the government that says that the General Electric is a monopoly and the managers of the company shall go to prison.

The General Electric was forced to give their innovations to other companies and the managers paid fines for their "grave" mistakes and anti-American activities. Their gravest mistake was—to think that what they invented is theirs.

<u>Thinking out loud</u>:

Q1 - Do you think those people from General Electric shall be awarded or punished?

a) I think they shall be made examples of American spirit and persistence. For many years they were attempting to create better product that would bring them profits and would make the lives of so many others better.

b) I think they shall be punished for wanting to keep their trade secrets to themselves. It is not important who did it, everything shall belong to everybody.

c) Life is good and I can live without all those innovations. I do not care either way.

<u>Comment of a Progressive / Socialist</u>: It is obvious that if a product was used by the military, it shall belong to the government. No one can have a right to keep to himself anything that can help in our country's defense efforts.

<u>Comment of a True Liberal / Capitalist</u>: The government can't take my money even if they badly need it. The government can't take my belongings even if the President dreams about them. The government, the state, the mayor, the president are not the owners of my property. If they want something, they are welcome to politely ask, and if they have something I want, we will trade.

<u>Author's opinion—Right answer</u>: a

Alcoa was better than others and because of that everyone wanted to buy their products. The government punished Alcoa. Du Pont was better than others and because of that everyone wanted to buy their product. The government punished Du Pont. The General Electric was better than others and because of that everyone wanted to buy their product. The government punished the General Electric.

The government is telling us that if someone is becoming better than others, he should be unmercifully punished. Do you think it is smart?

Yes, I think it is smart because no one shall be different from others. First they produce good product that everyone wants to buy. Then the same people would want to live in better homes than others. Then they want to drive better cars. This is terrible, because I also want to have better home, but I didn't do anything to earn it. If I can't have it, I do not want anyone to have it.

If we punish people who do better things and who lower prices, we are stopping them from making our world a better place to be. If they win, we all win!

Looks like what they say is if you are running faster than others, you should slow down. If you look better than others, you should wear bad dresses and do not comb your hair. If you have a sense of humor and others do not, shut up, and laugh at their not funny jokes.

If you are striving to be the best in what you do, the government calls it un-American and creates laws to punish those who are better than others. Our own government is waging war on unique and outstanding. This is what America was all about—award unique and outstanding and give them incentives to make our world a better place. But socialists are always saying that everyone shall be the same! Not taller, not smarter, not sharper, the same! Everyone shall be equal to everyone! Hail to mediocrity! Hail to socialism!

Riddle #32 - Senior Citizens Hotel

Mark who was a freshman at a local high school lived near the senior citizens hotel and always said hello to all those old people who were either looking out of their windows or sitting at a bench by the hotel's door. From time to time he did something for them like run to buy a paper, or said what the time it was. He used to stop by one old man's window and talk with him about the local baseball team. It was this guy, Tom, who gave Mark this brilliant idea.

Why wouldn't you make some extra money for yourself, asked Tom once? I am sure many of us here need small things like an extra postal stamp here and there, or walk a dog, or even set up a video recorder. We the old people are not that good with the new technology. And you know it all, I guess.

Mark agreed to this assessment. Actually he prided himself as being very good with all this new technology. He frequently visited all the electronic stores and knew by heart what was very new or even just "coming" to the market. He didn't however have money to buy any of the innovations he dreamed about, but knowledge he indeed had.

Knock at the doors, introduce yourself and ask if the tenants want something you can do for them for a small fee.

This is exactly what Mark did and his life was changed forever. Every morning before school Mark ran to a supermarket and bought milk cartoons, dozens of fresh muffins and croissants, newspapers and fruits. On the way from school he walked two dogs, took some garbage out, changed bulbs and delivered letters that he took from the mail boxes downstairs. And in the evening he did some special orders like set up alarm clocks, re-programmed video-recorders and took care of other "modern technology" problems.

Mark was a good student and his parents were happy with his academic accomplishments and allowed him to make some extra money to buy himself things he wanted so much.

Mark bought himself the best phone ever. He earned enough to buy himself an apple computer and was now eyeing a very good bike. He even made some long term plans like putting money aside for college and buying a small boat, but everything was changed when the school authorities learned about his activities.

Mark was invited to the principal's office where he saw three members of the school board. They all looked very concerned.

Tell us what you are doing in this old people's home in your own words, the principal said.

I am helping those old people and making some money for myself, answered Mark. There is no one else helping them, and I charge a very small fee, so everyone can afford it. I for example can charge only twenty five cents for walking the dog, because at the same time I am delivering a prescription to a pharmacy also for twenty five cents, getting a package from a post office for another lady also for twenty five cents and maybe doing ten other things at the same time. What I am getting paid is OK for me and they are happy. I thought I was doing good thing, don't I?

Do you know that our country has a law that such a good think as competition shall be preserved at all cost, asked one of the board members? I am an attorney and my colleague here is a retired judge. Together with the principal of this school we are quite knowledgeable in the matters of law. And we want to tell you that you broke several laws by doing what you call a "good thing."

First of all, you do not have any one who is competing against you in the hotel. You alone are offering those services and this is called monopoly. Secondly, you work for much less than minimal wages that are established in this country. You have to start charging more. Third, it looks like you work overtime. If we will count your school time, your preparation of the homework and all your efforts at the hotel, in total your workday exceeds eight hours. After eight hours you should charge twice as much money and this is the law.

First you are punished by a fine of twenty-five dollars that you need to pay us immediately. Second you have to find at least one competitor who will offer the same services as you do, and you shall make sure that he or she gets at least part of the orders from your current clients. Also you shall immediately start charging your clients more and be sure that they pay you for the overtime.

Mark found one boy who agreed to compete but quit after a day saying that this is a crazy job and he has no time for it. A girl, who agreed to be Mark's competitor said that she doesn't like dogs, will not clean their pup and will not take any garbage out. Mark agreed to do it instead of her but she quit anyhow. Another boy was willing to do the chores but not before school.

Many of the old people who lived in the hotel didn't want others to help them and didn't want to pay more and Mark finally was left with three or four clients who continued to call him and ask to do things for them. Finally Mark decided to talk to the principal. After hearing what happened the principal said "The important thing is—there is no monopoly anymore! It is good for the country!"

But this is not good for me and for the people, who live in the senior citizens hotel, thought Mark. Good for the country but not good for the people who live in the country. How can it be?

Thinking out loud:

Q1 - Do you think that the school board did the right thing?

  a) Government has an obligation to stop a monopoly the moment it occurs

  b) I think the government again did something stupid

  c) I want my chocolate ice cream and do not care for anything else

Comment of a Progressive / Socialist: Maybe from Mark's prospective it is good to get a small amount of money for his efforts and it is OK to squeeze competition out of their potential earnings. Yes, Mark is very efficient, and he works hard. But what about another child or adult who is not that smart and fast? Why we do not think about him or her. Maybe they also want to earn money but can't compete? What about their dreams about good life? Should they be thrown into the toilet just because they can do the same job as Mark? Mark shall start learning to live in a society and not to be such an individualist he is today.

Comment of a True Liberal / Capitalist: Mark can work for whatever amount he wants to work. It is his body and his time. No one owns him and no one can "manage" him (except his parents until he is eighteen). Mark did good to the older people in the hotel and they gave him their own property (money) in exchange. This was a fair exchange. It was good to him and to them. Mark didn't steal, didn't coerce and didn't damage anyone's property. Mark is good!

Author's opinion—Right answer: b

Riddle #33 - Party Goers

This small town loved parties. And they invented all kinds of reasons to party. Celebration of the day when the Forest fire was stopped seventeen years ago—and they danced all night. Celebration of the thirteen years from the day when the Mayer's dog barked for the first time—and they had a carnival. The sun rise was beautiful—and they had a pool party. The sunrise was especially red—and they had a salute.

Everything can be a reason for a party they were saying.

The town folk loved to put on costumes and decorate their parties. Especially they loved all kinds of balloons. There were several stores that sold party stuff and tons of balloons every day. But one girl made especially great balloons. They were the best colors in the world, larger than at other stores and with beautiful artwork she herself designed. Her balloons were so beautiful that no one wanted to buy any other balloons. And when she began to sell them for lower than others prices, she became the only balloon seller in the town.

And there her trouble started.

Members of the city council were approached by other balloon makers who complained that this girl by the name Ana stole all their business, and the councilman decided to "look into this matter of balloon monopoly."

No, said Ana, I didn't steal anything. My balloons are better than other balloons, and my prices are lower. People want good and inexpensive products, she argued.

We shall make sure that there is no monopoly in our town, the members of the council told her. Monopoly is bad. Monopoly raises prices. Competition is good. Competition lowers prices. You should make sure that other balloon makers can sell their balloons as well. Since we can't force customers to buy their products we instead will force you make your products not as good as they are and sell them for higher prices.

Now Ana makes balloons that are not as good as they were before. She is also charging more for them. Since her balloons and her prices are the same as at all other balloon makers, people buy balloons from them as well.

When Ana was working hard to make beautiful balloons and sold them for lower prices, the town folk were buying them cheap. Now with the new rules of competition established by the government they buy them for more money and they are not as good as before.

Isn't it the exact opposite of what the government wanted to achieve by passing the anti-monopoly laws? Is it possible that fair competition becomes unfair the moment the government attempts to regulate it?

Ana went to the Mayor and told him that things got worse, not better. After hearing her story the Mayor said "The important thing is—there is no monopoly anymore! It is good for the town!"

But this is not good for me and for the people, who want to buy balloons, thought Ana. How can it be good for the town if it is not good for the people? Then she remembered—her grandmother warned her about progressives and socialists who put the country first and the people distant second. It is time to fight, she decided and on that day she started her campaign for the Mayor of the island. It time to save us from those thieves and robbers was her winning campaign slogan.

Thinking out loud:

Q1 - Do you think that the city council did the right thing?

a) Government has an obligation to stop a monopoly the moment it occurs

b) I think the government again did something stupid

c) I want my vanilla ice cream and do not care for anything else

Comment of a Progressive / Socialist: It only looks like it is unjust. In real life it is the only way people shall co-exist. If Ana will be the only seller of the balloons, many other balloon sellers will suffer. They will not be able to feed their families. Ana will have all the money, will build herself a castle, will buy the best cars, fly all over the world ... and others will have no food on their tables. Is it just? Since it is not, the government shall stop monopolies the moment they see them. Monopolies are bad!

Comment of a True Liberal / Capitalist: Three hundred years ago the only way to travel was in a horse carriage. There were no phones and television. We didn't have calculators and computers. We didn't know plastics, air conditioners and flushing toilets. If people wouldn't strive to make their product the best, we wouldn't have drugs to cure illnesses, and would still live on average not more than forty years. The progress is achieved because of people like Ana. And better life to everyone comes because she and others like her strive, innovate and push the society ahead.

Author's opinion—Right answer: b

Riddle #34 - Clothing Stores

In a city called Ai people loved to dress up. Actually they loved to dress so much that they spent almost all their money at clothing stores buying new dresses and accessories. This is why the world famous chain of clothing stores Bud-Nud opened a thousand and one stores on every corner of the city and all were doing really well. The stores were filled with a variety of clothing of many different styles and were selling everything really inexpensive. This is why the stores were always filled with happy customers and this is why Bud-Nud "killed" all the competition in the city. There were no clothing stores except Bud-Nud in Ai anymore.

The management of Bud-Nud sat down and said to ourselves "We got rid of all the competitors; it is time to raise prices." And they raised prices. First they were doing really well—the prices were up and they made more money selling the same clothing as before. Then the city folk noticed that the prices went up and they began to buy much less clothes. They bought so much before that they didn't actually need anything.

The Bud-Nud began to lose money and they decided to raise prices again, and again. And they lost more and more customers. And that the worst Bud-Nud's nightmare happened. When they were selling cheap and offered a lot of goods, no one was able to compete with them. From the moment they started selling for more many competitors saw an opportunity and re-opened their stores. The competition offered new fashionable designs from around the world for better prices than Bud-Nud. Most of the stores were small, each selling one line of clothing. But later some of them moved to larger spaces. A group of local investors opened a new chain of stores to sell clothes made in Ai.

Bud-Nud now wasn't the biggest store in the city. It lost many of its loyal customers, and the new generation didn't even consider buying their clothes there. Soon Bud-Nud decided to change their name and re-shape their image. The President of the company quit and new managers took over.

There is no Bud-Nud anymore. They made a small mistake. They thought that if they are a monopoly, they can raise prices, lower their services, shrink their product line and not worry about the competition. They didn't know what they were doing. They didn't know how the market can punish you for making such mistakes.

Thinking out loud:

Q1 - Can a business that has no competition raise prices and reduce services and still have sales?

    a)   Yes, it can—if it is a monopoly

    b)   No, because the moment they offer to customers what the customers do not want, the customers start looking for someone else to get what they want. And usually when they look, there is someone who will provide them with the product or service they want. And the monopolist loses its customers and profits.

Comment of a Progressive / Socialist: Sometimes there is a possibility to find an alternative source of the products, and sometimes not. We the people can't be dependent on a mood of one seller for things that are essential for our survival.

Comment of a True Liberal / Capitalist: There is one and only one thing any company in the world is after, and it is called profits. This is the only reason people start businesses and the only reason for any business to exist. Only a person who has no experience in conducting business will think that a company will start damaging its profits. If I sell good and inexpensive dresses I can sell a hundred thousand and get maybe ten dollars profit from each. Total I will get a million in profits. If I raised prices, less people will buy my dresses. I will sell twenty thousand and will make twenty five dollars from each. It is a half a million in profits. Do you think the head of the company says to the board of directors—I have a very good idea! Let's make less profit! Do you think they will be happy with this idea?

Author's opinion—Right answer: b

The absence of competition in capitalism doesn't mean that the winner can provide bad services or sell expensive products. Only by making customers happy the monopolist can continue to be a monopolist.

If he offers the best product for the best price, why is it bad? It is good for you and I. It is good for the monopolist as well. It is bad only for those who made inferior products and were trying to sell them for high prices. Let them think how to outperform the monopolist and if they do that, we will come to them to buy their product, right?

If the best producer is forced by the government to raise prices or to reduce quality of service to match the others, this is bad. That means we will get a poorer product and poorer service.

We the people shall decide by ourselves whose product we want to buy, not the government!

In short, when the government is trying to regulate the business, the results of its actions is always the exact opposite of what the government intended to do. This is why so many people tell their governments "Get off our backs! This is the best thing you can do for us and the economy."

Chapter XII

Blame capitalism first—or—
A fool and his money will soon part

Riddle #35 - Tropical Island

GARY LOVED THIS island. From the moment the boat with his tour group came to the shore he understood that this is the place he was dreaming about all his life. The island center was small but nice, with stores, movie theaters, restaurants, pool halls and bowling alleys. The trees were exotic and beautiful, the ocean was warm and magnificent, and the people were friendly and always ready to help. This was so much different from Chicago that Gary immediately decided that he will move to the island to live for the rest of his life.

He was a civil engineer but dreamed about opening his own business.

Gary found a space for rent on the main street and shook hands with the owner of the building. The location was absolutely the best and Gary already envisioned a huge banner over the entrance that would say "Trader Gary's store."

The owner of the building happened to be the island's Mayor and in turn he introduced Gary to who is who on the island. Everyone welcomed Gary and confirmed that business is booming here and that life is easy and absolutely beautiful.

Gary went back to Chicago. The winter was in its coldest. Gary was counting days and hours to the moment he would come back to the always warm island that had no winters or even cold days. He looked at the businesses that had more clients and produced larger profits. He didn't want to sell anything that would perish or rot. He didn't want to deal with fashion since fashion might change every year or sometimes even more often. It took him more than a month to find the product of his choice. Gary sold everything he had, purchased and packed his products and everything else needed for the store in a container and took off to the island. Forever and ever, he said to himself.

Gary arrived two weeks prior to the container and immediately began to prepare the store for the grand opening. He hired island's natives and decorated the store exactly as he envisioned. He prepared the grand opening the likes of which the island didn't know. He hired musicians, dancers and ordered a great amount of food and drinks.

When the container arrived Gary moved his merchandise in secret. He didn't want anyone to know what he will have in the store. He wanted it to be a surprise to everyone.

And finally the big day came. The entire Island population came to the main street to see what's in Gary's store. The party was a smashing success. The speeches were long and warm. The tropical drinks were long and hot. Finally Gary opened the doors and the islanders entered the store.

On the shelves, on beautiful mannequins, on posters everywhere the astonished public saw fur coats that were an absolutely smashing success in Chicago.

The islanders loved Gary's store. They loved the fur coats. They loved the air conditioner, the coffee he served to his clients, the music that was softly played at the store. They brought children there and even invited guests from the neighboring islands to come and see the store by themselves. However they didn't buy the fur coats. Not one of them. Never.

Gary was devastated. He lost all his money. He said that he now hates capitalism. He said that from now on he is for equality and will always vote for progressives and socialists. He said that capitalism is bad and under capitalism people are becoming selfish and egotistic. He is married with two children, works for the city of Chicago and hates everything about his life and his job.

Thinking out loud:

Q1 - Why did no one purchase Gary's coats

   a) Because capitalism is bad

   b) Because people on the island didn't like Gary's store

   c) Because they didn't like Gary

   d) Because they hate music and air conditioning in the stores

   e) Because no one needs fur coats on the tropical islands

Q2 - Which government will Gary will vote for?

   a) The one that helps businesses grow and protects producers

   b) Those that do not produce?

   c) The government that takes from producers and makes all people as equal as possible

   d) The government that helps businesses grow and awards those that work hard, create businesses and innovate

   e) I do not know

Comment of a Progressive / Socialist: a person worked all his life, received salary and benefits, and his life was secured. He was charmed by the "opportunities" of capitalism and risked everything he had. And lost. This is a good lesson for him and others like him. He should come back to Chicago and try to get his old job back.

Comment of a True Liberal / Capitalist: if God wants to punish a person he messes with his brain. It took Gary years to become an engineer. Why did he think that to become an entrepreneur will not take any preparation, study and thinking? He acted as a fool and he is the only one responsible for his failure.

Author's opinion—Right answers:

Q1 - e

Q2 - b

Simple Business Stories:

Baby Store

Jenny and Sue decided to open a store that will sell everything a baby needs. They found a great place, negotiated a good lease with an option to stay at the place for years, painted the store in pink and blue colors, designed all the features and brought many great things a baby and a mother might need. The store looked fantastic. It was definitely the best looking baby store in the whole region.

Jenny and Sue hired two people to help them in the store, brought a cash register, installed video cameras and put out a flashing sign "open."

Like with every new business, customers came to check it out and many people looked around and complimented the new owners taste and choice of products. There were however very few sales. At the end of the month the manager of the mall came and asked for the monthly rent. Jenny said to Sue "Please pay the rent." Sue said to Jenny "I do not have any more money. You pay the rent." "I do not have any more money either, "said Jenny.

"If you do not have money you can't stay in the store," said the manager: "I will rent it to people who can pay the rent."

The two store employees came to Jenny & Sue and asked to pay them for a month work. "We worked for a month and we need the money we agreed upon," they said to Jenny and Sue.

The electrical bill came by mail. And the garbage collectors bill. And the hot water bill. And the gas bill. They all said "you used our services, now pay."

But we do not have any money left, said Jenny and Sue.

The store is no longer open. Jenny and Sue are now looking for jobs and telling their friends that capitalism is a very bad system. It is not fair. It takes all your money and doesn't give anything in return.

Jenny and Sue now receive money from the government. The government takes money it give to Jenny and Sue from the store owners who did everything right and now because they were planning their businesses and were careful in their work, have to pay for Jenny and Sue's apartments, food, medical bills and re-education. Jenny and Sue now will vote for the government that takes as much as possible from smart producers and gives to those that didn't conduct their businesses right.

Q1 - Who is to blame for the store failure?

a) Capitalistic system is bad and it is responsible for Jenny and Sue losing all their money

b) The workers, owner of the building, people at the electrical plan and garbage collectors didn't like Jenny and Sue's store.

c) The customers who visited the shopping center were all racists and wouldn't buy anything from a salesperson of a different race

d) Jenny and Sue didn't think their business through and started it without enough money. If you didn't put aside some money for ongoing expenses, your business will go broke very soon.

Author's opinion—Right answer: d

Giant Furniture

Carl worked at a furniture factory in a large city. They were producing fashionable large sized wooden furniture. Carl decided that he will open a similar business in some other place and found a small town on the other side of the state. He rented a barn over there, purchased all materials needed for making furniture and brought his tools to the barn. He worked hard for three months and made a great collection of gigantic wooden furniture even larger and better than what his old factory did. After three months of hard work he invited the owners of the local furniture stores to view the collection. He was absolutely sure that they will scream with joy and fight over his huge tables and chairs, gigantic sofas and shelves.

Can you imagine his surprise when not one single store owner placed an order or even asked him about the prices of the furniture. All of them expressed an admiration and even awe of the quality of the furniture and all of them left without saying a word about doing business with Carl.

The next day not one of them called and Carl decided to visit one of the stores and find out what happened.

In our town, said the owner of the store Carl visited first, the ceilings are quite low and your furniture simply will not fit.

Carl lost all his money and now hated capitalism. He decided that from now on he will vote for the government that takes from smarter producers and gives to those that do not do research, do not think through their business and foolishly waste all their money.

Q1 - Why did Carl's business fail?

    a)   Local dealers didn't want competition and they conspired not to buy his furniture and kick him out of town

b) Capitalism just doesn't work for small business. The government shall tell people what kind of furniture to produce and at what prices to sell.

c) Carl started business without really knowing his market.

<u>Authors opinion—Right answer</u>: c

Pork Farm

Joanne's family owns a pork farm. They are always looking for new places to sell pork and one day someone told Joanne that there was a small town two hundred miles from their farm, with a farmers market every Sunday, and there was no pork sold anywhere. Joanne raced there on the next Sunday and confirmed there was no pork. She quickly secured a booth for the next week and went home to make preparations.

A week later she and her younger brother Jim took a small refrigerator, mounted plenty of pork in it and went to the fair. They were first to arrive and had enough time to prepare the booth. Joanne went through the market one more time and saw again that there indeed was no pork sold anywhere.

When customers started coming Joanne and Jim noticed that they were a bit different from the usual customers they saw on other farmers markets and fairs. Many women were wearing scarves on their heads, some covering everything except their eyes. It didn't bother Joanne how they dressed but those people were not that interested in the pork. In fact for the first two hours no one even came close to the booth. At the same time other sellers were busy making money.

After hours of wasting their time, Joanne turned to an old vendor who was selling vegetables and sold almost everything he brought with him. What the hell is going on, she said, why does no one buy from us?

This is a Muslim community, said the old vendor, they do not eat pork. It is prohibited by their religion.

Q1 - Why was Joanne's business trip to sell pork on a farmers market unsuccessful?

a) Muslims do not buy anything from non-Muslims

b) Joanne didn't do her job right. She didn't check the market before she rented the booth and brought her products to the fair.

c) Capitalism is a bad system. People are forced to think about money all the time.

d) Capitalism shall be abolished and prohibited, together with money.

Author's opinion—Right answer: b

Christmas Decorations

Bob wanted to get a new photo camera with the greatest optics in the world. But the camera he wanted wasn't cheap. The price was twenty-five hundred dollars. And Bob had only three hundred. Bob knew that he can't even think about this camera, but he loved it so much that he couldn't resist and kept looking … and found one on Internet that was selling for seven hundred dollars. Someone who purchased it never opened it, never used it and now wanted to get rid of it.

I have to find the remaining money. I just have to, said Bob to himself. I need to find something I can buy with my three hundred and sell for seven hundred.

One ad on the Internet caught his attention "Christmas decorations at 10% of the price. For a dollar you will get ten dollars worth of wonderful Christmas décor."

This is it, he said to himself. I will buy decorations for three hundred dollars that is now worth three thousand. I will offer them to people for half of this amount and will get fifteen hundred. Hooray! I can buy the camera and have another eight hundred dollars for myself. What a great thing to live in capitalism!

Bob purchased the decorations and went from door to door to sell them. No one wanted to buy anything. People were saying to Bob "This is January; we just took those decorations off our trees and our homes. We will not need them for a year. Come back in December."

Bob lost all the money he saved. I hate capitalism, he said to himself. It is an unfair system of robbing people from their belongings. He threw the decorations into the garbage and went home to dream about his camera and hate capitalism. Bob now tells all his friends to vote for the government that is anti-capitalism, the government that takes money from those that think before acting and gives it to those that act before thinking.

Q1 - Why did Bob lose all his money?

a)   Bob's neighbors didn't like him playing loud music late in the evenings

b)   Bob didn't think his business through. He didn't make any research as when his product is needed.

c)   Capitalism is a bad system. The neighbors shall be forced to pay Bob money for him losing money in a bad deal. If the neighbors are successful and smart, and they have money, they shall now pay for Bob's food, medical expenses and home rent.

Author's opinion—Right answer: b

Good Job!

Karina had a pet grooming salon. It was the best pet grooming place in town. Karina was herself a very good groomer and she taught three assistants to help her in the store. They assisted her at the cash register and in pet preparation, with every aspect of grooming and anything else the animals wanted. This was the best crew in town.

Karina however was always unhappy with their performance. She often yelled and cursed them, calling them names and threatening to fire them all on the spot.

One day Karina saw a sign across the street that there soon will be a new pet grooming salon. She wasn't happy that day and her assistants felt her unhappiness the hard way. The whole day they have heard that they are lazy and ungrateful and that she is thinking about getting rid of them all and hiring better people.

Next day all three of them quit. They were offered to work in the new salon and even though they were offered less in wages, they all agreed to work there. Karina quickly hired new people but they were not trained as well and Karina lost many of her customers who went with their pets to the new place. Karina lost so many clients that she had to close her salon.

I hate capitalism, she said to herself. It is a very bad system that allowed all of my assistants whom I trained to leave me at once. They shall be fined for leaving me or even imprisoned.

The day she finally took off the sign she met one of her past employees. How could you do that to me, she asked her?

I worked for you for two years and you not once told me "Good Job" she answered.

Karina is getting now paid by the government. She lost all her money and needs help to pay for her apartment, medical expenses and food. Since the government doesn't have its own money, it takes it from the people working at the new pets grooming salon and gives to Karina. Karina says that she will now always vote for the government that takes from the working people and gives to the ones that lost their businesses and sources of income. Karina can find work, but says that since she gets enough, she will not bother.

Q1 - Why did all of Karina's employees leave her?

  a) Because she had poor parents

  b) Because her dad left her mom when she was a child

  c) Because she paid them very little

  d) Because the other salon was brighter and bigger

  e) Because she was rude and ungrateful

  f) Because capitalism is a bad system.

Author's opinion—Right answer: e

Permits and Licenses

Paul got a small inheritance from his parents and decided to open a restaurant to serve breakfast and lunch. He envisioned a place surrounded by tall office buildings with no restaurants anywhere around. He had not much experience in running restaurants but didn't think it was a big deal to organize and manage one. So many people are doing it and I am not dumber than they, he thought.

It took him almost three months to find a good spot, remodel the space, buy and install all the equipment and hire people. And finally the restaurant was ready and after extensive marketing in all of the surrounding buildings he was open.

Many people came to check it out and were happy with the food and with the prices. Paul was very happy and proud as well.

At the end of the day he was arrested for opening a food outlet without proper permits.

Paul paid a huge fine and applied for the permits. In a month one inspector visited the restaurant and said that Paul needs to change the ventilations system. An inspector from another department told Paul that there is a requirement to have a back door for evacuation of customers in case of fire. Another inspector told him that his refrigerators are not installed in accordance to the regulations and he can't open the restaurant until he does it right.

I do not have money to do all that, said Paul. His restaurant was closed and he lost all his money. Paul was very angry. He cursed capitalism and said that this is the most unjust system in the world. He said that he will work on elections trying to elect people who will take as much money from producers and distribute them among all others like himself.

Q1 - Why was Paul's restaurant closed?

a)   Because he was a high school dropout

b)   Because he had a stumbling problem

c)   Because the inspectors hated him

d)   Because he didn't think through his business

e)   Because capitalism is a bad system.

Author's opinion—Right answer: d

Print Shop

Mary and Yvonne wanted to open a print shop together, but they came to a conclusion that they can't work as a team and split. Both decided to open shops of their own. Both purchased needed equipment and both hired people to work for them. Their shops were quite similar and they immediately became competitors.

In order to find clients, Mary hired two sales people and offered them good salaries. The sales people were very happy and grateful. The got nice desks, great new phones and computers and had gas in their cars paid by the business. You shall not worry about money, she said. I will take care of your needs, and you can now concentrate on the work. The sales people were grateful to Mary and promised to work hard for the business.

Yvonne found two people whom she offered commissions for their work. You will get a percent of the money we will earn with your help, she told them. If you work hard and well, you receive more. If you do not sell a lot, it is a waste of time and you will be fired.

Her sales people had to run fast and work hard to get the money they needed for living. It was not an easy job for them, and one of them quit. Yvonne hired instead two more, and then another person who had a lot of experience in sales. Yvonne made him the company's sales manager who in addition to what he would get from his own sales, he would get a percent of the sales of the others. For that he was supposed to teach them, supervise them and help them to sell.

Mary's people were coming to work at nine and leaving at five. The moment they would leave the shop they would put the thoughts about their work aside until the next business day. They were doing their jobs, but when a client wouldn't answer their calls or would reject their proposal they moved on to the next task.

Yvonne's people were fighting for every deal and every client. They worked longer hours and never forgot about their jobs.

When the economy was strong, both shops were doing OK, although Yvonne's shop had twice as much sales as Mary's. But when economy began to stumble and the situation in the whole country became bad, Mary's shop died. She had to let go her salespeople and other workers, and closed the shop down.

Yvonne bought her equipment and moved to a larger space. She said that her people were getting orders despite anything that happens in the economy.

I hate capitalism, said Mary. I would want to live in some other system. I want to change my country so other people wouldn't suffer as I did.

Mary's fired employees began to receive government's help. The government has no money of their own. They take it from the people who work hard. The government made Yvonne pay for Mary's and her workers' food, rent and medical expenses. Now Yvonne and her crew worked and provided not only for their own families but for Mary and her crew.

I wouldn't want to receive government assistance, said Yvonne; I prefer to earn my own bread. She decided to always vote for the government that helps business people to grow their businesses.

I am tired of all this competition, planning, and marketing and selling, said Mary to herself. I want others to pay for my needs and I will always vote for the government that takes as much as possible from those that produce and give to the others who are not.

Q1 - Why was Yvonne was doing OK when Mary had to close her shop? What do you think?

a)   Because Yvonne's parents were rich

b)   Because Mary was short with red hair and green eyes

c)   Because Yvonne had better printing equipment

d)   Because Mary didn't give incentives to her sales people

e)   Because capitalism is a bad system.

<u>Author's opinion—Right answer</u>: d

Multi—level Marketing

Randolph never heard about multi-level marketing before. But now he was really excited. Really excited! He attended this seminar and they told him that if he will sell a thousand dollars worth of food supplements and vitamins every month ... and if he will convince four people to became a sellers of the same company and they also will sell a thousand dollars each month ... and each of them will convince four people to sell a thousand dollars worth of food supplements a months, he will get his first million in about a year and a half! That was cool! No need to go to college, no need to learn any useful profession, no need to plan, invest money, even not much to do. Definitely, this thing they called for short MLM was the way to go!

Randolph went to all his friends, but they were a bit skeptical and said that they will pass on this golden opportunity. They told Randolph that they were already taking the vitamins they need, and that if those would be drugs to cure cancer and other terrible diseases, than they would buy and sell those products. Otherwise, there are many other products in the drug stores and supermarkets that they can buy when they need and for less.

This was a huge disappointment, but Randolph decided that he is not a quitter. This is what all those MLM people were talking about—people quit just before great things begin to happened to them, and they miss their chance.

Randolph wasn't about to miss his chance. He decided to become a millionaire no matter what. The sick people are those that will listen to me, if I will tell them that I have a cure for their illness. The sicker the better, thought Randolph. Especially good to sell to those people who are sick with terminal illnesses. They will listen to anyone who will bring them hope. They and their relatives are my potential customers. They will pay ANY money for a glimpse of hope.

He began to think where he can find names and addresses of sick people. When he asked himself this question, he immediately knew the answer. In two weeks Randolph got himself hired as a part time clerk in a hospital. The hospital had thousands of records of sick people, with their names, addresses and phone numbers.

The first two weeks were just tremendously unbelievable. Randolph called the first hundred people from the archives, and lied about the products he had. To everyone he was saying exactly what he found from their files they need. Everyone bought the vitamins and food supplements he was selling. People whom he visited were happy to see him and very thankful. The asked him to come by any time, took his phone number and said they will recommend him to all other people sick with similar illnesses.

During those two great weeks Randolph sold his supplements and vitamins for more than five thousand dollars. He became the best selling representative in his MLM company and got a lot of praise of his superiors who were making money from each sale he made.

Then it stopped. One day just before Randolph was about to leave for work the head of the personnel department called him and asked not to come back to work. Randolph didn't even ask why. He already copied all their records into his files and had all the addresses and names in his computer. When I will finish with this list, he thought, I will get into a different hospital and copy all their records. Life ahead was looking bright and happy.

Since he didn't go to work, Randolph began to call new clients from the list. They were not friendly as others before. Actually a couple of them told Randolph that they were warned that a scam is going around. They said that they were told to report him the moment he calls.

Randolph called some of his best customers. They hang up on him. One old lady said that she doesn't want to hear his voice ever. She added that she already agreed to be a witness of the law suit against him.

When Randolph called the MLM company, he was asked not to call anymore. You are no longer associated with this company, he was told. Randolph started yelling at the secretary that he hates the company and hates capitalism, but she hanged up on him.

As a result of the court trial the hospital and the MLM Company were forced to pay damages to the patients. Randolph was told by the judge not to do anything like that in the future, or he will be punished. Since he didn't have anything there was nothing to take from him. He got six months in jail, but all jails in his area were full and he was dismissed.

His attorney spent countless hours with his case and had to be paid by someone. Randolph didn't have money to pay him, and the public attorney was paid by the government. Since the government doesn't have money of their own, they come to people who make money. The patients whom Randolph conned and other people who work and earn money were forced to pay for his attorney, judge, prosecutors and clerks in the court, electricity providers and garbage collectors. All that and more were paid by the people who worked and honestly earned money and whom the government punished for that.

After the trial Randolph was out of work and applied for the government help and now good people who earned their money the old fashion way without lying to their customers are paying his medical bills, rent of his apartment and food. Randolph doesn't have time to work. He is planning his next big scheme to get his million dollars in eighteen months.

Q1 -Why people didn't want to talk with Randolph and were filing a law suit against him?

    a)   Because he wasn't brushing his teeth

    b)   Because he had abusive parents

    c)   Because he cheated the place he worked at and lied to his customers

    d)   Because they found a place to buy similar products for less?

<u>Author's opinion—Right answer</u>: c

The Boat Factory

Gordon considered himself a very smart man. He worked at a boat factory and knew exactly how to make boats better than his employers. He saved money, went to a small island near Greece and built a boat factory there. He employed dozens of islanders to work at the factory. His boats were much better than the boats made by the islanders themselves, and every islander wanted to buy his boat. The problem was that the islanders didn't have enough money to buy Gordon's boats and Gordon wasn't able to sell any of his boats. He lost all his money and had to close the factory and go home to try to get his job back.

Q1 - What did Gordon not do before he started his business?

a) He didn't check the weather on the island

b) He didn't talk with the authorities

c) He didn't check if his products will fit the size of the customer's wallets

Author's opinion—Right answer: c

Riddle #36 - Fair Competition

This was a small town slowly growing from a very tiny town. This small town needed a Main Street with a couple of coffee shops, a movie theater, a city hall tower with a clock and a bookstore. Two people at the same time decided to open book stores and as sometimes chance does it, they rented spaces on the same street one across another. And as again sometimes happened, they decided to open their stores at the same day.

Oops! Two book stores were opening on the same street across each other on the same day! And the town barely needed one book store. The owners of the stores immediately recognized the problem and realized that they are at war. One of them will win and another's business would die. Simple as that.

The owner of the north side of the street store (we will call it North Store) decided to sell everything so inexpensive that his competitor wouldn't be able to make profits and would go out of business.

I will offer huge inventory in my store, thought the North Store's owner. The computerized system will allow people to find everything very easy and efficiently. I will have text books that people would be able to borrow for a small fee. I always will have something related to books on sale. Like book covers, or lamps people will be using to read the books with. I will train my staff the way they will always be willing to answer to any questions the customers might have.

At the same time the owner of the South Side store was thinking about his business model. I will make my store beautiful with large selection of children's books, with places in the store people can sit and read, with a coffee shop and music section, the South Store's owner said to himself. People will be drawn to the store, with children, and all those that do research, and people who just want to sit and read magazines, and have a cup of coffee with their morning paper. This will be the best place to meet in town. I will have writers come here and read their stories, meet with their readers and sign books.

The stores were built exactly as the owners of the stores wanted. Both had a reception prepared and it was a day to remember. Many of the town folks came with entire families, guests arrived from the nearby towns and villages, and even several local dignitaries such as a congressman and an aide to the senator came to wish both of them luck. All those people went first to one store, then to another, congratulated the owners and left. And the waiting started. Both owners were hoping that their store would win, and both feared that they will lose.

The other store has great selection of books, thought the South Store's owner. Their prices are great. It is a very good store and it will be very hard to compete with it.

The other store has so many great services, thought the North Store's owner. They have a coffee shop, and place to sit and read, and a special section for kids, and a music section. There are computers connected to Internet and they can check their emails or send messages to friends while they are in the store. It is a very good store and it will be very hard to compete with it.

Both stores did OK the first week. They both did OK the second week as well. Actually during the third and fourth week they did even better. They were always full of customers who seem to like to come back to the stores and shop there. And two months later the business exploded. People came from the distance of thirty or even fifty miles to check the bookstores. The South Side store added an outside coffee shop and a kid's playground. The North Side store opened the basement and expanded its variety of books. Now they had a special travel section, and a cooking section, and a philosophy section, and a self-help section. They sold books almost at cost, but sold so many it brought the store good profit.

Actually most of the money I am not making not on the books, mused the North Store's owner. It is the additional services that make us profitable.

People from all over knew now that the best bookstores in the region are in this small town that wasn't famous for anything. Since so many people were coming to the town, the business people began to open new businesses to cater to their needs.

There were now several restaurants on the main street of this small town. One of the best pet groomers in the region moved there. Two hair salons and three shoe stores brought the best and most fashionable footwear to the thousands of customers that now came to shop and enjoy the town.

Musicians and clowns performed on the street during evening hours, the very best ice cream was sold at four different locations, and in the middle of the street that was now closed for traffic and is a "walk in only" many vendors were selling anything from funny hats to jewelry and cell phones.

There were several portrait artists offering customers to paint them or their children. And above all, there was now a huge temporary tent with a circus that might soon become a permanent feature of the town.

There is a lot of construction goes on in the outskirts of the town— many people who never heard about it now want to live nearby and are planning to open their businesses to serve all those customers. There is a rumor that a large hospital is considering opening their new state of the art medical facility. Every person in the town is employed and there is a constant need for more and more helping hands.

Thinking out loud:

Q1 - Why didn't the competition kill the book stores?

a)   The government ordered town folks to buy books from both stores and this is how they survived

b)   People bought books from both stores out of pity

c)   The business in both stores was thought through. The business models were different but both prepared very well. This drew people not only from the small town but from all over.

Q2 - Why did so many businesses come to the town?

a)   They all came because a lot of people visited the book stores and the owners of many businesses saw an opportunity to sell their products and services

b)   The government ordered them to

c)   They came by coincidence

Q3 - Why did the town grow so much and why did all the people who lived there found themselves jobs?

a)   It all happened because of the government orders

b)   It just happened, like rain or wind

c)   When government is not interfering with the business, the towns grow and people are getting good jobs instead of government assistance

Comment of a Progressive / Socialist: It is very good that the book stores were built in town. More culture to people is good. However the salaries that are paid by small business owners to the workers are far from being good. The owners of the business receive much more than the workers and this is inequality. This is actually an exploitation of people by the capitalists. Everything should belong to the government, or at least controlled by the government. The government will make sure that no one gets exorbitant profits, and everyone will be covered by a reliable health insurance and gets enough money to cover all expenses. If in this town the business is booming, possibly that in other towns, cities or villages people are starving. Profits or no profits, but all the people are supposed to have food, shelter and medical help. It is not important they are working or not, sick or not, thieves or honest people, no one supposed to go to sleep hungry.

Comment of a True Liberal / Capitalist: The most important people in the capitalistic society are not kings or politicians, but innovators, entrepreneurs and investors. Those people make discoveries, innovations, create new businesses and make things happen. If not them, we wouldn't have cars and planes, phones and radio, and people would be dying from many illnesses that now are easily treated by modern drugs. When governments do not interfere, the businesses are booming. When government does not interfere the people create, produce and live better lives. The town is booming because no government regulations stopped the process of people attempting to build better lives for themselves and in the process they make it better for everyone.

Author's opinion—Right answer:

Q1 - c

Q2 - c

Q3 - a

Chapter XIII

If you will be able to choose—which societies you can find on the market?

"The trouble with socialism is that you eventually run out of other people's money"

Margaret Thatcher.

AS FAR AS historical records go, there always has been a person in any group of people who would try to take from producers what they would make and would give it to someone else, himself included. Let's call him "strongman."

Producers would work hard, would spent countless hours to grow food or make things and this person would force them to give him for free the fruits of their hard labor. It is an exchange, he would say to the producers. In exchange for what you might ask? Most of the times those things this "strongman" would give producers in exchange for their products were not something that the producers really wanted or needed.

Regular folks were producing barely enough food and goods to survive. Then bullies with weapons would come and take part of what those good folks made, giving them in exchange their promise to protect the producers from other robbers.

Q1 - Do you think the life of the producers would change if another strongman (not the one that robbed them) would be robbing their belongings?

a) I think their life would be much worth under a different strongman

b) I think their life would be much better under a different strongman

c) I think their life wouldn't change at all. They would be still producing and either one of those strongman would rob them.

Q2 - Do you think it would be less robbery, more robbery or about the same robbery if a strongman would be a midget?

a) More robbery

b) Less robbery

c) About the same amount of robbery

How about if he or she who robs the producers would be from Indonesia—would it be more robbery, less robbery or about the same amount of robbery?

How about if he or she would be a Buddhist? Or a Pagan? Or a giant with two heads? If someone would rob your family, would you care how he or she looks, what language they speak or what Gods they pray to?

Would you feel better about starvation of your entire family if you would be robbed by a person who speaks your language, who dresses the way your family dresses and who has the same color of skin as you?

a) Yes, I would feel better if my family would starve because this person and not others robbed us

b) I do not care how those people look. Let my family and our belongings alone! Only then I will feel better.

The citizens of those cities and countries that were "protected" by their rulers had no idea if they would be worse, better or the same under another guy, because no one asked them what they want or think. If you will not give, you will die they were told. It was a good alternative and after much thought the producers usually gave whatever the strongmen wanted.

Occasionally they revolted and died. Seldom had they prevailed and the throne would be than taken by one of them, who in turn would become the Strongman, would come to them and demand their products in exchange for protection.

But the robbery didn't stop there. Another portion of their goods was taken from the producers by people who promised them protection after death. If you will give enough, they were saying, you will be having good life after this life ... for a thousand years. If you do not give, you will be burned on a frying pan for about the same amount of time.

Since even to question this promise was scary and dangerous, the producers gave to those people who were scaring them with afterlife tortures as part of what they produced as well.

The first way to extract goods is called force and the other is called fraud. Usually the approaches mix and match and there is a lot of fraud in the first approach and a lot of force behind the second approach.

Under the influence of Thomas Paine whom some credit with the actual writing of the Declaration of Independence (or at least whose influence is evident there), and who started the American Revolution with his famous book "Common Sense," the six thousand years rule of monarchies around the world began to decline. Paine was the first to declare that people can survive without a king and actually will be doing much better not having one.

You probably think that this is not a big deal to envision a word without a ruler, a monarch, a Great Father who gives or takes at will, who resolves disputes and send armies to conquer additional territories and kill other monarchs. But at the time Paine wrote his book no one thought it is possible.

In times past, most of the kings were thrown out of their countries, and three different systems of co-existence emerged. All of them proclaim that they are a democratic system and are good for the majority of the population.

One system we call International Socialism and the believers say that it has a goal of building a society where everyone will be getting from a state an equal amount of everything. It will be even better in the future they say. Soon everyone will work as much as they can or will not work at all, but will get from the State anything they want, those socialists promise to the people. The socialists call this ideal (they say they want to achieve) Communism. I hope you understand that "work a little and get anything you want" is a bit unrealistic, but many people who didn't read this book believed in it.

Their symbols are red flag, five-ray star and a song called International. The best known country that adopted socialism and said that it is building communism was called the Union of the Soviet Socialist Republics (USSR).

The second system is called National Socialism with a goal of building a state managed society, equal to almost all. This system we usually call Fascism. In the past it associated with Nazi Germany, with the swastika as its symbol, but it is much wide spread than just one country. Elements of fascism are evident in many countries, including the United States of America, but the proponents always disguise them under a different name.

The third system is a Free Society that we called Capitalism. Under this system the equality is not in distribution of belongings, but in opportunities. Everyone has an opportunity to become someone. It is good and scary at the same time. If you failed, it is not because someone didn't allow you, but because of you and you only. The best known capitalist country in the world is the United States of America (USA) with stars and stripes over the flag.

The main difference between the three systems is in who owns and controls our belongings. Socio-communists say that the State shall own everything; socio-fascists say that people can own them but everything shall be controlled by the State, and capitalists say that people themselves shall own and control their belongings.

The first person, who attempted to analyze all three of those systems, was Karl Marx, who hated Capitalism most probably because he didn't succeed in it.

Marxs was a German philosopher who lived in the XIX century and who wrote two major works on the subject of hatred of Capitalism. One is called "The Communist Manifesto" and the other one that he wrote nineteen years later called "Das Kapital" (Capital)

In the Manifesto Marks defined communism as an "abolition of private property". In plain English it is when "no one has anything of his own."

Andrew Galambos, the author of the "Private Property Theory" defines freedom as "total protection of private property."

We just learned that Communism is total abolition and Freedom is total protection of private property, of your belongings. By comparing the two definitions it looks like communism is the direct opposite of freedom.

Well, we discussed in this book what the direct opposite of freedom is? Do you recall? It is called slavery! Let's put the two and two together—Communism equals Slavery.

Capitalism is simple—if I created something like thoughts, ideas, things, or if I purchased something with the money I earned, this is mine. Whoever touches it without my permission is a thief. If you want to take it by force or coercion, you are robbing me and you are a robber even if you are Karl Marx or the President of my country. Get off my property, is a cry of every good American! Get off my property or I will shoot ... this of course is if the government wasn't smart enough and didn't take guns from their owners.

Apparently Karl Marx wanted things that others had and he didn't. His definition of "happiness" was to take <u>everything</u> from the people that produce, and distribute among those that do not produce or do not have.

Taking absolutely everything that you produced from you without your permission is called "total and absolute theft" and it is creates a society of total stealing. Would you want to live in a society where nothing is yours, everything can and most probably will be taken from you without your permission and given to someone else?

a) Yes, I would love to live in such society. I would work very little (actually I will pretend that I work) and will get for free many things that others produce.

b) No, I would hate to live in such society. No one would work hard and we will always have shortages of everything.

Since it is very difficult to take everything from people who do not want to give up what belongs to them, the idea Marx had was to take it away gradually. You might know that as a "frog example" from school, but I will repeat it to you just in case you missed this lesson.

If you would throw a live frog into a pan with boiling water, he will immediately jump out of the pan. If you put the same frog into slightly warm water and start heating it bit by bit, the frog will not notice temperature changes and will sit in the water until he will lose consciousness and will be boiled to death.

This is exactly what Karl Marx meant by gradually introducing communism into the society. If you would come to a person and say "give me all you have" he will probably call the police or fight. But if you come to him and say "Let's help sick children and I need merely one per cent of your earnings and many children will live," most people would say "sure."

Wouldn't you give a small amount of what you have to cure sick children? The problem is the governments do not stop at "one small thing." Then there is another cause and another. The government wants to be in charge of your money. Guess why?

This would be OK if you donate voluntarily and for a cause you believe in. But the strongmen of our world do not come to us and do not ask us when time they think of another use of our money. The strongmen sit in very comfortable armchairs in capitols and talk between themselves. They decide to take our money because they can, and because they think they know better than we do what to do with our money. We are smart enough to earn but not smart enough to spend.

Q1 - Do you think they know what to do with your money better than you?

   a)   Yes, I think the government knows better than me what to do with the money I earned

   b)   No, I think I know better what to do with the money I earned

   c)   And you, what you think?

People like you and me do not revolt because every time the government increases what they take from us by "a very small amount of money" and we believe time after time that this is the very last increase and this is it.

In 1861 the US government for the first time in the US history imposed a personal income tax of 3%, and in 1862 the congress decided that rich people should pay 5%. Six years later because of the revolt of the taxpayers the congress repealed this tax.

The congress agreed that it is "not the American way to take money from producers" and abolished all income taxes ... they thought forever.

Thomas Jefferson once wrote this about taking from one in order to give to someone else: "To take from one, because it is thought his own industry and that of his father has acquired too much, in order to spare to others who (or whose fathers) have not exercised equal industry and skill, is to violate arbitrarily the first principle of association, 'to guarantee to everyone a free exercise of his industry and the fruits acquired by it.' "

Is it clear? It is clear to me like a whistle. Do not take what is not yours! It is NOT YOURS! It is called theft. You take my money; you take my time I invested to make the money. You are enslaving me. I do not want to be your or anyone else's slave. I want to pursue happiness the way I want to pursue it. I do not want yours, but do not take mine.

In 1913 the then-government of the United States decided to take what is not theirs. An income tax was again introduced as the 16th amendment to the constitution. The robbery was made legal and it was only a matter of time the amounts taken from you and I would go up.

And here it was—in 1913 the Congress passed an income tax law with rates beginning at 1 percent and rising to 7 percent for very rich people. If you would make one hundred dollars a day, you would pay one dollar to the government. It is still robbery, but a sly one.

Less than one percent of the population paid any income tax at the time. What do you think would happen if the congressmen would offer to Americans in 1913 to give a third of their income to the government?

The enraged citizens would probably throw all of them, including senators, presidents, congressman and the like out of their offices and opt for the king to rule.

What do you think would happen if the Congress would offer Americans in 1913 to give half of their incomes to the government?

The citizens of this country would probably hang everyone who ever passed by the White House.

How about if I will tell you that in 1963 the income tax on the top earners in the United States was 92%?

Republican presidents Ronald Reagan and George Bush lowered income taxes, and the government under those presidents stole less than under Carter, Clinton and Obama. So we all say, thank you Presidents Reagan and Bush for stealing less than the Democrats.

Karl Marx thought that in order to achieve communism, a country needs to go through a preparation stage called socialism. During this stage he was proposing to use workers' powers to gradually take away all properties of the owners of all businesses, small and large.

As a result of robbing business owners and taking their properties away from them, Karl Marx wrote, the workers would become a new ruling class. All properties will be gradually confiscated and given to workers to control and operate. If at the latest stages the business owners will start resisting, the workers shall be prepared to take the rest of the properties by force.

Do you now see that Marx is a robber and a thief who teaches other robbers and thieves how to rob people from their belongings in a way they will not notice it. Sounds like a school of thieves and robbers, right? Marx wrote books about how to get to people's pockets the best and easiest way.

If a progressive or socialist will tell you that capitalists are "thinking about money only" tell them that you guys are thinking about the same thing—and if they will start denying it, ask them to read their dear teacher Karl Marx. The difference is that capitalists are thinking about how to make money by selling goods and providing services and socialists about how to rob those that made and sold goods and provided services.

As we already learned, those ideas were articulated in two works by Marx. First one, The Manifesto is the base for the Socio-Fascism; the second one Das Kapital is the base for the Socio-Communism. Two major social structures and one Founding Father for both!

The results of the implementation of those great ideas was hundreds of millions people were killed; the world experienced two terrible wars, cultural setbacks and starvation of nations. Marx was enormously successful. There probably wasn't any author or philosopher that had such an impact on civilization in such a short period of time.

And now the United States of America that was leading others on the Capitalist path is gradually changing its ways to become a socialist country and after that—who knows which of the two ways (socio-fascism or socio-communism) it will chose?

You do not believe me? You say, America and especially the Republican Party are for capitalism. They will not allow America to go the Socialist way.

Well, how about Abraham Lincoln, a Republican who introduced Income Tax and Federal Reserve System? How about Teddy Roosevelt introducing anti-trust laws? It is a pure socialism and a giant step toward the "equal" society.

This is the Republican Party that comes up with outrageous ideas taken from the Communist Manifesto, but it is the Democratic Party that is enforcing those destructive laws and regulations.

Not surprisingly that the six times a Presidential candidate for the Socialist Party of America Norman Mattoon Thomas said "The American people will never knowingly adopt socialism. But, under the name of 'liberalism,' they will adopt every fragment of the socialist program, until one day America will be a socialist nation, without knowing how it happened ... I no longer need to run as a Presidential Candidate for the Socialist Party. The Democrat Party has adopted our platform."

OK, let's say we understand what socio-communism is all about— take everything from producers, force them to work and distribute what they produced to everyone in the country. But how to distribute? Who and how will decide what to give to this or that person or family? If you eat more than a neighbor, does that mean that you shall receive the same amount of food or more? If Jim is two sizes larger than Tom and needs more fabric for his coat, will he get more or they shall get equal amount of fabric? If Tom wants more expensive fabric for his coat that Bill, how and who will to decide what is equal?

Socialists answer to this question with a slogan—"from everyone according to his abilities, to everyone according to his needs." In other words they say you shall give everything you produced to the government and you will receive from the government everything you NEED.

We already talked about how people work when they can't be fired, when they have their job guaranteed forever and when they will not be compensated for their efforts. Now let's talk about the second part of the socialists' main principle—how to distribute according to everyone's needs?

Hello! Do you have NEEDS? I do. I have a NEED to fly in a private jet to Paris to view the Eiffel tower and from there to India to ride the elephants. And what do YOU need? Aha, you NEED to have a sports car called a Lamborghini! Good. You worked a little (actually pretended to work) and you can get Lamborghini or Porsche or a couple of Mustangs. Would you want ... sorry NEED anything else?

Q1 - Do you think this system will work?

   a)   Yes, it might work

   b)   I do not know, I need to think about it

   c)   Of course it will not work!

Do you think the socialists believe that this system will work? Of course they do not believe it will work. So why they tell other people that it will work? Maybe they have something up their sleeves?

Yes, they do.

They say "you will be getting according to your needs, but <u>we will decide what you need</u>."

What a wonderful idea, right? If they will decide that you do not need meat, you will not get meat. There is no way you can get meat because you gave everything to the government and there is nothing you can sell or exchange for even a piece of meat. Do you understand that? If you give all your property to someone else, you are not free anymore.

They can decide that you do not need fruit juices, or you do not need to go on vacations, or that you do not need such a "large and luxurious" apartment as what your family has now. They might bring a couple of more families to live in your home with you. They can decide that you do not need television or that you do not need to see action-adventure movies. Then you will not be able to see them. No. None. Nada. Nyet!

I am not joking. The socialists did it many times in many countries. The Soviet Union, Cuba, East Germany, Vietnam, Poland, Hungary, Cambodia ... and the list can go on and on. There is nothing you can do to get what you really want in a socialistic country, except to steal it.

They steal from you, you steal from them. Until they capture you. If I would be you, I wouldn't advise you to be captured stealing in a socialist country. One thing they know how to do and it is how to punish people.

But who in such case needs socialism, you might ask?

This is a very good question. The people who think they will be members of the committees that will decide what you need; only those people really want socialism. They know that what they promise is impossible, but they want to be in charge forever, and lie.

If you are in the socialist government all you need to do is to oversee that everything is taken from the producers and delivered to the government storages. In the Soviet Union they killed those that didn't want to give up their belongings. In Vietnam they sent such people to die in the "labor camps," in China they starved them.

Then part of those goods shall go to "small people" who are waiting for giveaways, and part will be used to indulge those that "govern."

The rulers can make it even simpler. They can give the people they rob a little money to run to the government owned stores and wait for something the government will decide to sell there. One day they might decide to sell a little more, another day a little less. One day they might decide to raise prices, another day to give people something for free. The people will cheer the government for that and call the leader their savior.

If you work for the socialist government and you like someone, you can give him more. It is not yours, you do not care, and you can be generous. If you do not like someone, you can make him crawl to you and kiss your feet begging to give him something he really really needs. Such as medical drugs for their children. What do you think parents will be ready to do for you if saving their child's life will be totally in your hands?

If you are in a socialist government, people will give you anything you want—their survival depends on YOU.

Q1 - But what if it is you who needs to crawl to ask for something you need, would you like it?

a) Yes, I would love to beg the government to give me something that my family really needs and can't live without

b) I would prefer to work and earn, and have nothing stolen from me.

Q2 - How about waiting in line in a store not knowing what the government will bring today for you and your family to eat? Would you like it?

a) Yes

b) No

c) I do not know

The bigger the government, the more aspects of our lives it controls, the more you and your family depend on it.

Q3 - The question is—do you want to depend on the government or do you prefer to depend on yourself? Do you want socialism in our country or do you want freedom?

a) I am weak. I will wait for giveaways

b) I am strong. I want to be in charge of my own life.

c) This is one of the questions each person in your generation will have to struggle with by yourselves.

Q4 - Progressives offer us socialism as the best way for everyone. They call it "equality." Personally I do not like it. How about you?

a) I would love to live in socialist country

b) I would hate to live in socialist country

c) I am sure that many people who didn't read this book will tell you—what about socialism in Europe? They are not complaining.

Those who tell you that do not understand the "frog" principle. There are no more scientific breakthroughs that are coming from Sweden. There are no innovations that were originated in Norway. There are less and less medical drugs that are created in the Great Britain.

Gradually. Slowly. Pleasantly. Step by step. Bit by bit. The moment that people take others' people property without their permission the decline starts.

OK, this is socio-communism you say. But what is the other alternative—fascism?

There is a book called The Rise and Fall of the Third Reich, by William Shirer that sold millions of copies worldwide. It is one of the best books about history, theory and the practice of German and other fascistic regimes. This is what this book tells us: "Fascists quickly arranged for public works and hired all unemployed people to do a variety of public projects."

Does it sound good and … familiar? Do you remember what question we always should ask in order to check if this good is an absolute good? The question we need to ask is—where did the fascist government take money to pay their salaries?

The answer is simple—from the producers. The producers of cars, railroad equipment, furniture, jewelry and everything else paid not only salaries of people who worked for them, but also salaries of the people who worked at the government projects.

Q1 - Did it lower the cost of cars and furniture? What do you think? We already went through a series of exercises together and you should be able to make up your mind.

    a)   Yes, it made cost of all products lower

    b)   No, it made cost of all products much higher

    c)   It didn't affect costs of goods manufactured in Germany

The producers were told by the fascists what to produce and what amount of money they can charge for that. Do you remember we were talking about a price control?

    a)   Price control is very good for the economy

    b)   Price control brings devastation to the economies … Rome was destroyed because of the price control attempt.

The fascists' government wanted more and more money. They needed to support an army of people working on the government projects. The only people that had money were the producers, and the government was taking and taking and taking from them as much as the government needed. Those that didn't pay were severely punished.

Did they pay you might ask? I think they did. You see, in fascist countries not abiding by the government rules meant prison or at some cases execution. Yes, they paid.

Do you think German producers received enough profit from their factories and businesses that allowed them to re-invest and start new businesses? Do you think the producers were happy? The governments of the fascist countries didn't take away people's properties (except properties of people they arrested or murdered) but they controlled them.

This is what fascists learned from Karl Marx's Manifesto—impose huge taxes on producers, tell producers what to produce and where to invest, take over factories in several key areas and establish "industrial armies" of unemployed people. This is NOT socio-communism. This is socio-fascism, and it also was originated from the Karl Marx's ideas.

Below is a list of similarities between Karl Marx's Communist Manifesto and Adolph Hitler's National Socialist (Nazi) German Worker's Party:

Communist Manefesto: Prohibit private ownership of land.

National Socialist German Worker's Party (fascists): Land reform in accordance with the national needs, and when the States wants confiscation of land without compensation.

Similarities: Only State can own the land, and the land can be taken from people without paying them anything.

Communist Manefesto: A very high progressive income tax—to take large amounts of money from people who produce and do with the money what the government wants. If the government thinks that they need more money, take as much as the government feels is needed.

National Socialist German Worker's Party (fascists): Profit-sharing in large enterprises. Nationalization of all enterprises converted into corporations.

Similarities: Take from the rich as much as possible.

Communist Manefesto: Confiscation of the property of all rebels (if you are against the government, all your belongings will be taken from you.).

National Socialist German Worker's Party (fascists): Ruthless battle against those who harm the common good by their activities. Persons committing base crimes against the People, usurers or profiteers are to be punished by death.

Similarities: Punishment of the people who are against the government and the state by harshest means necessary.

Communist Manefesto: Prohibit all rights of inheritance—if your grandfather worked all his life, bought a house, bought a car, and left some money in the bank for you, and then died, the government takes everything he earned away. Everything. You or your family will receive nothing from him or other relatives.

National Socialist German Worker's Party (fascists): The abolition of all income obtained without labor or effort.

Similarities: If it wasn't you who earned the money or the property, it will be taken from you disregarding how you got it.

Communist Manefesto: Confiscation of the property of all emigrants.

National Socialist German Worker's Party (fascists): Only Germans can be citizens of the State and the State can provide opportunities of employment only to citizens.

Similarities: Those who are not by blood same as the main population of the country will be discriminated upon, their property taken from them and they will not be able to find jobs.

Communist Manefesto: Public Interest before Private Interest.

National Socialist German Worker's Party (fascists): Public Interest before Private Interest.

Similarities: Public Interest before Private Interest.

I hope you now understand that the two (socio-communism and socio-fascism) is really faces of the same coin? They want the same things but use a bit different means of achieving it. Both social structures mean control over your property which means control over your life. You are 100% enslaved or 99% enslaved is not much difference for you. In any case you lost your freedom.

Do you remember how the person who has no control over his belongings is called? If you forgot I will remind you—a slave.

Both social structures want to make us slaves. The people who advocate them hope that THEY will be the slave masters in the new social order. They can't become new Kings; they can't be new Shahs or Caesars. So they are trying to become Fuhrers, Party Chairmen or Duces.

After they create such order, how do you think they can stop you from demanding to give you your life back?

Q1 - How in your opinion they can shut up people who demand better products and services or want to hold on to what they produced?

a) Scare you to death so you are afraid to raise your voice

b) Create an arch-enemy and blame conditions in the country on this enemy

c) Take over TV, radio and newspapers and feed us their lies 24/7

d) All of the above

Q2 - How can those who are in power shut up political opposition?

a) Outlaw them

b) Kill them

c) Take over TV, radio and newspapers and feed us their lies 24/7

d) All of the above

Hitler was a socio-fascist. He called himself National Socialist (Nazi for short).

You probably think that if he was that close to socio-communists he was supposed to love them. Do you know that French Christians killed a lot of British Christians during one hundred and thirty years of wars between those two countries? Do you know that Muslims kill more Muslims than they kill Jews or Christians? Do you know that immediately after the French Revolution one wing of the revolutionaries began to murder another wing? Do you know that the moment the Soviet Revolution happened, socialists of different groups began to kill each other by thousands?

Here is the example that will show you the difference between the socio-communists and socio-fascists (both groups now call themselves "progressives"):

Socio-communists want to take your car from you and then force you to drive it at the speed they want, to the direction they want with the radio tuned to the only station they will allow you to listen to.

Socio-fascists do not take your car from you. The car is yours, but you ... can't touch it without their permission. When they will allow you to drive it you will have to go with the speed they want, in the direction they want with the radio tuned to the only station they will allow you to listen to.

We are very lucky that they were killing each other like spiders in a jar. If socio-communist Stalin and socio-fascist Hitler would have formed a united front, we would be in trouble.

Q1 - Do you think that workers in those countries that implemented either socio-communism or socio-fascism were happy that they do not have enough food and goods at the stores?

a) Yes, they were happy

b) No, but they were scared to show it

Q2 - Do you think that producers were happy that they can't get profits from their businesses or even keep the products they themselves
produce?

a) Yes

b) No

Q3 - Will producers or workers spend sleepless nights thinking how to
do their jobs better under those conditions?

a) Yes

b) No

Q4 - Do you think those countries will have many innovations, new
drugs, new and exciting products developed?

a) Yes

b) No

Q5 - So why do you think Franklin Delano Roosevelt (FDR) liked
those ideas so much that he started implementing them in the United
States of America?

a) Do not ask me, I do not know.

Q6 - Why do you think Carter liked FDR so much that he said that
he is one of the most important presidents in the history of the United
States?

a) I have no idea

Why do you think Barack Obama likes FDR and Carter so much that he now tries to repeat what they were doing and implement the same policies?

Do not look at me. I do not know. I think it's crazy, but this is my own opinion. Maybe he wants to fundamentally change America and make it a socialist or fascist country? He likes to take from producers and give to other people, usually to those that helped him to get elected.

Can you please remind me what taking from people without their explicit agreement is called? And how people who do that are called? Hmmm, if you forgot, please start reading this book over and over again.

Do you think all those presidents didn't understand what they were doing?

Or they did understand what they are doing and were doing it anyway?

Personally I do not know which answer scares me more. How about you? What do you think?

Chapter XIV

Capitalism is there. Is it good? Is it bad? What is in it for me?

I WANT TO share with you a story that I heard from Jay Stewart Snelson, whose lectures and written works shaped the direction of this book. The story goes as follows. Two brothers received a huge inheritance from their very rich relative. Each of them got a hundred million dollars and both were thinking hard about what to do with the money.

The first brother thought about all those poor people who had so little in life and his heart went out for them. He was a progressive person and wanted to live up to his ideals. Actually he was a "closet socialist" but he didn't know that.

He asked the government to give him names and addresses of a hundred thousand of the poorest families in America and one day each of those hundred thousand families received an envelope with a check for one thousand dollars.

There were so happy to get the money! Some bought new television sets, others furniture or clothes, some spent it on booze and fancy food, still others on house repairs and kitchen upgrades, on new teeth and cosmetic surgeries. In about two weeks the money was gone. And the poor people came back to the same welfare checks and food stamps, government assistance programs and the thrifty stores they used to buy from before they received the checks.

This brother was hailed in the media as a hero! He was named the person of the year by a dozen of magazines and in one small town the citizens named a square after him. Hail to the brother! But I would withhold my judgment for a while.

The second brother decided to invest the money. He looked for some innovative ideas and found a revolutionary plastic product that he instantly loved. After careful investment and good management he built a billion dollar industry that directly or indirectly employed exactly one hundred thousand people across the United States.

Each of the employed people received salaries of several thousand dollars a month, good medical coverage and other benefits. They didn't have to go to the government offices to beg for assistance or food stamps. They were earning their leaving and their families were proud of them. Hundreds of thousands of families were working and producing something that other people needed.

When the press learned that this brother received so much money in inheritance and didn't give anything to charity, everyone was outraged and called him a "capitalistic pig" and a "fat cat." One magazine compared him to his charitable brother and called him the "most despicable person of the year."

This brother made a lot of money for himself, and again invested them in new technologies where he employed another twenty thousand people. When asked by a newspaper correspondent, why he doesn't help oppressed and needy he had an audacity to answer that "the best way to help an unemployed person is to find him a job."

Which brother in your opinion helped people more?

    a)   The first brother who gave everything he had to the poor people. His intentions were honorable. He is a very good person.

He helped hundred thousand people to have two good weeks! He didn't benefit from the money he gave away.

b) The second brother who used his capital to create new jobs. He made a lot of money for himself. At the same time he helped hundred thousand families have better life! The first brother's intentions were honorable, but his actions were stupid.

You would think it is an easy to understand this story. It might come as a surprise to you that many congress people, senators and even some of the presidents of this and many other countries do not understand it. Otherwise why would they raise taxes (money that they take from you and other producers) instead of allowing you and me to invest them in the businesses that might bring prosperity to America?

They do this illogical thing of taking money from the people who can organize factories and start new businesses and give that money to poor who enjoy them for a week or two and immediately after that go back to ask for additional assistance.

Or maybe our congress people and presidents are smart and they understand that the money they take from rich will not really help the poor? They say to poor that if they will not vote for their party, the other party will not give them any assistance. Maybe the government people and even some of the presidents are ... selfish? Maybe they are thinking about themselves, but blaming others in the same sins? Maybe they do it in order to convince people to keep voting for them to continue to be in the government? Maybe they want to keep millions of people poor in order to keep their own jobs? Is it possible?

a) No, all government workers are very good people and they think only about the good of the country, never about themselves

b) Yes, and this is probably the only explanation why so many smart people continue to do the same thing that doesn't work for years and years. It doesn't work and they keep repeating it. Very strange indeed. They probably much more greedy and dishonest than any of the people they call "capitalists" whom they constantly badmouth.

Oops, I promised you to provide opinions of both sides. Here we are—opinions of the people who are opposing capitalism. This is what they are saying.

1. Sweat Shops. Capitalism, the progressives say, provokes poor working conditions, and as a most daring example they bring "Sweat shops." Did you ever heard about the Sweat Shops of hundred years ago? You didn't? I will tell you exactly what it is.

In small and large factories through mostly south and south east of the country, hundreds of thousands of working people who had low level of education, in many instances no English to communicate with the authorities and whom no one provided food or shelter when they didn't work, were working at the Sweat Shops and where were sweating there like … pigs (I have no idea if pigs are sweating and how they sweating, but people say that and I just repeated). They were operating primitive machinery or performing manual labor in high temperatures and without any air conditioners.

Did you ever have a chance to visit Atlanta during any of the summer months? Do you know that everyone in Atlanta is sweating like … like people I guess? They sweat on the streets, sweat in their cars upon entering, sweat when run from their cars to the stores, film theaters or work places. They however do not sweat in stores, homes, cars and factories due to a little device known as air-conditioner.

Can you imagine, progressives and socialists tell us, that those terrible factory owners didn't care about their workers and didn't install air conditioners in their factories? They were unable to part even with small amount of money to make lives of their workers bearable, they are saying. Only when organized labor began to push for improvements at the workplace, continue socialists and progressives, those capitalistic sharks began to change conditions of the employees.

What a bunch of baloney!

First, there were no air conditioners at the beginning of the Twentieth Century.

Despite the fact that the idea of lowering temperatures of objects by exploring the principles of evaporation were introduced by Benjamin Franklin and John Hadley in 1758, only in 1902 the first modern electrical air conditioning was invented by Willis Carrier in Syracuse, New York. Carrier's technology was applied to increase productivity in the workplace, and The Carrier Air Conditioning Company of America was formed to meet the rising demand.

So, those capitalists created the air conditioners … for factories. And the demand for them was so high, that at the beginning this one company and then many others began to produce air conditioners and sell to capitalists. And the price for them at that time was high! Those dirty and inhuman Capitalists parted with large amounts of money to improve working conditions for workers. It is just opposite of what socisilsts tell you, right? But why those sharks did it?

Maybe they cared for workers … or not?

What do you think—if it is very hot, people sweating and feeling bad, do they work well and fast? Or they work better and faster when they are in a cool atmosphere?

Do you think capitalists in the business of making people feel bad, or in the business of making money?

Do you think capitalists are making more money when their employees work slow and bad, or when they work good and fast?

a) I think capitalists want workers to feel bad and do not care about profits

b) I think capitalists think about profits, because this is the only reason they organize their businesses. And people who feel good work better.

Now let's talk about how those newcomers who worked at the sweat shops really felt.

The emigrants were coming to the United States and most of them settled in large industrial centers, where they were able to find work. Most of the work was in those factories. So the poor emigrants went to work to factories, worked for a month or two and began writing letters to their families back in Poland, Italy or Russia. And their families, their brothers and sisters, their mothers and fathers run after those letters to the ships with all their belongings and boarded them in order to get to this great land called America.

What do you think was written in those letters that increased emigration tri fold every year? Do you think the sweat shop employees wrote to their families "It is terrible over here! I am overworked, underpaid, do not have enough even for food ... please send me money to buy a ticket to come back home," or they wrote "This is the greatest place on earth! The streets are paved with gold! Come quickly and bring everyone you know with you!"

Which of the two letters would bring such huge emigration that the United States of America was forced to restrict it?

Today we are in a shock when we talk about sweat shops ... but it was the best thing ever happened to thousands of emigrants who came here to build new life. Many of them went on to become educated people, owners of their own businesses. Andrew Carnegie who himself used to work at the sweat shops once said "Blessed he who was born poor ... he is charged for the life time of achieving success."

Capitalism didn't create sweat shops. The sweat shops were long before capitalism. Capitalism illuminated them all together by inventing and implementing air conditioners and other better for productivity conditions at the workplace. Capitalists are not in the business to make slaves out of people. They are in the business of creating profits. They want workers to work better. And workers work better in a cool air. Hence capitalists installing air conditioners in their factories.

2. Child labor. Progressives and socialists say that capitalism provokes child labor. What can be worse than that, they say.

First of all I can name plenty of things that are worse than that.

Second, do you think Capitalism invented child labor or it was there for centuries? I think we can safely assume that it was there for thousands of years. Children worked on their parents' farms from sunrise to sunset, starting at a very early age. Children worked for other farmers if those other farmers would hire them. The work was very tiresome, the food was scare and children run by hordes to the cities where it was possible to find work and survive. To run from home was a survival instinct for many.

If capitalists wouldn't hire children, those children would DIE or would have to steal food to survive. So the alternative wasn't between a nice place where children can study, live and play electronic games and the sweat shops, but between working at a factory and starving. NOW tell me the capitalists did good thing for children or bad?

Working at the factories was much much easier that working in the fields. The hours were shorter and the pay was better. Much better. It was still terrible by all modern and any other standards, but it was better than the alternative.

Why do children run from villages? Working on the farms offered very low pay and no perspectives. Working at the factories offered them a chance to survive and build their lives. They grew together with capitalism, some became skilled labor, some got education, and some became capitalists themselves.

Capitalism didn't create this problem. Capitalism resolved this problem.

3. If not for the unions, the workers would be getting very small compensation for their work.

Socialists often say that business owners and workers are on the two opposing sides of the "barricade." By that they mean that owners of businesses want to pay workers as little as possible and the workers want to be paid as much as possible. They also say that the only way to resolve this dispute is to fight each other.

Socialists believe that when workers organized into unions they can fight with the business owners more successfully and make wages rise faster.

For the last fifty years of the nineteen century there were practically no unions in the United States. According to what socialists and progressives say, the salaries of the workers were suppose to stay the same or maybe change a little? Not true! Wages rose and doubled during this period. Oops, dear socialists, you are ... misinforming us again!

In 1900 unions began to play larger and larger roles in negotiations between the owners of businesses and the workers. Now we shall expect (if you still believe socialists) a huge rise of wages, right? Oops, the rate of rise in wages from 1900 to 1916 was less than half that of the previous comparable period. Hmm ... Looks like unions are not doing their job. Or maybe it's not them who make wages rise?

OK, the best way to check if the unions have something to do with bettering workers salaries is to find when a lot of workers join them, and the unions began to dictate what business owners should do!

During 1936 to 1945 millions of workers joined the unions. The unions gained power, pushed business owners hard ... and the wages went up, right? Oops, during those years the wages were increasing exactly as before that and after that. Oops, Oops, Oops!

The question is—if unions are not the deciding factor in the increase of wages, than what?

Union Story #1

Jim works at a furniture factory. He makes one dinner table a day. The dinner table sold for $100. Jim gets for each table $50.

Bobby works at a coat factory. He makes one coat each and every day. The coats are sold for $100. Bobby gets for each coat $50.

Jim can buy one costume that Bobby makes with his two-day wages (he gets $50 a day and a costume's price is $100). Same with Bobby, he can buy one table that Jim makes with his two-day wages.

Enters Jim's union and demands from the business owner to pay Jim more. After back and forth negotiations when ten union representatives meet each day for a month with the business owners' lawyers, they reach a compromise and from now on Jim is getting $60 a day for making the same table. Jim is happy. He is very proud of his union representatives.

But Bobby is unhappy. He goes to his union representative and demands to negotiate on his behalf wages similar to what Jim is now getting. After a month of negotiations, when business owners' attorneys meet every day with the union representatives, Bobby gets his pay raise and also gets $60 for his day's work.

He is happy. He celebrates and praises his union representative.

Now the table manufacturer calculates his costs. Cost of his worker went up 20% (from $50 to $60). Cost of all materials went up 20% because all other workers demanded their unions to match the wages to the furniture manufacturer workers. Cost of energy went up because of the same reason ... So he also raises price of his tables by 20%. Now price of one table is not $100 but $120.

Bobby's boss made the same calculation and raised the price of the coats he makes by 20% ... and they now sold for $120 each.

Let's put our thinking cap for a moment. Jim now gets $60 a day. It is much more than before, right? How many days shall he work in order to buy one costume that is now sold for $120? He has to work the very same two days to buy one costume. Did anything change?

Bobby gets $60 a day now. It is much more than before, right? How many days shall he work in order to buy one dinner table that is now sold for $120? He has to work the same two days to buy one dinner table. Did anything change?

Q1 - Who won because the unions demanded to raise wages?

a) Workers

b) Business owners

c) Union representatives who were getting paid for their hard work of defending workers, and attorneys who worked hard to defend factory owners

What is your opinion?

Union Story #2

On a meeting of all unions in the capital the union bosses made a decision to demand that the government would make a law prohibiting paying workers less than $11 an hour. The unions helped government to be elected and they knew that their voice will be heard.

The government quickly said YES and ordered all business owners to pay workers a minimum $11 an hour.

The workers who were receiving less than this amount were happy and praised their union representatives and the government.

On a boat factory ten friends were getting $10 an hour ($80 a day) each. Together they were earning $800 a day. The factory was doing boats and made and sold one boat a day. They were able to pay $800 to the workers and not a cent more. Otherwise the business didn't make sense to them.

Everyone was happy, but of course when the ten friends heard that they are getting a raise that union demanded, they became even happier.

The boat factory owners were unable to raise prices for their boats because they knew that their customers would stop buying their boats. On the other hand they didn't have enough profit to pay the ten friends $880 a day (up from previous $800 a day). The only way to keep costs of the boats under control was to fire one of the workers.

The manager of the company fired one of the workers and began to push the rest of the workers to do the job without the tenth person. The workers now were getting $11 an hour, but one was unemployed. The workers were angry with the company that fired one of them.

The government came to the boat manufacturer and said that from now on he will pay additional money to help the unemployed worker to buy necessities such as food, medical expenses and rent. The manufacturer didn't know where to take this money from and fired one more person.

Now eight people were working for ten, getting $11 per hour. The manufacturer paid their wages plus sent money to the government to cover necessities of the two fired workers. The manufacturer paid a total of $704 to the employees and send $94 to the government to feed the two fired workers. They were paying $800 a day as before. Eight workers were getting better salary and two were getting bare minimum to survive. It all came from the same sales of the same boats as before.

Q1 - Who won because the unions demanded to raise wages?

a) Workers

b) Business owners

c) Union representatives who received salaries from dues paid by the workers and government representatives who received salaries from taxes paid by the same workers and by the factory owners

What do you think?

The eight workers were unable to do work of ten people. The boats now were not the same quality as before and the customers began to complain about it. Several boats were returned and some of the

distributors stopped working with the boat manufacturer. The manufacturer now thinks about either closing down the factory or ordering
boats abroad, from a country that doesn't have unions. The unions
were very angry and called the manufacturer who was thinking about
shifting job oversees an anti-American." The union representatives
recently called for nationalization of the boat manufacturing industry
in order to keep American jobs from fleeing overseas.

Union Story #3

Jim's son works at a furniture factory and makes one table a day. He
gets $50 and a table is sold at $100. The factory owner buys new equipment that allows Jim to produce five tables a day. Now the cost of the
table is less because Jim worked on each table fewer hours. Each table
now sold for $50 instead of $100.

Bobby's daughter works at a costume manufacturer and makes one
costume a day. She gets $50 and a costume is sold at $100. The factory
owner buys new equipment that allows her to produce five costumes
a day. Now the cost of the costume is less because Bobby's daughter
worked on each costume fewer hours. Each costume now sold for $50
instead of $100.

Jim's son gets $50 a day, and can buy a costume with his ONE DAY
wages. Bobby's daughter gets $50 a day and can buy one dinner table
with her ONE DAY wages. This is a real improvement! Now Jim's son
buys a table and can buy something else for the $50 he saved. Same
with Bobby's daughter—she can get a costume for $50, and can put
aside the other $50 for her vacation or college fund.

Who won now?

   a)   Workers

   b)   Factory owners

c) Consumers

d) All of the above?

Who is unhappy?

a) Union representatives

b) Government workers

c) Attorneys

d) All of the above?

I want you to understand that the "quantity" of money that people get is not the most significant measure of what are your wages. The "quality" is much more important. Sounds strange, right?

You probably would prefer to get ten thousand instead of two hundred, right? Not so fast please. Paul gets two hundred <u>dollars</u> per day and Abba gets ten thousand <u>dinars</u>. Who gets more? I guess you have no idea.

How about what is better—five dollars in 1927 or ten dollars in 2006? If you said that ten dollars in 2006 is better, you are wrong.

The most important thing is how much your day of work can buy. For example if a rail road engineer was able to buy one shirt using one day wages in 1905, and his great grandson who is also a rail road engineer is able to buy two shirts with what he earned in 2005, than the real wages grew during this period two times. It maybe misleading to use as a measure one product, but if you consider a "basket" of different products, you can get a pretty clear idea about how the standard of life changes from country to country or from one decade to another.

I want you to know that the wages of the American workers grew by nearly five times from one hundred years ago. As recently as a hundred years ago a person had to work hard during most of his waking hours in order to provide himself with the food and protection required to keep him alive.

If each of us were forced to do everything we need to survive, we barely can produce the food we need and the shelter to hide under. I for example do not know how to grow food or how to make shoes and it will take me a long time to learn. I am bad in any work related to building or repairing. But I am relatively good with teaching and writing.

If someone else will make repairs in my home, cook my dinner and grow my food, I can teach their kids and write stories for the daily newspaper.

The exchange of goods and services enables each of us to do what we do best. Technology we use now allow us to make a lot of things, much more than what we need for ourselves—so we have something we can exchange for the things we do not know how to do.

We exchange those surplus products for money and are using that money to buy other things we need. One crazy scientist counted that all the machinery and equipment each of us are using in are daily lives is an equivalent of 33 human slaves of the past.

In other words those tools and machinery help each one of the productive people like 33 assistants. How much better it is to have these silent, non-complaining servants than to have 33 human slaves! They far surpass slaves in efficiency, and with minimum maintenance costs. They don't rebel or run away.

There is 8766 hours in a year. Your great grandfathers were working 3500 hours each year and practically all of great grandfather's leisure hours were needed for eating and sleeping. We now on average work 2,000 hours, or even a little less, per year.

In order to feed ourselves and provide bare necessities we now need to work about two thousand hours in a year. We can work as much as our ancestors did, but we CHOSE to work less. We work less and we can buy five times more they were able to buy working harder and longer hours. Actually the work week they had was about 70 hours—compared with our 40 hour week.

If you need ten dollars to go to see a movie on weekend, and you are offered to do a job that will bring you twenty, what would you chose? Would you chose to go to a movie (leisure) and not to earn more money, or would you forget about the movie and the weekend with friends because you can earn more money?

If you are starving you would chose money. Most of the people today chose leisure time over additional money. That means they are earning enough to survive and now want to have a good time.

This is why people stopped working 3500 hours a year and gradually reduced it to 2000 hours. Otherwise they would find additional jobs and work, work, work all the time. Unions or no unions, we chose to have good time over more work. So the shorter work week would have come anyhow, with or without unions. The trick is to increase productivity. Increase of unions does nothing to raise wages and shorten our work time.

John & Mary - a non-union story

At the time this story starts there were no electrical chain saws in the world. A wood cutter would use a regular saw, would cut five trees a day and would sell them for five dollars all together. He had not only to cut the bunks but also cut off all benches. By the end of the day all wood cutters were tired and would come home to eat, sleep and get back to work. No time to spend with the family, no time to talk to neighbors, no time for hobbies. The money the wood cutters were earning were barely enough for the family to survive.

John Smith invented an electrical chain saw. He was now cutting twenty trees a day and easily cleaning them from the benches. He was now receiving five times his previous earnings. He also was coming home not as tired as he was before. His kids loved it. From time to time John was now skipping the evening's work and coming to baseball games or school events his children took part in.

John made four electrical chain saws and hired four wood cutters to help him. Each of those woodcutters was bringing him twenty dollars and he paid each ten dollars. This was twice as much as they made before John hired them, when they were working with regular saws.

John was now a business owner. He had great tools. He supervised four workers and he brought plenty of money home. His children began to think about colleges. His wife now stopped doing laundry and ironing. A woman that had laundry business took it over and did a great job.

Two of John's old friends asked him to open a restaurant together. They had this idea of "everything from the forest" diner, but didn't have money. They offered him an ownership in the restaurant in exchange for his investment. John agreed and made his friends' dream possible.

A local charity was preparing a concert to benefit orphans. They came to John and Mary and asked them to participate. The Smiths became honorary chair people of the event and donated money to the needy.

Was this chain saw invention good for John?

Was this chain saw invention good for Mary?

Was this chain saw invention good for their kids?

Was this chain saw invention good for the wood cutters John hired?

Was this chain saw invention good for the wood cutters' kids?

Was this chain saw invention good for John's friends who wanted to open a restaurant but didn't have money?

Was this chain saw invention good for their kids?

Was this chain saw invention good for orphans?

Was this chain saw invention good for the customers?

There is a simple YES to all those questions. Better tools enabled John to produce MORE. He produced more and was able to get more money. With this money his life improved. He was able to employ other people and THEIR lives improved. Since he had some surplus of money (he didn't spend all that he made) he was able to finance another business and help two more people to make more money. Now THEIR life was improved. Many customers came to the restaurant. They loved it. THEIR lives were improved. John was able to help others, something that he wasn't able to do before.

Are there any unions in the picture?

Heartless & Selfish Capitalism

So many people say that we need to regulate banks and big corporations ... otherwise they will make us all poor ... capitalists is oppressing workers ... goal of capitalism is to enslave everyone.

You and I already know that this is not exactly true. Many people however continue saying those words and they seems to believe in what they are saying. Why they do it? What is the reason they hate capitalism so much? They live a good life, have cars, television sets, cell phones and computers, they go on vacations to other countries and see how poorly people live there ... they have many freedoms people were even not dreaming about ... they work in comfortable offices, enjoy air conditioners at work and at home, watch movies, go to restaurants ... So, why?

Imagine you live in an ancient Rome ... and you are a slave. You look at beautiful homes of the patricians and you dream about living there and having slaves. You are not responsible for being a slave. It was your luck. You hate the slave owners, and ... want to be in their place.

Or that you were born in Russia during the Ivan the Terrible reign ... and you are a peasant. You do not know how to read or write, can't even talk to the aristocrats without their permission and sometimes wonder how it is to be in a Tsar's guard. It is not your fault you are not up there. It is not your failure that you at the lowest level of the society. You were born a peasant.

Throughout the history of the humankind, in almost all countries in the world people were born into castes. Except few very lucky or very unlucky individuals most of the people were remaining in their caste for life. It was not their fault they were unable to become army generals, live in palaces, kiss princesses or commission symphonies for their birthdays. It was not their fault!

In all those countries and practically in all societies of the past you were a prince only if your father was a king. You lived in a palace if your parents left you this palace or if you conquered this palace from another person who lived there because his parents left him this palace.

Now, what makes you a baron or a prince in capitalism? If you will not tell it to anyone, I will share with you this secret. If many people buy a lot of something from you, you will be a prince. You can live in a palace, you can kiss as many princesses as you wife will let you and you can commission symphonies for your birthdays even twice a year.

But beware, if those people who made you a prince will stop buying what you produce or create or sell, you will lose your throne. Those people are your kings and queens. Serve them better, offer them products they need and at a good price, and they will crown you. If someone will start selling better products and offer better prices, he will become the king and you can lose everything you had.

It is the common man who determines what will be produced and in what quantities and qualities. It is the common man who determines if you will become a success or a failure.

They do not care if you are tall or short, blond or brunette, talking with an accent or have perfect Cambridge English. They do not care what paste you brush your teeth and how you comb your hair, were you born a Duke or a street sweeper, you are Indian, black, Jewish, Muslim, male or female. If you offer them good products they will come to buy your shoes or toothpaste. If you are not that good, they will come less and will be ready to pay less.

If you are an actor and loved by millions, you will get many millions for your participation in the movies.

If you design interiors and they are spectacular, you will have many clients.

If you know how to market products, you will find many people ready to pay handsomely for your services.

If you are not paid well, if people do not want to buy your product, if they do not want to see a film with you as the star, you can't blame anyone except yourself. And this is the core of the problem. People do not like to blame themselves. Actually they would blame anything but themselves!

For example, when you get a bad review on your project, what do you tell your mom? Mom, it was the teacher's fault ... he didn't explain well ... everyone made the same mistake ... the teacher doesn't like me ... I did everything right, but ... a bird ... an elephant ... this stupid pen...

You are trying to shift the blame away from you, right? You probably think that your mom doesn't understand that. You think that you invented this lie. No, you didn't. In fact, I am almost sure your mom as a child did the same thing. She tried to shift the blame away. Ask her.

In capitalism what you achieve in life depends on you and you only. A woman can come to her husband and demand "Why didn't you go to this training like our neighbor Ron did? If you would go you would get the raise he got!" and the man knows that this is his fault.

"Why were we not putting aside some money? If we had then we would now be able to open our own business?"—is another good question, and this again is no one's fault except the person who didn't put any money aside.

What makes many people unhappy under capitalism is the fact that capitalism provides everyone an opportunity to grow. If you are a teacher, you can become a principal. You are a physician, you can have a line of patients at your door, or you can wait for one that would visit you by mistake. If you are a singer, you can sing at stadiums for thousands or in the shower for yourself only. Or maybe you should think twice before becoming one.

Those that didn't achieve what they would want to achieve saw their pals and classmates achieving it in front of their eyes. They feel that someone wronged them. Someone or some power that precluded them to become one of those who have it all.

Millions of people in America live as only Dukes live in many other countries but hate their life because they do not live the way other people live. Such people say to themselves "If those other people got more than something is to blame for that and they blame ... the system."

Ludwig Von Mises who examined this hate for capitalism in his brilliant book The Anti-Capitalistic Mentality says: "The fool releases these feelings in slander and defamation. The more sophisticated do not indulge in personal calumny. They sublimate their hatred into a philosophy, the philosophy of anti-capitalism, in order to render inaudible the inner voice that tells them that their failure is entirely their own fault. Their fanaticism in defending their critique of capitalism is precisely due to the fact that they are fighting their own awareness of its falsity."

I have been in many countries where people say they hate America. I asked them many questions trying to understand why this country that did nothing but good to them bring up so much emotion. I am convinced now after countless conversations that they hate America because they envy Americans. They want what Americans have. They say America didn't do that or did that, and because of what America did we are poor, uneducated, miserable and sick. They actually know that this is their own fault, their own doing, but for that they hate America even more. But they need to blame someone else, not themselves.

There is however an additional reason people who live in capitalist society say and write so much about "terrible capitalism" and people who live under socialism, fascism, monarchies or religious states do not say or write bad things about their rulers or social order. If you live in a capitalistic society there is no retaliation for almost anything you might say or write. You opponents who would disagree with you may call you names, will probably scream their lungs off, but will say hi when meeting in a dining room.

If you live in socio-communism, socio-fascism or a Muslim state, you will be killed if you would write an honest opinion about the rules and the rulers. Many were killed and many hide from fanatics fearing their retaliation for an opinion they voiced. I know people who spent years in prisons for a joke that offended someone among the ruling elite of their "just" countries. The mere fact that there are many critical articles and speeches by Americans about "the inhuman face of capitalism" is the best evidence that it is a just society.

Chapter XV
Laws of Human Nature

DO YOU WANT to drive fast cars, wear fashionable clothes, have interesting friends, go to great concerts, study in the best universities and have good health? Or you want to drive old clunkers, have one pair of dirty jeans, work at a junk yard, be friends with a group of losers and have dirty, smelly and rotten teeth? Would you want to gain or you would prefer to lose?

Let me safely assume that you would strive toward gain and away from loss. Exactly as it is postulated in the J. Stuart Snelson's Win-Win Theory: "*The law of human nature is the inborn drive of people to act toward gain and away from loss.*"

And this is his Law of Human Action: "*All humans act toward their perception of gain and away from their perception of loss.*"

In plain English this means that when you have a choice you will try to get what in your opinion is good and to avoid something that in your opinion is bad. Let's try to verify the validity of those laws. Do they work?

One evening you come home late. There is a shortcut through the park, but it is completely dark. You have a feeling that someone or something is hiding in the dark. Would you take the shortcut or not?

You might be hurt. I am sure you will <u>avoid</u> it and go the longer way.

You are a good math student. You have been selected to participate in a city-wide math competition. The very best mathematicians from different schools will compete on television to be chosen for the nation-wide competition. You need to study two additional chapters for tomorrow, but your friends invited you to play soccer. What would you do?

You will be on TV, you will have a chance to compete and win a great price, maybe to be chosen for the nation-wide competition. I am sure you will <u>do it</u> and will skip one evening the soccer practice.

Why you would avoid the dark shortcut. It will bring you home faster. You are not sure there is something harmful in the dark park. You however made a choice of the inconvenience of the long way. Why you would skip the soccer game—you love it so much? You are not sure you will win the math competition. But you perceive it as a great opportunity. There is something more rewording in studying math than to play soccer this evening. You constantly make choices and they are leading you to perceived gain and away from the perceived loss.

Dog House Builder Story

Your son purchased with the birthday presents money fifteen dollars worth of materials and built a doghouse. He went to the neighbors and convinced them to rent it for their dog for ten cents a day. Since that moment he began to get three dollars a month in rental fees. A boy next door laughed at him and said that he spent his day in a pool. He rhymed it with a word "fool."

Your son waited for five month, got fifteen dollars from the rent, purchased another set of wood and nails and built another doghouse. And rented it to another neighbor for the same ten cents a day. Now he is getting six dollars a month. The boy next door laughed at his efforts to make money. During all this time your son was working the boy next door was watching sports and enjoying life.

Your son waited for two and a half months until he got fifteen dollars (now he was getting money from two rental properties), bought new set of materials and built another doghouse. And rented it to a neighbor from around the corner. Now he was getting nine dollars a month. The boy next door was playing his game console and laughing at him out loud.

After a month and a half your son got from the rents fifteen dollars ... then in one month ... now every two weeks he was building new doghouses ... every week ... every three days...hundred dollars a month in rental fees ... three hundred dollars a month...

Finally your son had one hundred doghouses out there earning him money and was getting three hundred dollars each and every month. When one of his clients would call and say that he doesn't need the doghouse anymore, he would just go out and find another person who had a dog and would rent it from him.

Is it good? Does the doghouse builder like getting three hundred dollars every month?

     a)   Yes

     b)   No

     c)   I do not know

Would you vote for a government that will take from your son those three hundred dollars a month and give it to your neighbor, who all this time was laughing at him?

     a)   Yes

     b)   No

     c)   I do not know

Would you vote for the government that will take half of his earnings and give it to this boy who was doing nothing to earn them?

     a)   Yes

b) No

c) I do not know

What if this laughing boy's dad left him when he was a child—would you be happy if the government would be taking half of your son's earnings and giving the money to him? Would you think it is fair?

a) Yes

b) No

c) I do not know

I am almost sure you answered to those questions the way that will give you as much gain and as minimal loss as possible. And this is OK. This is called "Human Nature." We will talk very soon how we humans can have "Human Nature" and be human to each other at the same time.

New Society - Island of the Magnificent Ten

Ten friends, Peter, Marla, Tim, Rick, Carl, Andrew, Gabriel, Aaron, Mary and Sarah were on a boat tour with their school when their boat was suddenly lifted in the air by a twister and thrown on the uninhibited island in the middle of the ocean. After much cry and sobbing, the friends suddenly understood that they are alone on the island and being alone has its good sides. From now on they could do whatever they want and no one can order them around. The life was totally theirs and beautiful!

All ten were really happy. They were running around, climbing trees, swimming in the ocean, fighting and playing. Until lunch. Or to be exact until the lunch time, since there is no lunch.

Why there is no lunch? Simply because no one prepared it. A couple of kids sampled some berries but still were hungry. This is it. The rest was really hungry. After several hours of perplexity all ten come together on a shore and started discussing the situation. It didn't work at the beginning because they didn't know how to listen to one another and how to respect one another. Hunger however was a good teacher and soon they started communicating.

Marla said that she knows how to cook, but she needs what to cook. Andrew and Gabriel said that they know how to hunt rabbits and birds. Aaron from being a boy scout knew how to make and keep fire running all the time. The arrangements were made and the work started. In no time two rabbits were hunted down, some wild but tasty vegetables found, a salty tree juice collected and fire was set and everyone was seating around it waiting for the food to be eatable. Life was beautiful again.

Then someone asked where Tim and Rick are. No one saw them since the food preparation started. They simply disappeared. But when the food was almost ready and smell of cooking was all over the island they came out of nowhere and said that they are terribly hungry. Where you been, you all ask.

Oh, we found this great beach really close to here, they answered. After we eat, we will go there again. The waves are really something there, they say.

We need to decide who does what for the breakfast said Marla. She was happy everyone liked her rabbits and her fire-burned vegetables.

OK, we are going back to the beach, Tim and Rick said getting up. Call us when the food will be ready.

The rest of the ten began feeling overwhelming anger. Hey guys, said Carl, everyone should participate.

Why, asked Tim, and it was obvious that he doesn't understand.

Because, if you do not want to help, Carl continued, you are not getting any food.

Tim and Rick considered it. Then Tim said, I can whistle for your entertainment after you eat. Now the rest were considering this proposition.

Mary said, I am OK with that. I will let him eat if he will entertain us after that.

Sarah said, I hate when people whistle. I am not giving him anything for whistling. I rather give him something for not whistling.

No one knew what to do, until Gary came up with an idea. The eight people who will be participating in making food each will get an equal share of the food and can do with their own shares what they want. Mary will give a bite to Tim who will whistle for her. Jack said that he will listen also and may give Tim another bite.

Carl who eats a lot offered to others to wash their clothes in exchange for part of their food. Two kids took him up on his offer.

There always will be people who wouldn't want to work, or would try to get something for free. This is also a part of Human Nature. The rest will either work to feed them and will hate them, or will refuse to share. You can't convince people to do something they do not want to do. But in many countries the rulers forced people to share. They did it in Monarchies, now they are doing it in Communism, in Fascism and in partly even in Capitalism. They say: "You work and share or we will throw you off the cliff to feed the sharks." When two or three producers punished, the rest will work and share. They hate the ones that make them share but they will share.

Next day the eight made enough food for the whole day and divided it into eight equal portions. Some of those that made food and got their share gave a bit to Tim for the entertainment; some gave a bit to Carl for washing clothes. Rick did nothing and received nothing. At the end of the day he was upset and hungry. He was angry as well. The others had food and no one wanted to share with him. They are pigs, he thought, even his best friend Tim who was eating the great looking rabbit stew and said that he did not have enough for the two of them.

Rick was very hungry indeed. He looked around and saw that Peter is alone and preparing to have your meal. He jumped Peter, grabbed his food and ran away.

Now Peter was without food. And angry. What to do? Rick disappeared and most probably already gulped all his food.

Peter now had three options: Rob someone else, Beg someone to give him food, or Offer someone something they might need in exchange for food.

I can make beautiful island jewelry from the seashells; Peter said to himself, girls like those things. He quickly made several necklaces and in no time exchanged them for food. He had enough to engage Carl to wash clothes. Life was great again. The only thought that bothered Peter was what Rick will do tomorrow?

We need to defend ourselves from robbers, Peter said to his friends. All of them agreed. Together they built a small storage where they brought all the food, jewelry, and everything they considered valuable. Andrew became the chief keeper of the goods. Everyone agreed that he will not hunt anymore, but for keeping goods safe he will get an equal share of food and everything else that others get.

Rick tried a couple of times to get to the food, but couldn't. Everyone felt safe again.

Under a new order everyone was coming to the storage three times a day and Andrew was handing each one his or her portion of food and other goods. Andrew now called this place "the center."

Soon everyone noticed that he was giving Aaron more than others. Did he work more, you asked. No, was Andrew's reply, but he needs more.

This was not what the friends agreed, but no one protested because Aaron was quite large and maybe he needed more. They thought that maybe he was suppose to work a bit harder and make more if he needs more, but since there was now enough food for everyone they didn't say anything.

One morning Mary said that she doesn't feel good and can't work, but Gabriel saw her picking mushrooms in the woods and then drying them in a hidden place. At the time to have the meal she came to the center and had food with the others who did work on this day. After lunch both she and her best friend Sarah disappeared and when Gabriel checked on them he saw them hiding sweet berries and nuts they found in the woods. Then again, they came to the center to share the food that others prepared. And again everyone noticed that the food portions became even smaller.

There will always be people who would pretend they work for the group but secretly would do something for themselves. They steal their time from others.

At night Marla saw Andrew getting into the storage and coming out chewing something. This wasn't what the group agreed to and she told Andrew that in the morning she will raise this question in front of everyone.

In the morning however there was a surprise that changed things a bit. Andrew and Rick were standing shoulder to shoulder at the entrance of the storage.

We can't allow things to continue the way they are, said Andrew when everyone was present. Some people need more, some less. Some can't work at all, but we are not animals and we have to take care of them. Also sometimes you do things that are not needed, or do more than needed. I remember how food was spoiled because no one thought how much shall be cooked this day, he said. Someone shall be in charge; otherwise there will be mistakes or over production or under distribution. From now on you all bring everything to the storage, and the Central Committee that is comprised of me, Rick and Aaron will decide what to do with the food and goods you make. To be sure that you bring everything you do to the center, Rick will be checking on you and will not let you cheat. If you cheat you will not get food that day at all. If you continue cheating, you might be punished even more. We own this island together. It belongs to all of us. I will make sure we take good care of the island. To preserve its beauty, there will be area on the island that you will be prohibited to visit. It is done for your own good. Also, from now on I will tell you what you will make, when and in what quantities. Is that clear?

First thing the committee orders others to do is to build a high fence around the storage. They said it was needed for protection of the food, but it wasn't really clear whom they were protecting it from. Near the fence there was now a place Andrew called "jail" for people who would not do their share.

This now was looking like socialism. The committee said that they will take everything from everyone and will make sure there are no cheaters. They will tell others what to do; they will take everything from everyone and then will decide whom to give what. Without doubt they would give to themselves a bit more than to others. Or the best pieces. Or much more than a bit more.

Andrew told Peter to bring dry benches to burn. When Peter went to the woods he saw bees and soon found the beehive. And by a heroic deed he got out some honey. The moment he was at a secure distance from the beehive, Rick appeared. He pushed Peter, grabbed the honey from him and ran. He did exactly what he did a couple of days earlier, Peter thought. Nothing changed. But this time Peter decided to give him the fight of his life and ran after him.

Rick ran to the center and disappeared behind the wall. The moment Peter reached the gate; Andrew was standing in the entrance. This is a restricted area, he said.

He robbed me from my honey, Peter said.

Yours, asked Andrew in a surprised tone of voice. I thought that everything on this island belongs to everyone. You should know that he didn't take it for himself. He brought it to the center.

This is robbery, Peter said. This is not fair. I demand you give the honey back to me. It is mine. I was risking my life to get this honey! Why, just because three of you said he can do it, the theft and robbery suddenly is OK?

Peter couldn't finish even half of the sentence. Rick and Aaron came out from behind the fence, grabbed him and threw him in the jail.

Now Peter had plenty of time to think. He was the smartest kid in his class or maybe in the whole school. Socialism doesn't work, he said to himself. It doesn't work because it is against human nature. Some people would want to work, some do not. Some people would use their heads and hands and others do not. You can't take from the ones that make things and give to others. The ones that make things will stop working. We all want things that are good for us and run from things that are bad for us. If our work is producing results and good for us, we will work. If work is not producing results, we will pretend that we are working.

In the beginning it looks good but those of us that really do something useful are forced to give larger and larger parts of what we do to those that do not produce. Those that do not produce are getting things without much effort. Plus they hate and envy producers because the producers still have more than what they are getting. The working people will work less and will try to do things on the side and cheat. Their Human Nature makes them want to keep more and to give less. The central committees will punish them. People will cheat again and again. The central committees will punish them again and again. Not good.

Peter's thoughts were interrupted by sounds of a meeting at the central place. Peter heard that Aaron was talking but he couldn't understand the words. Then Aaron's voice grew louder. "I give this island back to you" he was saying: "Andrew is no longer our leader. He never consulted with the other members of the central committee and because of that he made a lot of mistakes."

The door to the jail opened and Rick motioned Peter to get out. "Here is our friend Peter" continued Aaron: "Life will be different from now on."

Nothing really changed, except it was now Aaron who was telling others what to do and handing food to them. Every day in the evening everyone had to be present at the central square to hear Aaron talking about the beautiful life they all now had, about terrible times when no one was in charge, or about mistakes that were made when Andrew was the leader of the group. Only after this talk the food was served.

No one except the Group Leaders (this is how they called themselves) were allowed to enter the "inner place." Sometimes Sarah was going there to discuss something, but everyone knew that she was spying on others and telling the Group Leaders who among islanders did or said what. For that she was getting some extra food and other valuables. She was the only one of the girls who was allowed to have and wear two necklaces at the same time.

This was a new thing on the island. The Group Leaders told others what to wear and how to behave, especially when meeting and talking to the Group Leaders.

No one was showing any initiative in preparing new foods or creating new things. The food became dull and no one expected anything exciting to happen. A couple of times there were beatings always happening in the darkness of the forest and always when a person who was beaten was alone. The Group Leaders called it "just punishments." The islanders even stopped talking between each other. The only subjects of conversations were weather and hate for the previous regimes. Andrew was nowhere to be seen, but no one asked about him. Asking can be punishable by the new law.

One day the Group Leaders told the islanders that there is an enemy out there that wants to destroy them all. They said that they suspect that Andrew went somehow to other islands, amassed an army and they are planning to attack. The Good of the Island, the Group Leaders said, demands sacrifices from everyone.

From now on we will all have rations, the Group Leaders said. That means that everyone will receive small and equal amounts of food that will be enough to survive, and everything else will be stored for an emergency and the future war efforts.

After the enemy would be defeated, they said, life will come back to normal. But before this wonderful thing will happen everyone will have to work every day and work more hours. If someone will not work or will steal from the Group, such person will be punished by lashes and a jail time.

In order to make islanders work those long hours the Group Leaders made Marla and Gabriel supervise them. The Group Leaders assigned watch hours to each of the workers and everyone except the Group Leaders had to stay awake at night guarding the camp from the invaders.

Now every Friday the islanders sang a song that Sarah wrote about greatness of the Group Leaders blaming the arch-enemy Andrew for all the bad things that were happening on the Island.

"We have a great vision for our future" said Aaron during one of the Friday meetings, "And we will bring you there whether you want it or not."

Now it looks and smells like fascism, Peter thought. We are told that we are the owners of everything here but at the same time we can't do what we want with what we own because of the good of the island. I want my own vision of happiness, not Aaron's. Maybe his will be ten times better than mine, but I want to reach mine. I want what I perceive to be good. And maybe what he sees as good is bad for me.

And one day Peter talked to his friends and they all left the camp and went to do what each of them wanted to do.

Aaron sent Marla and Gabriel to find everyone and bring them back, but Marla and Gabriel didn't come back either. Then Aaron decided to come out himself while being flanked by Rick and Sarah.

They saw that two of the kids were building a house with several bedrooms and a large kitchen. The kids thought that the fall is coming and everyone will need somewhere to stay. They thought that they will be able to rent rooms to others and get some good things from them in exchange.

Marla was making dry foods and thinking about opening a small diner. Gabriel and Peter were teaching others how to build boats. At the same time Gabriel was starting a chemistry lab because he thought that there is a good possibility to make great pots and pans from the tar he collected from several trees on the island. He was sure he will be able to exchange them for many good things he himself needed.

Everyone was busy doing something. No one was pushing anyone to do or not to do anything. Rick immediately offered Marla to use her diner at night as a music and dance club. Then suddenly Aaron saw Andrew who was busy creating clothing designs from fur and linen. "I was hiding and feeding Andrew all that time" said Marla to a bewildered Aaron.

"But what I can do? Will you accept me? Will you punish me?" kept asking Aaron: "And if I will do something, will anyone trade with me?"

"Here it is" Peter told him, "If you will do something that someone needs, he or she will be happy to trade with you for something you need. If you can offer me something that will make my life better, why would I punish myself for not trading with you? Or if you can offer me something that will help me to avoid danger or any other bad things, I would want to get it. Why would I think about who you are? If you do not ask too much for your goods, I will trade with you. Anyone will."

"You might need a judge" said Aaron: "If people do things together, and make agreements, there is a need in someone who would help to resolve disagreements."

"You might need a doctor"—said Sarah: "Of course I am not a doctor yet. I will need to learn a lot. But I can start as a nurse helping anyone in need."

"Great," said Peter: "I just want you to know that Gabriel was planning to become an attorney and a judge, but if you will be better and less expensive, I am sure people will go to you. It is a free island. Everyone does what he or she wants to do, if of course it causes no harm to anyone else. We can vote for you to judge us or for him. And we vote the only effective way—each can hire you or him and pay for the services. If someone wants Marla to teach them, they pay her. If they want you to judge a dispute, they hire you. If an islander wants someone to guard his property, or they want someone to repair their shoes, or they want anything else, they will hire people who can do that.

"If they want someone to govern the island, they can hire such person or such people like they hire a dry cleaner or a taxi cab driver. If however they do not like the government they hired, they can fire the government like they would fire a dry cleaner or a restaurant by not paying them anymore. If the government doesn't do something it was hired for, I will not trade with them my goods in exchange for their services. There are plenty of other governments that would jump on such an opportunity. The best and the least expensive government shall govern our island, not the one that wants to steal our money and make us do things we do not want to do.

"If there is a need for something that no one does on our Island, then immediately someone will jump on an opportunity to offer others this product or service. No one on our island can tell that he wasn't 'given' an opportunity. Because no one 'gives' opportunities here. If you succeed, we are happy—that means that we are getting something good in exchange for what we ourselves are making. If you fail, this is not good for everyone else as well. That means simply that we are not getting new products or service. You can do things yourself, or you can offer someone to work together with you, or you can be a helper in someone's business, if they hire helpers. Welcome to the world of the free, home of the smart."

Do I care, thought Peter, how this system is called? No, I do not care even if it is called "Pumpernickel." If a system works, if I can do what I want without being punished for that, this is a good system. Our Human Nature is to go for the good as we see it and avoid bad as we see it. The only rule of the land shall be not to harm anyone's belongings. This shall be punishable by law and enforced vigorously. I am sure there will be plenty of us who will provide help to those in need.

Marla showed it by hiding Andrew from harm even after he did so many bad things to everyone. This is the only system that works with, not against the Human Nature and allows us to be "human" at the same time. This is how I would want to live my life.

The Island of the Magnificent Ten, as it was soon known throughout the world, became a magnet for thousands upon thousands of people who wanted to live their lives free and live them without anyone who would tell them what to do and how to behave, what to make, how much to charge, whom to sell. And especially what to do with the earnings. The Island of the Magnificent Ten became a model for many countries and showed future world leaders what to strive to be.

Chapter XVI

Scientific verification

TWO POWERFUL TRIBES decided to pick some wild forest berries to make jam for the upcoming winter. The leader of one of the tribes assembled his tribesman and announced that he prohibits them to eat berries while picking them. He said that anyone who will eat berries will be severely punished. The berries, he said, shall be used exclusively for the jam, and when time comes he will divide the jam between all of them. There is no taking berries home, he also said. If I will find that someone took berries home, such person will be severely punished.

The other tribe's leader told his people that each of them should bring from the forest as many berries as they want. From those berries they together will make jam and each will get his share according to the amount of berries he brought. I would advise to get as many as possible and have jam ready in case someone in your family will get sick, he told them.

Q1 - Do you think people from the first tribe tasted berries during the time they picked them?

a) Yes

b) No

I think they did. It is a natural thing to eat one or two berries while picking them. I think it is stupid (not smart) to tell people to do things that are contrary to their nature.

Do you think they liked to eat those berries in secret thinking that if they will be caught they will be punished? They probably were eating the berries hiding behind the bushes and at the same time watching another tribe eating berries and enjoying life. What do you think they were feeling at this time? Love to their leader, or something else?

Do you think they might have wanted to bring some berries to their children at home? Do you think they liked their leader who prohibited them to do what they want? Do you think they trusted each other not to tell the leader that they tasted berries and took some home despite his prohibition?

I think they would look for another tribe to join if they had a chance.

Now the other tribe—did they have to hide while doing things they wanted to? No, why hide if you can do it in the open? If they wanted to have berries at home they would take some and no one restricted them. If they wanted more jam, they would bring more berries to the leader. If they wanted less jam, they would bring fewer berries. If they didn't want any jam, they wouldn't bring any berries. They probably had more friends and were not afraid of them like the people in the first tribe.

They were free to do things they wanted to do. Free people are happier than the not-free. Do you remember what non-free people are called? They are called slaves.

Some people in the free tribe picked a lot of berries. Some picked a little, but enjoyed the forest and took some berries home. Some didn't do anything. They just walked, watched birds, and had a good time.

If you want people to be happy you can't force them to do things that are against their nature. You can't force them to do anything period. The rules of any society that really want their people to be happy must be harmonious with the human nature, or they are doomed to a certain failure.

People will eat berries while picking them and will bring them home to their children despite anything any leader will do to stop them. It is dumb, dumb, and dumb to order them not to.

All socialist societies are built on ideals that do not take into an account this "insignificant" thing called Human Nature. Since humans usually do not fit into those societies, leaders of those societies force them to fit by punishing them for disobedience.

People usually do not like to be punished, so in order to keep them in the groups the leaders punish them even more.

Here is an example.

A Smoking Prohibition Story

Everyone knows that smoking is bad. There are two ways to convince people not to smoke. One way is to teach them that smoking is bad, what it can do to their loved ones, tell them real stories and show films about what smoking does to their bodies. It is a very long way, but many people will quit by consciously making this wise decision.

Another way to make people stop smoking is to prohibit smoking and punish those that smoke. You can also prohibit stores to sell cigarettes. This is a much more efficient way to immediately have many people stop smoking. They will not be able to buy cigarettes anywhere and even if they would buy some, they wouldn't be able to smoke anywhere in public.

But they will find a way to make or buy tobacco and smoke it in secret.

Once upon a time the government in America tried to do the same thing with alcohol. It didn't work because people didn't want to quit. They were ordered, but they didn't like it and they began to look for a way around it. Many people started making alcohol on their farms, others smuggled it from abroad, and others sold alcohol secretly. Gradually consumption of alcohol rose and people began to drink as much as they drunk before but in secret and for much more money.

The way of prohibition looks easier, but it doesn't work. Why? Because it is against human nature. When you force people to do something they do not want to do, they resist. They hate oppressors and are trying to do whatever they are forbidden to do in hiding.

People will start growing tobacco in their own backyards, they will smuggle it from abroad, and they will find other ways to get nicotine into their bodies.

Smoking is not good. I wouldn't advise you to smoke. This story is not about good or bad smoking, but about good or bad prohibition instead of teaching and convincing.

Let's now examine and find out in which of those societies we discussed in the previous chapters we would want to live, but this time let us use the Scientific Method.

First let's find out if the society in question is against human nature or if it takes human nature into consideration. Let's check if the good that is offered to people in those societies is not bad for others. Let's find out if there is a majority that is oppressing the minority in those societies, or maybe there is a minority oppressing the majority? Or maybe no one oppresses anyone and life is beautiful.

People live to pursue happiness. The question is not "which country is stronger" or "where the greenest fields are" or "how much steel this country produces" but "where people are happier?"

Let me remind you what this Scientific Method is and how it works. You were studying it at school. It is usually wads and is applied to physical sciences, such as physics, chemistry, astronomy and math. But the scientific method can be applied to social sciences as well.

When scientists want to find an answer to a question they are trying to resolve, they:

- Gather data by observation,

- Formulate an idea (called "hypothesis"),

- Make predictions based on the hypothesis, and

- See if those predictions are come true.

- If it works in 100% of the situations, then the hypothesis is right. If it works only in 99.9% of the situations, it shows that the hypothesis maybe wrong, and scientists usually go back to their books, drawing boards and hot showers they usually think.

While reading this book you very possibly were thinking—is it true that life in capitalistic countries is better than in other social structures? The most capitalistic country in the world is the United States of America. How can I prove to myself and my friends that this is really the best place to live? Now you start your observation and thinking process. You asked yourself—people tend to be happy when they have total freedom and they themselves are in total control of all their belongings?

You <u>observed</u> that people's property is safer in the capitalistic society than in any other contemporary society.

You <u>formulated a hypothesis</u> that people live better under capitalism.

You <u>predicted</u> that since people (natural law) act toward their perception of gain and away from their perception of loss, they will tend to emigrate to the countries that have capitalism and away from countries that have socialism, monarchy or fascism.

Now let's observe and find out if this is true in 100% of the cases.

The United Nations Secretary-General Kofi Annan said that emigration is an expression of an individual's will to live a better life. There were 191 million international migrants last year, with most of those migrants living now in just 28 developed countries that have either a capitalistic society or a partly capitalistic society.

The United States leads the world as a host country, with over 38 million migrants as counted in 2005, constituting almost 13 percent of the country's population.

That means in plain English that people from all over the world are trying to get into the United States by all legal and illegal means. They try to get to the US because they want to live a better life. They want to leave their own countries because life in those countries is worse than in the United States. The United States has the largest number of emigrants in the world, and that simply means that life in the United States is the BEST IN THE WORLD.

Your Hypothesis (see above) is now becoming a <u>Confirmed Truth</u>—it is better for people to live in a capitalistic society than in any other known society of the contemporary world.

And now please see the chart that clearly shows the difference between what is available to your societies:

In which society people have more freedom?

- Socialism – No
- Fascism – No
- Monarchy – No
- Capitalism - Yes

Which society protects people's properties the most?

- Socialism – No
- Fascism – No
- Monarchy – No
- Capitalism - Yes

Which society enslaves people the least?

- Socialism – No
- Fascism – No
- Monarchy – No
- Capitalism - Yes

Which society creates more medical drugs, innovations, new products & ideas?

- Socialism – No
- Fascism – No

- Monarchy – No

- Capitalism - Yes

Which society has a wider variety of shows, books, entertainment & is more fun?

- Socialism – No

- Fascism – No

- Monarchy – No

- Capitalism - Yes

In which society has more stores, restaurants, better roads, and more lights?

- Socialism – No

- Fascism – No

- Monarchy – No

- Capitalism - Yes

In which society are people afraid of the government the least?

- Socialism – No

- Fascism – No

- Monarchy – No

- Capitalism - Yes

Your homework for today is to decide in which society YOU want to live!

Chapter XVII

Symptoms of the illness

Case #1 - Government Rules

SOCIALISTS ARE AGAINST monopolies. They say that the anti-monopoly laws defend you and other people like you & I against those "greedy capitalists." If there will be a monopoly, they say, you will receive bad goods, bad service and will pay more than the product is worth.

In Chapter XI we talked with you about monopolies. We came to the conclusion that when a monopoly knows that the moment it stopped providing great products or services, and starts raising prices, there will be another company that would jump onto an opportunity and will start competing with the monopoly. Threat of competition is a good tool to keep prices low and quality high.

Let's talk about schools. If you send your children to private school you pay twice. You pay for the government to run the public school, even if you are not studying in one. And you pay for the private school where your children actually go.

If you sent your kid to a public school, you tossed a coin. If the principal and all teachers are exceptionally good, you are lucky. Because it is an exception. You can't move your child even if the school is really bad. You can't take the money you paid to the government and move your kid to whatever school you want. You are paying for it but you are not in charge. You and your kids lost your freedom. Do you remember what people who lost their freedom are called? Do you remember what the people who make others un-free are called? Do you like governments that do that to you, your friends and your kids?

I do not know about you, but I personally do not like such governments. In fact, I hate them.

When a principal knows that his salary and the money the school gets is coming from the government, and nothing is coming from the parents, who is the boss for such principle? The parents or the government? What do you think? I hope you are not that naïve.

Schools like everyone else should be competing for your money. Like shoe factories, like computer manufacturers, like hospitals and dry cleaners, restaurants, electronic game producers or attorneys. Only if they compete, they will try to be better and better, less and less expensive. Otherwise YOUR CHILDREN will not be well educated, will be bored on half of the lessons, and will not be able to compete with the workers from other countries where schools are working better than in your home country. A lot in your future life depends on how good your school and your kids' school is.

When a government manages schools, you are not getting one of the most important things in life. Simply put, because of their own political reasons (they want the teachers union to vote for them and give them money) they steal your future from you.

Q1 - Do you want your future to be stolen?

   a)   Yes

   b)   No

   c)   I do not care

Do you think it is OK to steal your and your kids' future if the government is comprised of people whose fathers left their mothers when they were young?

Do you think it is less theft or more theft if the government who steals your future is comprised of the people who have very good intentions? Do you think it is OK to steal your future if the people who are stealing it mostly are good people?

Would you prefer good people to steal your future or you would prefer bad people to steal your future?

Would you prefer people with PhD in gymnastics to steal your future, or you want people who drive red cars to steal you future?

Or you say, I do not care who you are, my future is MINE! My kids' future is THEIRS! Do not touch it. I want to make my own choices in life!

Case #2 - Kibbutz Dining Room

A group of pilgrims founded a new village they called Kibbutz. There were some pilgrims that were old, some were sick; some families consisted of women and children only. For every working person there were two who weren't able to work.

The pilgrims didn't want anyone to starve and organized a large dining room to feed everyone. People who were not able to perform hard work were assigned to the diner to cook, serve and wash dishes. The villagers calculated that to feed each person they need one hundred dollars a month. Since for every working person there were two that didn't work, every working person was to pay three hundred dollars.

From time to time some of the villagers had guests, and they were always welcomed by others to share their food. The dining room was large and no one asked any question when they saw a new face.

One day however the cooks said that they need more money to buy food and more helpers to serve. They said that there are much more people eating now than when the diner started.

The villagers counted how many people were coming to the diner and were astonished to find out that there are twice as many as the pilgrims that lived in the village. They saw many people that no one knew. After a short investigation they found out that there are several dwellings around the Kibbutz filled with people who come to the diner every day, eat there and take a lot of food out.

The villagers had an emergency meeting to discuss the problem. Some said that they have to build a fence around the Kibbutz to stop the intruders from entering the diner. We shall have one gate and let into our village only those who came to visit us or work here, they were saying. Others said that this will be a restriction on the personal freedom of the intruders, and offered to call them not an intruders but "wandering guests" in order not to offend them.

There were others that said that some of those people were coming to do small jobs here and there in the Kibbutz and the villagers have an obligation to feed them and their families.

Let's start asking everyone whom we don't know who they are, said several villagers, and kick those that no one invited out, they insisted. We can't do that, said others, because if we will start asking who they are, we might offend those that are invited by our fellow villagers.

You can't kick out a person who reached to you for food, some others were saying. We are humans, they were crying out loud.

The villagers didn't know what to do and turned their anger to the cooks. You shall start watching the cost of the food supplies, the villagers said to them. Since there are many more people who are now eating in the diner and you are buying more food from the suppliers, you can force the suppliers to sell you everything for less. From now on you shall feed more people for the same amount of money. If you can't do that, we will kick your behinds out of the diner, they told to the cooks.

The food slowly became really bad. The portions became smaller, and the ingredients of lesser and lesser quality. Soon the food in the diner was really bad.

Q1 -Why did the quality of food go down?

a) Because the village cooks became tired

b) Because when you have more people coming to the diner and you have a limited amount of money for buying ingredients, you have to either make portions smaller or use cheaper ingredients, or do both.

c) Because the cooks in the diner were racists

Q2 - How did the villagers resolve their problem?

a) They shall build a fence around the village and let only those that are invited in

b) They shall have someone at the door of the diner asking all unknown people what are they doing at the diner and who invited them.

c) They shall make the diner a commercial restaurant and stop taking monthly fees from the villagers.

d) They shall take more money from the rich villagers, and take nothing from poor villagers and the "wandering guests."

If you read this book with attention, and were thinking about what you read, then you have chosen "c."

But now let's talk about millions of illegal emigrants who now live in our country. Millions of people entered the United States illegally. Some of them lied that they are tourists and didn't go back home. Others come inside of ocean containers, refrigeration trucks or even gas tanks. Hundreds of thousands cross our borders during dark nights. They come here looking for work and a better life. We understand and appreciate their desire to live in America. They however have not chosen to wait for a permit to enter, like many of your ancestors did, and decided to break the law in order to get here. We are flattered that they want to live here among us, but how about respect for the laws of the country they want to live at?

Those people are not paying for the education of their kids, but their kids are studying at our schools for free. You pay for their education.

The amount of teachers is the same. The amount of schools is the same. The budget is the same ... but there are many more students to teach. Two things are happening at the same time—the classrooms are becoming overcrowded and the quality of education goes even lower.

Q1 - Do you want your kids to study at schools with many kids in a classroom and less attention to each student?

   a)   Yes

   b)   No

   c)   I do not care

Those people are not paying for medical expenses for their families, but they go to emergency rooms and are getting medical treatments for free. With the new laws (some call this new law "Obamacare") there will be many more people at the hospitals and much less services for each.

Q1 - Do you want more people in the doctors' offices, less time to visit with your doctor and less services?

   a)   Yes

   b)   No

   c)   I do not care

Some of the people who came to this country illegally came here to steal and rob, and if they are caught they sometimes go to prisons in America (and you pay for their attorney, transportation, food, and policeman who are catching them and holding them in prisons) or they are deported and two days later they are back on the streets of our cities.

There are many cities in the US that are not allowing even a policeman to ask a person if he has documents or he is an illegal emigrant. They say that it is because the police can by mistake ask an American citizen this question and this can be offensive to an American citizen. They are calling those illegal emigrants by another name—they call them "undocumented emigrants" in order not to offend them. I personally will not be offended if someone will ask me for my documents. I am not offended when I am searched at the entrances to the airports. I thank people who do that—their job is to prevent terrorists from entering our planes and killing American citizens, you and me. Why I should be offended?

It is better for all of us, the new progressive US government is saying, to have more people in our health system. If all illegal emigrants will start coming openly to the doctors, we will be able to buy drugs cheaper and that will reduce the cost of healthcare, they are insisting.

In other words they are saying that to buy five computers is cheaper than to buy two computers. Or that to buy two tickets to a baseball game is cheaper than to buy one ticket. Or if really listen to what they are saying it is cheaper to have two kids than one. Interesting math, I would say.

Q1 - Why do you think the US government is saying that to buy more will cost less money than to buy less?

a) They say it because they are stupid

b) They say it because they think we are stupid

c) We elected them to serve us but they do not care about you, or me. They just want illegal aliens and their relatives to vote for them on the next elections.

I personally think it is "c," but I might be wrong.

Case #3 - The Fair Pay Story

The island called Fair was divided into two equal parts. Once the island was uninhabited, but after the discovery of a special fruit that wasn't growing in any other part of the world which had an exceptional taste, two food companies came there and stared producing from it great tasting juices, canned fruits and jams.

As usual where people are, the government comes and the island soon had a mayor and several other people who were pretending to be helpful to the citizens of the island.

The Left part of the island became known as LP and the right part as RP. The factory workers on LP organized a committee that soon began to call itself the Fruit Workers Union. The union approached the RP workers, but they never decided they wanted to participate in this organization or not and each was negotiating his own salary and benefits.

Very soon the LP workers were getting more money than the RP workers. They were also getting longer holidays and more benefits. Because of that the price of the products they were making went up and buyers stopped buying their juices and canned fruits. The management of the LP factory came to the union and suggested to lower the salaries. The union refused and organized workers to strike. All the work on the LP factory stopped. The fruits that were already purchased were spoiled and the company had so much loss that the management decided to close the factory. All the workers at the LP factory lost their jobs.

The RP factory got many more orders and in order to make their workers happy and working faster began to give them nice bonuses.

Q1 - Do you think the workers at the LP factory are happy not having jobs and money to buy food?

a) Yes

b) No

c) I do not know

Q2 - Why did the LP workers lose their jobs?

a) The fruits weren't as tasty as before

b) Unions demanded higher pay and that affected prices of the products

c) Factory management made many mistakes

d) Buyers didn't want to buy at the LP factory because they didn't like color of the eyes of the general manager

The United States universities and scientific labs create new ideas, technologies and products. The United States companies want to make the products based on those technologies here in the US, but can't. They can't do it because the wages of the workers are so high, that it makes the products very expensive. The products are now produced abroad, in the countries that do not have unions. Now their workers have money to buy food, pay for the rent, buy cars, phones, dresses and presents to their children. American workers who demand higher salaries are not getting anything, and are begging the government to help them and give them something to survive. This is why America borrows money from the countries that do not have unions.

The same workers, who do not want to work for less, blame companies for "taking jobs overseas" and demand government assistance for not having jobs. The government as we already discussed many times has no money of their own. They can (a) borrow money and make our children pay interest on those loans, (b) print money and make dollars worthless thus stealing from the people who worked all their lives and saved, or (c) tax those that have more and stop them from investing and starting new businesses.

Case #4 - Endangered Salmon

Two fisherman's villages were on the opposite sides of a large Laguna. In one village everyone was red haired and in another village everyone was green eyed. The villagers were good neighbors, coming to each others' birthdays and spent most of the holidays together, competing in different sports, dancing and singing.

Most of the men in both villages were salmon fisherman and spent lots of their time fishing. Many women were preparing salmon for sale, conserving it, smoking and drying it. The business was good, and villagers were happy with their lives.

Sometimes the villagers took their fish and fish products to the nearby town, and sometimes the townsfolk came to the Laguna to buy those wonderful salmons from the villagers.

One day a young red haired villager by the name Tilly went to the town and met a nice group of people that called themselves environmentalists. They told him that they are studying an impact of fishing on the Laguna and that they found out that there is less salmon now that was before and that the villagers have to stop fishing or the salmon would be extinct.

Tilly was so impressed and taken by their story that when he came home he immediately organized a group of young people who opposed fishing. From the beginning no one took them seriously but two years later Tilly was elected to be the Red-haired village mayor and he ordered to stop any and all salmon fishing by his fellow red haired villagers.

When older fisherman refused, the Salmon-watchers (this is how they called themselves) made holes in all their boats and they were unable to leave the shore. At the same time the green eyed village continued to fish salmon, make and sell products made from salmon.

The older villagers tried to talk sense to Tilly and his Salmon-watchers, but every time on the town meetings they attempted to discuss this issue, the Salmon-watchers yelled so loud, no one was able to hear anything. The red haired village stopped fishing for salmon and the people didn't know how to make money. They began to buy salmon from the green eyed villagers, prepare it and sell to the town people. Of course now they were buying salmon instead of getting it for free and they were unable to make as much money as they were making before. They now didn't have enough money to repair their houses, to buy new appliances and to send their children to good schools and colleges.

In order to make any money, the red haired villagers were performing all kinds of manual jobs for the green eyed villagers. They washed dishes, cleaned houses, took care of their gardens and repaired their houses. The red haired village looked like a very poor village, and actually it now was a very poor village.

All this time the green eyed villagers were fishing salmon and asking each other why those crazy red haired people are not doing the same? When they were told that there is less salmon in the Laguna than before, they were laughing and saying that it is called migration and every seven years the Laguna is getting colder and the Salmon goes away. Then during the next seven years the Laguna is becoming warmer and the salmon returns. This has nothing to do with you or us, they were saying to the red haired villagers and to their Mayor Tilly. But Tilly and his Salmon-watchers didn't really listen. They now there thinking about an impact of fish smoking on the surrounding forests and were preparing a new law to prohibit any kind of smoking in the village.

Q1 - Who is more important in your opinion—salmon or people?

   a) Salmon

   b) People

   c) I do not care for any of those species

Q2 - Did Tilly make the red haired villagers life better or worse?

a) Diversity of life in the Laguna is of paramount importance to the red haired village people

b) Tilly ruined the village and lives of many people. Most probably if the danger were real, the villagers would find a way of how to replenish the salmon population like we here in America are doing with the forests. Its plain stupid to buy Salmon from the neighboring village and not to fish themselves. Looks like the environmentalists were socialists or progressives.

The United States economy is based on oil. It is used to produce energy, move our cars and airplanes, make plastic and rubber. It is the most essential element of the American industry and we are not able to survive without it. America buys huge amounts of oil from foreign producers, and pays unbelievable amounts of money to Saudi Arabia, Venezuela, Mexico, Nigeria, Russia and Iraq. We are becoming more and more dependent on those countries and are constantly afraid they will become hostile to us and would stop selling us oil and gas.

At the same time the United States of America has huge resources of oil. Oil is in Alaska and Off-Shore, in Montana and North Dakota, on the border with Canada and on the border with Mexico. Possibly America has more oil than any other country in the world. But it continues buying oil from other countries, spending huge amounts of money and losing its independence.

The reason is that American environmentalists are now allowing us to drill oil, build refineries, or even build nuclear reactors to substitute for the lost oil. They say that we will endanger the environment. They are OK with Chinese drilling in our waters. They are OK with Canadians drilling the same oil fields. They are OK with half of the world refining oil and making gas for us. They are not OK only when it is done by Americans and for America.

Don't you find it strange?

I do.

Case #5 - Post Office Saga

In the old days of your grandfathers in a great state called Kalifornia was a medium size town called A on the South and another medium size town called Z on the North. When people traveled from one town to another they told their friends and relatives that "I am now going from A to Z", or when returning, that "Today I am going from Z to A."

When someone in Z had a birthday, people from A would go there and wish him or her Happy Birthday and give presents. When someone in A was sick, people from Z would come to A to wish him or her speedy recovery and would bring juice and fruits they grew themselves. They however never brought chocolates to each other because in both A & Z chocolates were considered unhealthy.

Then one day someone invented mail and people stopped coming to each other's birthdays or wishing a speedy recovery in person. Everyone was now writing letters and sending them with the mailman who was then called a "mail runner." People in A would bring mail to his home and the mail runner would run with the mail to Z. Then in Z he would take all their mail and deliver that back to A. He did it every day but Sunday, because he was a religious man and went to Church every Sunday, rain or shine.

The citizens of A were happy. They paid a little for each delivered let-ter or parcel and knew everything will come to the addressee in time and in good condition. The citizens of Z were happy for the same rea-sons. The mail runner was happy. He was making a living and helping people at the same time. Almost everyone was happy except the gov-ernment. The government was not happy because the government is not in the business of being happy, but in the business of taking money from one group of people and distributing them to another group of people who didn't earn them.

The government invited the mail runner and said "Do you have a license to run mail?"— "No," said the mail runner. "Did you go through vigorous safety regulation training?" they asked. "No," said the mail runner. "Do you have an accountant that can tell us exactly how many packages were accepted, how many delivered and how much you got for them?" "No one complained," said the mail runner. "It is about time you hire an attorney" said the government, "We are going to sue you and put you in jail for a long time." And they did what they said.

The people of A & Z revolted. They wanted someone to deliver their mail, and the government told them "you will pay a little extra to us and we will take care of your mail."

The government hired twelve mailmen in A and twelve in Z. They built seven one-story and two three-story buildings in the cities and in the middle of the road. Two important government managers were appointed to be in charge of the government sponsored mail program. One was called Mail Governor of Kalifornia and another Mail Lieutenant Governor of Kalifornia. Three analysts were added to the department to study trends in the customers' mail tendencies. The government began to charge each citizen a sum equal to sending of three hundred sixty five letters a year, disregarding whether they sent those letters or not. They charged even new born babies and brain dead patients in hospitals.

The mail now wasn't delivered immediately but in two or three days, and many letters were lost in transit. The post office workers blamed it on bad weather and capitalism, organized a union and demanded an increase in salaries and benefits.

During the next three years the post office raised prices of mail five times and on the day the mail runner was released from prison, each citizen of both A & Z paid the government an equal of sending a thousand letters a year.

The mail runner learned his lesson. He hired an accountant, announced that he is again in business and offered to deliver mail faster and cheaper than the government service. He was arrested again even before he began accepting and delivering letters. The official explanation was that he interfered with the governments business. No one knew exactly what that means, but everyone understood that it is dangerous to cross paths with the government.

Q1 - Do you think the government cared about people's needs?

a) Yes, they had people's needs in the hearts and minds when they terminated the mail runner business and established the government run business

b) I do not know what intentions the government had, but as usual if the government does something the results are just opposite of what they said they wanted to do.

According to the US government, no other system for delivering mail—public or private—can be established absent Congress's consent. Congress has delegated to the Postal Service the power to decide whether others may compete with it, and the Postal Service has carved out an exception to its monopoly for extremely urgent letters. In other and simpler words, the Postal Service can allow someone to compete with it or decide not to allow competitors. Isn't it interesting? Is it called Capitalism? Is it called a well-earned monopoly?

Let's for a moment imagine that someone by the name X is the only one who by law is allowed to sell eggs in your city. People need eggs and they will come to stay in line to get them. This Mr. X can raise prices and people will still come to him. He can make them dance and sing songs while standing in line, and they still will come to him. Mr. X can give them terrible service and they will still come to him ... And no one can compete with him and sell eggs because the Government prohibits anyone to compete with Mr. X!

Wait a second, you might tell, in this book you wrote that monopolies are not bad, actually you said that they are good ... why suddenly are they bad?

There is a slight difference between a monopoly by a company that is afraid of competition and attempts not to lose its customers and a monopoly created by a government. The earned monopoly is doing better and cheaper good then others, but the moment they start raising prices or lowering quality, there will immediately be others waiting for the opportunity to enter a lucrative market. When governments create monopolies, they are making sure that no one will be able to jump on the opportunity.

The US Congress prohibited anyone except The US Postal Service to deliver first class mail (letters) on the territory of the United States. The Congress doesn't care if they do a good job or bad, they do not care whether the service charges a lot or a little, or if there are long lines and the postal offices are dirty. The US postal service can do whatever they want and you can't do anything about it. You can't find anyone who would deliver your letters except for them.

OK, you can argue that Fed Ex and USPS are now delivering parcels ... but not letters. You can pay them twenty dollars to deliver one envelope with a letter, but this is not what we are talking about. We are talking about slavery, where the citizens of the United States are forced to buy services of a company that does an unsatisfactory job, does it very expensively and offers bad service ... and there is a prohibition on competing with this service and a fine and a jail term if you do. Yes, in the United States you can get punished or even get into prison if you do not have competition and became a monopoly (remember the Aluminum company), however you will be punished and may get into prison if you compete with a government originated monopoly (The Postal Service). Beware; we are well on the way to socialism ... or fascism.

Chapter XVIII

We identified the problems, but is there a solution?

SOONER OR LATER every Political Democracy reaches a point when more than half of the voters want to steal the belongings of the minority and now has the power to do it by voting for more and more taxes on the rich and more and more entitlements for themselves. The minority doesn't like it and the problems, often with violence and blood, start.

Once a lady friend told me "No representation without taxation." I thought that she got the famous Boston Tea Party slogan backwards, but she was serious. How a person, she said, can be allowed to vote on the use of other people's money if he or she does not contribute anything but only receive from the pot? Don't you think that such a person will always vote for taking money from others and giving to himself? And since we all know human nature they would want more and more and more of the other people's money and properties. The more votes they have, the larger piece of the other people's riches they would be able to take.

Sooner or later every Political Democracy paves a way for a repressive Tyranny. Sometimes the transformation is long, through socialism, i.e. through tyranny of the majority who are not happy with the riches the minority was acquiring. Sometimes it is shorter and direct, through tyranny of the minority who were not happy with the re-distribution of wealth the majority was imposing on them.

Sooner or later any repressive and bloody Tyranny destroys the society it oppresses. If the goal of a person is happiness, than Political Democracy is only a short term solution. Socialism in any way, shape or form is not producing happiness. Tyranny is not answering this question as well. What to do? Where to go? What to choose?

"By virtue of exchange, one man's prosperity is beneficial to all others."—C. F. Bastiat

Wow, what a weird statement, one would say. This C.F. Bastiat is telling us strange things—he is telling us that if some other person will have more money and belongings, it will be better for you & me. Is in your opinion it is a crazy idea or a very smart one?

We were always told that when someone wins, the rest of us lose. And the fair solution to our problem of not having enough money (the socialists and progressives are telling us) would be to take as much money as possible from the guy who has money, and divide this money and property among the less fortunate. Usually however when you find out that something was originated by socialists, you can be quite sure it is a lie.

When one person makes lots of money he invests them into either new technologies or into competing with someone who already sells you and me products or services. Some people do it directly, others through banks or mutual funds, where thousands of people pull their money together in order to have more "investing power" and to enjoy the help of professional money managers.

New technologies mean that we will have multi-functional cell phones and faster Internet, better medicine and quieter air conditioners, faster and more reliable cars and planes. And we will have all that for less. Is it good for you and me, or it is bad? So, please tell me what do you think—is it good for you and me if someone makes lots of money?

If there is no one with an excess of money, there is no one to invest in new businesses and technologies. And then comes what is called "stagnation" or paralysis of entire countries and continents.

Competition makes producers to produce more, better quality and sell it in more pleasant surroundings. Everyone gets better products, higher quality of life and everyone shops in more pleasant places. Availability of capital means that there will be competition. Do you think it is good for you and me, or it is bad?

When producers and investors accumulate more money, it is good FOR ALL!

A need to sell their products and services forces competing firms to lower their prices. Everyone can buy for less, and can buy more things with the same amount of money. For example if you got five hundred dollars for your birthday one year ago, at that time you could have bought with it one a 20" TV. This year you will be able to buy a 40" HD TV. When you will get your birthday presents next year, for the same five hundred dollars you probably will be able to get a SMART HD 3D TV with play station, plus a cellular phone and an ice cream. Is it good or bad? If it makes your life better, would you like producers to get more money or you want them to make less money and not be able to make new things and offer lower prices?

Yes, I want producers and investors to have more money, create new products and lower prices

No, I hate people who live better than me. Even if this person invented electric bulbs, I would prefer not to have light, but have everyone live the same or worse than I do.

What do you think?

When customers stop buying from a producer he immediately starts thinking about how to bring those renegade customers back. He innovates his products and services, adds new ones and if successful the customers are coming back and voting for his product with their money. This is how new products and services are born. Producers want to keep old customers and find new ones. Yesterday you had a cell phone that was only for talking, today you can send messages, see videos, make photos and do a million other things.

This is real democracy, when you vote with your money for the best product. You award the good producers with profits they deserve. If a producer is not doing something you want and like, you do not award him. Is it fair? I think it is fair. It is called Economic (Market) Democracy. It is the only really fair democracy in the world.

Q1 - Now tell me if you are OK if people who are making yours and my life better are becoming rich in the process? I am OK with that. If someone makes my life better, I wish this person all the money and happiness he wants.

How about people who steal your money and your property? I do not wish them to succeed in what they are doing.

There are two things that are standing on the way of stealing and cheating. One is called conscience, another is called law. We hope our government is guided by either both or by at least one of those safeguards.

The US Constitution gave the Congress an authority to take as much money from us as THEY deem necessary ... as they think they would NEED to conduct programs THEY think is good for us...and as you already guessed each of the congressman and senators NEEDS a lot. They do not buy Lamborghinis, but each spend much much more than the cost of Lamborghini on things HE or SHE deems important.

They can't stand the temptation. They have friends who helped them to be elected and those people want something in return for their support. Their families are large and many of their relatives need good jobs or opportunity to make business with the government. It can be very profitable and lucrative. Politicians have this unique possibility to take OUR money and give it to someone they like or need.

Hi, says one politician to another, let's build a wall that would separate Washington DC from Washington state. Good idea, says another. I will vote for this great wall that YOUR cousin will build with the money we will steal from the producers. I am however want you to vote for a project which two very nice people who gave me money for my re-election complain want to do—a research to find out if birds can fly. It will cost American producers two billion dollars but why would you care? The money is not yours and the answer they say is very important to the whole humanity.

The two politicians shake hands and vote in Congress for those great and important projects—to build a wall to separate Washington DC from Washington State and to research if birds can fly.

It really doesn't matter that DC and the Washington State are not even close to each other and that everyone knows that birds can fly.

Many members of congress have no idea about geography or ornithology (I hope you know what is it). Recently a representative of our government said publicly that "Arizona has no right to issue any emigration laws because they are not even close to the border." Again, I hope that YOU know that Arizona is a border state. I just wanted to show you the quality of people making decisions about our lives. Arizona has long mutual border with Mexico and through this border every day thousands of Mexicans enter this country without permission, but some carry drugs to sell them to you, other not-so-smart people on the streets of the American cities and yours and mine children.

Probably our Founding Fathers thought that politicians in America will be moral and will restrain ourselves from stealing and cheating. What a huge mistake it was!

Many of our contemporary politicians don't even know that they supposed to be moral. Many of them laugh when someone mentions word "moral."

One of the politicians or government functionaries NEEDS a yacht, another needs private jet paid by you and me, and still another needs Lamborghini. They really need it. And they get it the easy way. They create laws that take from the producers any part of what we earn. They either take your money, or borrow money that YOU will have to return with interest, or they print more money and making YOUR savings worthless. Then politicians divide those stolen from you money among those in greater need and ... build walls that would separate Washington DC and Washington State.

We are offered an alternative between politicians that steal more (Democrats) or steal a bit less (Republicans).

If you are one whom they steal from, then you most probably vote Republican. If you are one of those who receive part of the stolen money than you most probably vote Democrat. Some of us defending what is ours, others trying to get as much as possible of not theirs. Which position in your opinion is moral and which is not? What do you think?

Both major US parties offering us alternatives that involve theft of our belongings and distribution of our money among those that didn't earn them.

The real alternative shall not be between "those who still a lot and those who still a bit less" but between "those who steal" and "those that do not steal." There are other ways that the agreed by the producers programs can be financed. NO STEALING FROM AND ENSLAVING OF THE AMERICANS—this is what we shall demand.

As a society we will have to create a safety net for children, old and sick. We are humans and taking care of our own kind is one of the major distinguishes between us and the animal kingdom. However helping others is a moral duty, not a law based obligation. We need to teach our kids to help others, not to tell them that the government will decide what to do and whom to give, and the only moral obligation they have is to pay taxes. This is wrong!

Did you ever read the Declaration of Independence? I am sure you were asked at school to memorize it … but did you ever really read it?

Let's take a quick look on the most important provision of the Declaration "all men are created equal." You do understand it, right? But who gave men (you and I) such rights? Maybe a King or a strongman? In this case he can take them back, right?

But the Declaration says something different. Men are endowed by their Creator with unalienable rights, says the Declaration. What that means, you might ask? That means that NO MAN can take those rights from you, this is what that means.

What are those rights, you might ask?—Those rights are Life, Liberty and the Pursuit of Happiness.

Who owns you?—YOU!

Who can control you and your belongings besides yourself?—NO ONE!

Can you do whatever makes you happy?—YES, and no one should interfere with your pursuit of happiness, but you can't interfere with the other people's pursuit of happiness. Yours are yours and theirs are theirs.

How the Declaration proposes to defend those rights?—To secure these rights, governments are instituted among men, says the Declaration.

And who forms the government, who tells it how to govern?—The governments shall derive their just powers from the consent of the governed, says the Declaration. That simply means the governments shall listen to what we the people tell them and govern (manage the country) accordingly.

But what if such government is not doing what it is suppose to do, what if instead of protecting Life, Liberty and Pursuit of Happiness it attacks and steals our belongings?

The Declarations answers to that very simple. Whenever any Form of Government becomes destructive of Life, Liberty and the pursuit of

Happiness of the Americans it is the Right of the People to alter or to abolish it, tells us the Declaration, and to institute a new Government.

In other words, if the government attacks (takes without your permission, steals) people's belongings, we the people have a right to change it or to get rid of such government.

So, does the United States government attacks you belongings? Let's examine it one last time.

The Constitution gives the Congress a right to take portion of people's earnings when they are needed. When the Constitution was written, the people in the United States paid WHEN NEEDED a very small amount of money to the government. We already talked about it—sometimes 1%, sometimes 3%, sometimes nothing.

The US Government gradually, step by step, like Karl Marx proposed, began to take more and more and more—and in some instances took more than 90% of what the producers made. The new administration and the President of the United States who supposed to protect the belongings of all the citizens began to call producers not "the most honorable citizens of the country" but "fat rich cats."

When the government takes this amount from producers, can the producers invest in new businesses? Can they hire more people and pay them salaries? Can they create new products? Can they lower prices? No, now the money that they would use as investments went to the needy people and no new businesses will be built.

So, does the US government interferes with our freedom, belongings and pursued of happiness?

Yes, they do!

If the Government of the United States attacks our property—what we should do?

Maybe we shall start thinking about getting rid of such government and institute a new one? One, that will not have a power to steal from its employers—us?

International Socialism (in its final form called "communism") steals all people's belongings. Any form of Socialism is a step-by-step way of seizing control over people's belongings. If you fight with the socialist government, you will be punished. The further society is down the road to communism, the harder will be the punishment.

National Socialism (fascism) muscles controls over many of people's belongings, including freedom. If you fight, you will be punished. The further society is down the road to fascism, the harder will be the punishment.

Decent people usually hate fascism and do not have the same feelings about socialism for one and only reason. Fascism acts immediately when it is installed and it uses nationalistic phraseology.

Socialism on the other hand is creeping into people's lives almost unnoticed and its slogans look honorable. <u>The goals of the two are identical, but their methods are different.</u>

Political Democracy that is based on Capitalism steals some of people's belongings. You can fight. You can be punished, usually not as hard as under other systems. If Political Democracy is not protected by internal safeguards it may morph into socialism and eventually into communism or fascism.

Out of those three: lose all your belongings, lose a large part of your belongings or lose some of your belongings, I personally chose Political Democracy. I am choosing "the lesser evil."

But wouldn't it be wonderful to live in a society that does not steal from you?

Is it possible?

It is your turn to think how to do it. You can change the world. But please think about what kind of change you want to bring before you start. The one thing is obvious—the new America shall be based on Market Democracy. And the rules are simple: Do not touch my belongings. I will not touch yours. I shall be in command of my life and my property. I shall have a total freedom to pursue my own version of happiness. You too, you can pursue your happiness any way you want unless it interferes with my belongings or my freedom. I am not your slave in any shape or form. You are not my slave in any shape or form. I am 100% in control of my life and my belongings. I have 0% control of anyone else's belongings. You have 100% control of your life and your belongings. You and everyone else have 0% control of other people's belongings.

And be prepared to defend those rights from all those who would hate us for our riches and for our happiness and will try to destroy us attacking from outside and from within.

Chapter XIX
Epilogue - Shifting Paradigms

AT THE DAWN of civilization Cain used a stone and killed Abel. It is impossible to kill many people with a stone. It is a difficult task, especially if the people will resist. The best stone fighter can kill several dozen people a day and will have to rest.

It is possible to kill a bit more with an arrow. Especially if the targets are standing still and not shooting back. But I would be surprised if an average bow and arrow warrior would be able to kill more than one hundred a day.

When handguns were created, it raised the human ability to kill to many hundreds. An invention of modern artillery raised our abilities to kill thousands a day.

There were situations in the history of our civilization when a group of determined humans were able to exceed the mentioned above numbers. When Genghis Khan for example heard that one of the cities he already conquered rebelled and killed the governor appointed by him, he turned about eighty thousand of his horsemen from whatever important stuff they were doing and arrived at the walls of this rebel city of one million. His people were able to kill all the citizens of this city that was situated in Afghanistan in about ten days. It however took a determined effort of eighty thousand people and ten full days to kill one million.

Look at the current situation. We humans already have devices that might kill millions at a push of a button. For some time production of those weapons have been done by scientifically advanced countries only. Those countries were more or less democratic and had no intention of committing mass suicide or really intentionally murdering millions. They knew the risks associated with such devastating kill.

Not anymore. First of all the countries that are far behind in many other scientific and social developments are rapidly advancing in the area of modern weaponry. Secondly some of those countries have close ties to people who are determined to eliminate whole groups of humans, who differ from them by their beliefs.

It is now only a question of time until some of those weapons (chemical, nuclear or biological) would fall in the hands of those groups that call themselves either freedom fighters, or religious zealots, or just avengers for something that was done to them or their ancestors by ancestors of some other group of people.

It is now only a question of time until some deadly gas, or virus or either a "dirty" or a "clean" bomb would be activated in the cities of the enemies of those groups.

How much time do we have? Maybe two decades, maybe four. Not more than five. That means that during the lifetime of our children this civilization as we know it will perish. Or will perish completely. Unless we find a way to co-exist. Unless the paradigm of resolving differences by violence would be shifted.

You say it is impossible and we are doomed?

I am more optimistic than you. Let me tell you why I am optimistic. There was a guy by the name Giordano Bruno. You might know him as a crazy person who insisted that the Earth or even the Sun wasn't the center of the Universe. He was saying that the Universe is infinite and has no center at all.

Of course he was burned for that on a stake. Who wouldn't burn such a crazy lunatic? No one in the entire world thought that the Universe is infinite. What, people would say, there is no center, the Earth is orbiting the Sun, and the Sun itself is moving to some unknown destination? Where it is moving? Everyone knows that the Earth is immovable object and the Sun along with all other stars is orbiting Earth in perfect circles. Burn the bastard alive!

Do you think this happened five thousand years ago? Maybe one thousand years ago? Actually Bruno was burned alive in September of 1600. In about hundred fifty years after his death there was NO SANE PERSON in Europe who thought that the stars were orbiting the unmovable Earth. More than that—if a person would insist that the Earth is the center of the Universe he probably would end up in a psychiatric asylum. Or burned alive. People do not change, but beliefs do.

It was a major paradigm shift. From a handful group of rebels to the entire population of all the civilized countries is a giant step, and it was done in a very short period of time. In a very very short period of time.

We however have even less time. That means we needed to start yesterday and have to move very fast. And we need to educate ourselves and our children at the same time.

Is it possible? Yes, we are not changing laws of nature, so it is possible.

Is it difficult?

You bet! This is probably the most difficult task that ever was on the shoulders of men. There is however a simple alternative facing us "either change or die." A very simple one—we change or we all die.

It is your choice.

Choose whatever you want.

CPSIA information can be obtained at www.ICGtesting.com
Printed in the USA
LVOW08s1430260114

371022LV00008B/731/P